The Composer's Advocate

The Composer's Advocate
A Radical Orthodoxy for Musicians

Erich Leinsdorf

Yale University Press
New Haven and London

Published with assistance from the Kingsley Trust
Association Publication Fund established by the Scroll
and Key Society of Yale College.

Designed by Nancy Ovedovitz
and set in Times Roman type.
Printed in the United States of America by
Vail-Ballou Press, Binghamton, N.Y.

Library of Congress Cataloging in Publication Data
Leinsdorf, Erich, 1912–
    The composer's advocate.

    Includes index.
    1. Music—Interpretation (Phrasing, dynamics, etc.)
2. Conducting. 3. Music—Performance. I. Title.
MT75.L44   781.6′3   80–17614
ISBN 0–300–02427–4

10   9   8   7   6   5   4   3   2   1

Contents

Preface

Early in 1977 I held a seminar for young conductors that was arranged under the auspices of the New York Philharmonic Society and the Rockefeller Foundation. Among the guests for the opening session was the editor-in-chief of the Yale University Press, Edward Tripp, who had earlier proposed that I turn the symposium into a book. Partly to clarify the most significant ideas, I gave another seminar in July 1978, this time in Aspen, Colorado. This book is based on those discussions and also on an article of mine published in German. Its title was *Do You Read Music or "Aimez-vous Beethoven"?* The subtitle was *A Few Musical Thoughts for All Who Read Notes.*[1]

Although this book is directed primarily toward conductors, I hope it will prove equally useful to other performers who feel inadequately prepared to master the deeper complexities of music. Whether conductors or instrumentalists, all musicians who perform the great compositions of our heritage have the same advantage: they can reside in the company of the world's greatest musical minds at will. While the farmer, the clerk, the shopkeeper, and the broker usually must spend their days in dull routine, often under the orders of uninspiring bosses, the musician is privileged to make a living while dwelling each day with genius. No matter how many tales of woe told during contract negotiations, no matter how many hours spent on picket lines, most musicians do know that theirs is a unique calling and better than any in the commercial world.

Nevertheless, all too many members of our profession should know more about music. They have been trained to learn only those parts of a work written for their own instruments. It is as though they were espionage agents allowed to know only a tiny part of a grand strategic design. If it were in my power to arrange, every musician would possess and know the full score of every piece played and thereby come to appreciate wholly the beauty that he helps to create.

Only in recent years have I come to understand as a conductor that a short explanation of the content and sense of the music to be performed can make

1. Erich Leinsdorf, *Lesen Sie Musik oder "aimez-vous Beethoven"?: Einige musikalische Gedanken für alle, die Noten lesen* (Frankfurt: Henry Litolff's Verlag, C. F. Peters, 1976).

rehearsals more meaningful for most participants. Only in recent years have I realized how much a conductor can and should tell, simply because it is not common knowledge among musicians. Yet we cannot get close to the genius in great works merely by knowing more. Indispensable partners of knowledge are imagination, thoughtful intelligence, and ultimately the willingness to forget ourselves in the service of what we undertake to represent—the composer and his music.

To accomplish this goal we must agree on several premises. This book will expound three simple ones:

1. Great composers knew what they wanted.
2. The interpreter must have the means at his disposal to grasp the composers' intentions.
3. Music must be read with knowledge and imagination—without necessarily believing every note and word that is printed.

If these premises sound somewhat contradictory, I hope you will discover in the following pages why they are not.

One
Knowing the Score

Musical Literacy

Long ago, I spent several weeks in Salzburg, living at a modest inn on the outskirts of the city. I was thrilled when my next-door neighbor turned out to be an up-and-coming young conductor who was music director of an important American symphony orchestra. We talked a great deal, and when we retired after luncheons I could hear through the wall the music from his portable phonograph. Often the same side (four minutes and twenty seconds in those years) was repeated over and over. By the time my neighbor departed I had figured out that these sessions with the Victrola were preparation for his winter season's repertoire. I was twenty-two, green and provincial, and yet my original awe at having met a real chief conductor of an American orchestra turned into puzzlement. Why should a man of such eminence need to learn his music from repeated hearings of other performers?

Forty years later such a discovery no longer surprises me. When I began my first season as director of the Berkshire Music Center in 1963, I found in my conducting seminar twenty-eight candidates admitted by the previous regime's screening process. They were unknown to me. For evaluation I gave them a three-part quiz. In the first part they were to find a wrong note in a C-major triad played by the four horns in the slow introduction of Weber's *Freischütz* overture. (There is one Breitkopf and Härtel edition of the score that contains that misprint.)[1] Nobody spotted it, which meant that there was no connection between eye and ear, even in such an utterly simple harmonic configuration. After the

---

1. Searching for mistakes in scores can sometimes result in mere hairsplitting. Errata vary widely in importance. In 1958 a conductor traveled far and near to enlist support for his campaign to force the house of Ricordi to publish better-edited scores of Verdi's operas. He spoke darkly of twenty thousand misprints in *Falstaff* alone, but when I saw his list it showed that many, perhaps most, of the publisher's sins were dislocations of a crescendo or diminuendo by a sixteenth of an inch. These were quibbles rather than legitimate complaints about misprints of real importance. There *are* cases where a slight misplacement of crescendo-decrescendo can play bad tricks. A famous spot appears

1

unsuccessful search for a wrong note in Weber, my twenty-eight seminarists were asked, without scores for reference, in how many symphonic movements Brahms had used trombones. What followed resembled an auction rather than a seminar. Bids flew from all sides. They ranged from five to a dozen! By contrast, we had a *succès fou* with the third question, which lifted twenty-eight hands in the air. All voices answered correctly in virtual unison. What had the question been? "Where does Brahms use a percussion instrument?"

These reactions showed that my seminarists mostly had listened to recordings, on which a triangle can be heard far more clearly than the trombones playing inner voices in a mixture of lower-frequency instruments, which are not always distinguishable. To know with assurance what instruments were woven into the center of the music's fabric, these students would have needed the first-hand acquaintance achieved through reading the score. The ability to read scores accurately and fluently is the obvious first step to understanding what a composer has written and how he wishes it to sound. Yet an astonishing number of conductors have avoided taking it.

The following story, told often and with great gusto by Arturo Toscanini, concerns a maestro who was conducting a season of Italian opera in South America. Toscanini, then all of nineteen, played first cello in the orchestra. They were rehearsing Gounod's *Faust*. He noticed that the conductor used only a piano-vocal score, which, as the English would say, is "not done." To test the maestro's knowledge, he decided to double the violin solo in Faust's second act aria ("Salut! demeure chaste et pure") on his instrument an octave lower. The lack of reaction from the conductor proved that he had no knowledge of the instrumentation, so Toscanini kept playing the violin solo at all the rehearsals. At the first performance, however, he switched to the printed cello part. This brought furious glances and hissed remonstrances from the conductor, who by now was used to hearing the solo in octaves and thought that something was amiss. Toscanini described the scene quite dramatically, imitating the furious question of the conductor—"What are you playing?"—and his own reply, delivered with a completely innocent expression, "Maestro, I play my part." In the intermission he was ordered to the conductor's room, where the dialogue continued.

"What were you playing?"

"My part. But in rehearsals I was not playing my part."

Unfortunately the deficiencies of this ill-prepared conductor were not an exception; they reflect current standards of literacy among many would-be professionals. I have often noticed, when borrowing scores from publishers or orches-

---

at the beginning of the third *Leonora* overture (example 12). In every orchestra the strings make the crescendo immediately after arriving at the F-sharp in bar 5, whereas it should not be started until the bassoons enter. The strings here are merely supporting the bassoons, not leading them. A minute error in placement in the printed version has led to a habitual error in playing this and the following measures.

tras, that there are many crutches for poor readers, among whom are some experienced conductors of repute as well as lesser lights. What can be found in scores previously used is often startling. Large penciled letters are used to make a *ritard.* or an *accel.* more easily discernible, cues are underlined, and huge numerals remind the reader that here we must beat four and there eight. And all of this is written in a variety of colors, more closely resembling a map for a myopic boy scout than a score for a fully prepared conductor. For a performance of Szymanowski's Violin Concerto, the publisher's American branch sent me a score so smeared over with pencil marks that little of the printed music could be seen. No eraser availed. I refused to use such a score and had a new copy airmailed from Vienna.

A number of years ago I received from another library a score of the Prokofiev Second Violin Concerto in which the artwork was so original that it would deserve reproduction. If done by a beginner, the doodles would cause a raised eyebrow, even allowing for nerves and inexperience. But this score was decorated by one of the most important conductors in the United States. If one examines his markings with a knowledge of the music, it is even harder to imagine how the performance went. In a 5/4 section too brisk for anything but two unequal beats to the bar, the conductor laboriously beat each quarter note. Furthermore, in dividing the bar he made an error in assuming that the composer had planned a 3 plus 2 configuration, whereas a 2 plus 3 was clearly intended.

It is no mere chance that these two examples are both of concertos. It is evident that solo concertos are not taken as seriously nor studied as thoroughly by conductors as are orchestral works such as symphonies and overtures.[2] From the plethora of visual aids here one must conclude that a concerto by Szymanowski or Prokofiev is first underestimated, then hastily glanced at. Finally, with rehearsals approaching and no time for real learning, the score is wildly marked up with traffic signals, which, combined with reliance on routine, helps some performers to avoid a complete breakdown. One thing is certain: if scores were read carefully and thoroughly, such markings would be unnecessary.

In recent years a new kind of mental crutch has appeared in many a score I have seen. On every page vertical lines are drawn with thick black pencil, extending from the piccolo part straight down through the double-bass line. These lines are like the demarcations of a surveyor, separating in this instance musical periods of varying length. Over each musical parcel is written a figure indicating the number of bars in the period. At other points one finds incomplete multiplications, such as "7 x 3," which indicates to the conductor 21 bars divided into 7 periods of 3. These are *aides-mémoire* for those who memorize scores that would take too long to learn musically.

2. Compared to orchestral works, the standard concertos contain few rehearsal numbers—orientation points where one can restart after having stopped for comment and correction. This suggests that stopping for correction is not the usual procedure. Soloists invariably show surprise when I ask them for two rehearsals, being used to one run-through without much attention to detail.

The diverse symbols added to the printed text of scores remind me of phonetic spellings intended to ease the reading of a Hebrew text for bar mitzvah candidates who are not conversant with the old language but want to make their parents proud. There is a Japanese method of teaching violin playing by rote. There are very famous and great singers (I know some of them personally) who never learned to read music. And there are many people who play the guitar and other instruments "by ear." But if there is one peculiarity that distinguishes the conductor's task from other modes of performance, it is the proven need for fluent literacy.

If I have dwelt on the strange devices to which some conductors are driven by their lack of musical literacy, it has been to demonstrate an inescapable fact that should be self-evident: *The prerequisite to conducting any work well is an intimate knowledge of the score.* When my Berkshire students became aware of their shortcomings, their first question was how they might acquire fluency in reading scores. One way is to learn what to look for in a score and how to interpret what one finds, through a knowledge of the traditions and the cultural milieu in which a composer wrote. This is the subject of most of this book. A knowledge of languages is also important, for reasons that I will explain below. Learning the basic skills of score reading is, however, a subject for another book.

Here I will do no more than suggest that I found it effective to read and play (if one can manage a keyboard) four-part writing in different clefs. The best score to use for such a purpose is Bach's *Art of Fugue*. At least one contrapunctus should be read and, if possible, played every day, and the number increased as proficiency improves. In reading or playing it is of primary importance to set a tempo slow enough that one is not forced into ritards or complete stops in order to decipher what is coming next. Any self-imposed game rules will do, as long as one understands that the even continuity of the reading-playing process is the main concern.

Clefs may at first impose an obstacle, but it is an obstacle worth overcoming. The old clefs are the key to common transpositions in modern scores, and the strict polyphony trains the mind to hear several autonomous voices at the same time.[3] The sensible use of old clefs is as little understood as is the reason behind the transposing of instruments in full scores. In both cases the best range of voice or instrument is made instantly recognizable by the location of notes. The five lines of the staff encompass the natural tessitura of the voice and the central range of the instrument, while the auxiliary lines indicate less comfortable

3. Transpositions for instruments and old clefs are related as follows: If one has mastered the soprano clef, one has thereby absorbed all transpositions of instruments in A the moment when the C clef is replaced by a G clef. By the same token, the mezzo-soprano clef is the F transposition, the alto clef is the D transposition, the tenor clef needs no elaboration, and the baritone clef serves as the G transposition.

pitches. This is the main reason why the unit score in C is objectionable. To most musicians an F on the fifth line of the treble staff spells the first finger on the E string of a violin. It does not convey the impact of the first horn player's high C on the F-horn. When I see the original notation, I feel the force and brilliance in the same way as I do the "Hoi-He" of Siegfried in the third act of *Götterdämmerung*.

For this reason alone I can never feel entirely comfortable with the new Bärenreiter editions of Bach and Mozart, where the old clefs have been eliminated. The use of only G and F clefs for the voices is a regrettable concession to the growing illiteracy of which I speak. When I first had the opportunity to see unit scores, I ascribed my irritation to the inertia that rejects new ideas. Gradually, however, I saw that the reasons for scoring in transposing keys were doubly valid: not only is the visual impact of an instrument's range far stronger when it is written as played, but the communication in rehearsal between conductor and player is ever so much simpler when both see the same note in the same spot. When the score is entirely in C, the English horn part still in F, and the clarinet part in A, there ensues a never-ending chain of misunderstandings as conductor and player discuss corrections or phrasing.

The Need for Languages

Mastering the technique of score reading obviously requires recognition of the symbols peculiar to music—notes, clefs, and a few other curious marks. But scores also contain words. Although most of these words are confined to a small Italian vocabulary familiar to every amateur musician, some scores give more detailed directions for performance, in various languages. It is impossible to follow the composer's wishes in such works without a precise knowledge of what his words mean. No one should need to be told that a conductor cannot direct an opera or choral work without understanding the words. (Knowing only Italian or only German is sufficient for a career in the provincial theaters of Italy or Germany but not for anything else.) Beyond that, however, nothing enhances the understanding of a composer's culture more readily than knowing his language. No translation can ever accomplish all these things.

It should be evident, then, that a conductor is well advised to study several languages, regardless of his origin. Yet an innocence of languages is widespread among musicians. I became aware of this when I first taught at Tanglewood. I went one day to hear what the student orchestra was doing and arrived in the middle of a reading session for the three Nocturnes by Debussy. I stood at the back of the orchestra. When the conductor stopped to make an observation, I asked the trumpet players what they made of the words *un peu rapproché*. They did not know. When I included everyone else in the query, no one knew enough French to give a reply, including the conductor.

"What is so important about that?" some skeptic is sure to ask. Why wouldn't the translation "a little closer" do as well? Because there is a very large body of music printed with French markings that carry associative meaning in the very use of the language. Evidently Debussy preferred a comment like *un peu rapproché* to the conventional *meno pp.* or *un poco più f.* His three words conjure up a synopsis of the entire piece. As we know from the title of the second Nocturne, a festival is going on. During the dancing in the streets, the sound of a parade is heard suddenly from afar. It approaches gradually until, at the climax, an orgiastic crowd of bacchants thunders by. Toward the end the composer regales us with another most telling comment. It is not sufficient to write *pp* and *più pp*; he insists on *et toujours en s'éloignant davantage*, meaning "until the whole magic is lost in the distance" (the essence of the message, not a literal translation).

Of course all of this can be translated by the conductor into the native tongue of the musicians. What is irretrievably lost is the firsthand communication between composer and performer. Translation is as much an interpretation of words as a performance is of notes. There is no guarantee of its faithfulness. If one plays around with the three simple words *un peu rapproché*, one can soon see the possibilities of translation cum interpretation. One possibility is "a trifle closer": one can almost hear the English accent accompanying these words. Others are "a little nearer," "coming a little closer," or "approaching a little"— which is to my taste the best, because it preserves the French *proche* in *approaching*.

These are examples from only one language. If translation is needed by the English-speaking world, it must also be duplicated for the Italian and German, to mention only the most frequently encountered tongues. Then come the Spanish, the Japanese, and so on. It would be far more artistically productive to exhort performers to consider languages as an integral part of their professional equipment and to study them.

What happens instead I found out, once again, by accident. A young singer was scheduled to perform Mahler's *Lieder eines fahrenden Gesellen* with me. She came to a piano rehearsal and most thoughtfully brought me an extra copy of her music to facilitate our working session. When I opened the copy I was taken aback to find printed over the first song the word *allegro* and four bars later, where the voice starts, the word *langsam* ("slowly"). I did not even touch the keys but ran to my shelf, took out the pocket score, and showed the singer what it says there: *Schneller* and *Langsamer*. A world of subtle significance lies behind these two words, and a world of misunderstanding behind the translations, which are not even precise, let alone meaningful. *Fast* and *slow* are definite terms, while *faster* and *slower* refer to an inner mood that determines what we feel as fast or slow; such distinctions exemplify the relativity of time about which Mann writes extensively in *The Magic Mountain*.

The situation at the start of this song cycle is that the young lad of the title has lost his sweetheart, who is getting married. The "doodling" clarinets of the opening bars are surely the village musicians hired to play during the meal. They are gay and merry for the party at the wedding but sad and melancholy for our wayfarer. If a conductor takes the first four bars too fast it may ruin the entire mood that these few notes are setting for the vocal line and the text. The actual mathematical difference between the two sections is not great: here a little more, there a little less. (It is not a linguistic problem that the rhythm in bar 2 differs in the two scores, though it is unfortunate that the vocal edition contains no comment about that difference.)

As to why a translator would replace two comparatives of quite common words with positives, I can only surmise that this is one more case of limited literacy and lack of imagination. The main limitations are a prosaic mind, instead of a poetic one, and a resulting inability to follow the poem's and the music's meaning. This routine approach to making an English edition misses the point of the German words, which, in their vagueness, reflect the uncertainties of a tortured mind. In this case the tortured mind may have been that of the wayfarer or of the composer; the translator's mind was merely insensitive.

Long before the days of Debussy and Mahler the problem of language in composers' directions appeared in the works of Richard Wagner. It was part of his philosophy to replace the customary terms *allegro*, *andante*, and the like with German words. But as soon as it became evident that Wagner's works had international appeal, the publishers printed orchestral parts with the old conventional Italian terms, causing additional problems by dropping the German ones. Aside from all subtler difficulties, this presents the conductor with a technical barrier in rehearsal, since comments in his score, such as *Sehr mässig bewegt*, cannot be located by the musicians if a new start has been announced. Good time is wasted in clearing up unnecessary confusion.

But beyond this, Wagner had his reasons for replacing the common Italian terms. Over the prelude to the second act of *Parsifal* the composer set these words: *Heftig, doch nie übereilt*, which in the translation appears as *Impetuoso ma non troppo allegro*. This is as useful for a student as an approximately cited telephone number. *Heftig* is not *impetuoso*, and *übereilt* is not *allegro*. These attempts to reestablish Italian as an Esperanto for musicians extend even to an American printing of *Orchestral Excerpts* that behaves almost as if the English vernacular did not exist.[4] In dealing with a passage from *Tristan* there must have been great embarrassment: nobody found an Italian word for *merklich*, so an English word, *perceptibly*, entered the exclusive Italo-German club.

These *Orchestral Excerpts* are, in fact, filled with linguistic gaffes. On page

4. Richard Wagner, *Orchestral Excerpts for Violin* (rpt. New York: International Music), pp. 38, 39, 52.

38 violinists will find a passage marked *Allegro, con elevazione*. Ostensibly, *elevazione* is a translation of Wagner's *Steigerung*. Although this word involves the idea of climbing, it does not, in music, imply the alpine variety. Instead it connotes an increase in tempo or in dynamic strength, or both, and it is always intended to produce more tension. Thus, in the context of this passage from *Tristan*, the original *Lebhaft, mit Steigerung* means "with vitality and mounting excitement."[5]

The truth is that Wagner's directives are untranslatable. When he writes *heftig*, he is revealing to the conductor, the musicians, and the baritone the main expressive quality of Klingsor's phrases. When he writes *doch nie übereilt*, he is cautioning that this vehemence (not impetuosity, which is very different) shall not be produced at the expense of the right tempo. A general vigor of expression must not be driven in too high a gear.

Let Wagner himself explain the problems he faced with translation. Speaking of the prelude to *Die Meistersinger* he wrote:

> The main *tempo* of this piece is indicated as "sehr mässig bewegt"; according to the older method, it would have been marked *allegro maestoso*. . . . This moderate 4/4 time can be interpreted in many and various ways; it may . . . express a true animated *Allegro* . . . or it may be . . . made up of two 2/4 beats . . . and assume the character of a lively *Scherzando*; or, it may even be interpreted as *Alla breve* (2/2 time) when it would represent the older, easily-moving *Tempo andante*. . . .[6]

The editor of the orchestral material believed he knew better than Wagner. If one opens the prelude to *Die Meistersinger* in any opera library, there is at the beginning the explicit directive *moderato sempre largamente pesante*, though Wagner preferred to call this *allegro maestoso*, if the conventional terms had to be used. This could cause inestimable confusion. What would happen if anyone really believed that the prelude to *Die Meistersinger* should be *sempre pesante*?

The need to understand the composer's first language is especially strong in music in which romantic ideas prevail. Even the finest translators would need many explanatory words to represent properly the original meaning. Take Wagner's use of *bewegt*, for instance. In *Die Meistersinger* this word has to do mainly with motion, but in *Parsifal*, when Wagner writes *Feierlich bewegt* at the onset of the Good Friday spell, the same word has to do with emotion. For Debussy, Mahler, Wagner, and any other master whose music has tangible association with poetic or pictorial imagery, the tempo indications more closely resemble stage directions than anything else.

---

5. Another error in *Orchestral Excerpts*, most shocking in a volume that aims to be of service as preparatory material, prints this direction one line too high in the violin studies. It should appear over the metrical and other changes six bars later.

6. Richard Wagner, *On Conducting*, trans. Edward Dannreuther (London: William Reeves, 1897), pp. 94–95.

From these short phrases or mottoes it is but a small step to a vaster field: comprehension of the poetry that inspired composers. There is hardly a composer of importance between the seventeenth and the twentieth centuries who does not present us with a body of music set to words. Past that stage of immediate connection comes the inspiration that composers drew from poetry for nonvocal works. Is it not axiomatic that such texts should be known and understood by any musician who aims to lead, correct, or exhort other musicians?

It is not only in opera that a conductor is faced with language problems that require decisions of a well-informed mind. In Bach's *St. Matthew Passion*, Jesus sings the words of Luther's translation. In two key phrases delivered at the Last Supper the final words are *Leib* and *Reich*. The voice ends together with the instruments on a first beat, producing the strong effect that linguists call a masculine ending. In all English-speaking countries, however, the King James version has become standard, and music publishers, such as Novello in Britain, have adapted Bach's melos to suit the words. Thus, the two phrases of Jesus end with the words *body* and *kingdom*, producing a weaker, feminine ending on an unstressed beat. Here a conductor will find a most delicate conflict to resolve: Which is more sacred, Bach's music or the King James text? One of them must give way.[7] Also in Latin masses and requiems decisions on the pronunciation of the language must be made, for there are always several opinions to be reconciled. If the conductor will not or cannot arbitrate, somebody else will surely step forward—and not without inflicting a tiny scratch on the delicate skin of the conductor's authority.

Any work with important poetry in German and French poses grave problems of casting. Most singers have mastered the Italian operatic vocabulary well enough to deliver and even understand what they are singing. This is by no means the case when they have to interpret texts by Goethe, Schiller, Stefan George, Nietzsche, or Baudelaire, or those by Verlaine and Debussy in the *Proses lyriques*. French imposes a nearly insoluble vocal handicap, because its proper pronunciation demands certain nasal sounds that are quite detrimental to good vocal production. German too has some traps, especially for Americans, who have difficulty negotiating the umlaut, expressed by the two dots over a vowel. I have seldom held a rehearsal with chorus or soloist without hearing ö and ü come out like "ay" and "i," which is the earmark of a fine Yiddish enunciation. To hear Goethe in Yiddish may be a rare treat for aficionados of the theater on the Lower East Side of New York, but it is less so for the public attending a Mahler or Schumann performance. Perhaps one reason that choral works are unpopular with American symphony subscribers is that their texts are

7. Even a great composer can show his Achilles' heel, when he, like Schönberg, ventures into the treacherous mine fields of a foreign language without sufficient depth of knowledge. Let any experienced actor recite the words of *Ode to Napoleon* in the composer's rhythmic version, approximating the speed he requires, and the problem will be painfully evident.

mostly unintelligible, written in unfamiliar languages, and sung by people who have learned the pronunciation by rote. Such performances fall far short of the great impact that a well-recited voice part carries. A conductor sensitive to the meaning and sound of languages will be discriminating in casting and will be able to correct lapses that often make the difference between good and bad delivery.

Useful though a knowledge of languages can be to a conductor in dealing with such technical problems, the ultimate reason for acquiring it is to understand the poetry itself and what our great composers took from it. The composer of instrumental works such as the Piano Concerto and *Kreisleriana* also wrote *Frauenliebe und Leben*. A person who cannot appreciate Mignon's "Kennst Du das Land wo die Zitronen blühn" is indeed deprived. The pianist playing Beethoven's Sonata in F-sharp, Opus 78, will play it better if he thinks of Opus 75, *Mignon*, which opens with music so similar that the composer must have still had Mignon on his mind when the sonata was conceived. Poetry will always be one of the best bridges into the land where great music originates.

The reader of poetry will discover a new dimension of musical symbolism through associations traceable in related compositions by the same master. Almost any lied by Schubert, Schumann, or Brahms could serve here as an illustration. Let us consider "Nachtigall" by Brahms, among many beloved songs one of my favorites (example 1). Like other great lieder it is short, thirty-three bars, and contains some obvious symbolism. It starts with the main motive—the sound of the nightingale—in the piano part. Where the words speak of how that sound "penetrates into my marrow and bone," the voice has an octave that, when sung with the right portamento, is bound to have an urgency and drive that can be felt in one's heart like a knife. I use the word *drive* because it would give a singer in search of the exact meaning of *dringet* an onomatopoeic idea of the sound for which to aim.

The subtlest of all the allusions in this piece is in bar 23,[8] where the poem speaks of *verklungenen Tönen*. Literally this means "faded tones," but the phrase is untranslatable, because its cadence retraces the gradual disappearance of an emotion—which often has a way of decaying like the tone. How does the composer express this feeling? There are four notes for these syllables: E, D, D-flat, E-flat. We all are familiar with that oddity of acoustic sensation when a source of sound moves away and there appears to be a flattening of pitch. Here, in the D-flat–E-flat, we have it in the composition itself.

I do not see how such excursions into the inner meaning of a work (and this is only a tiny example) can be made except through a thorough acquaintance with the language of these poems. Similarly, without knowing and reading the

---

8. The bar count used in the examples from classical works corresponds to an edition where the first ending is included in the count. A reader with a different edition may find the bar count off by as many digits as the first ending contains bars.

poems involved, it would be difficult to trace the development of the vocal section of Beethoven's Ninth Symphony. In Schubert's work the connection between lieder and chamber music is staggering. I will have more to say about musical symbolism in my discussion of composition. For now, it should be clear that in order to follow or even to recognize the meaning of musical formulas, knowing the language of the composer is most helpful, whether he be Bach or Ravel. I stress Bach because he used to great effect a series of symbols that were adopted by many composers up through the late nineteenth century.

It is obvious that practitioners of opera—especially in our age when the trend toward cultivation of the languages in which operas were originally written is strong—must know other languages in addition to their own mother tongue. It occurred to me long ago that the great void in the repertoire of most opera houses, the lack of Slavic works, can be attributed to our ignorance of Russian. Many works that are certainly as interesting and as musically sophisticated as *La Gioconda* or *Adriana Lecouvreur* are unknown to the West, mostly because their language is a barrier. There is no point in entering here into a renewed discussion of the long-controversial question as to whether opera should be sung in the vernacular or in the original. This subject has too many side issues to be enlightened by more debate. One factor must be stressed, however: the language used in opera is of great importance to the performers, greater than to the public. The conviction of the performer is strongest when he or she is fully at home with the language. When the words have been learned by rote, the singer's mechanical delivery, recalling recitations at year-end school ceremonies, mars their effect. Somehow the public understands intensity and real meaning, even if the language itself is foreign.

If I ever doubted this truth, it was beautifully confirmed by the film *Die Zauberflöte*, directed by Ingmar Bergman. The Swedish text did not disturb or detract from the original because the actors and singers were in complete identification with it. The antithesis of this success is the current vogue of performing *Boris Godunov* or *Eugen Onegin* in Russian with a cast composed of one or two singers who know the language and all other performers, including the chorus, who have memorized the text phonetically. Caring for diction, controlling and correcting it, always involves the conductor and the stage director, particularly in those works that have librettos by noted poets. Everywhere in the world of opera, companies have to be formed from a multitude of nationalities; hence language barriers and problems plague each one.

On several occasions when I stressed to young conducting aspirants that a broad education was an essential part of their equipment, I encountered not only skepticism but outright challenge as to how anyone could have enough time to acquire a deep acquaintance with a great deal of music and at the same time learn two or three languages. Possibly the reason for such skepticism is the regrettable American idea that education is a strictly pragmatic endeavor that should give the learner what he needs, and nothing more. Even using that nar-

Example 1. Brahms, "Nachtigall," Opus 97, No. 1

was in mir schafft so sü - sse Pein, das ist nicht dein,
das ist von an - - dern, him - mel - schö - nen,
nun längst für mich ver - klun - ge - nen Tö - nen in
dei - nem Lied ein lei - ser Wi - der - hall,
ein lei - ser Wi - - der - hall!

row definition I can assure any doubter that every one of the important conductors I met in my younger years was conversant with several languages and that every one of today's prominent international directors speaks and writes Italian, French, English, and German. To suggest the need for a thorough knowledge of these four languages is not unrealistic. The root of the problems encountered by many conducting candidates is that the entire concept of the conductor's role has been much too narrowly defined. The emphasis is mostly on what one does with hands and arms. But these gestures merely reflect other faculties and abilities, some of which can be taught, though not all.

The Problem of Music Editions

Having emphasized the prime importance to a conductor of acquiring an intimate knowledge of each score, words as well as notes, I must now warn of the snares that lie in wait for those who trust scores uncritically. As every conductor knows, a favorite formula with which instrumentalists and singers justify a questionable performance of some part of a score is "I only play what's printed." I shall have many occasions in this book to show how often this phrase reflects an inadequate knowledge of music and its traditions, rather than the faithfulness to the composer's wishes that it purports to express. Above all, however, this attitude ignores a basic fact: *What is printed is not necessarily what the composer wrote.* In the case of music by contemporary composers who were able to supervise the printing of their own works, one may assume that the scores are relatively accurate. The works of earlier composers, on the other hand, are performed from editions that may be removed by several stages from the composers' holographs. Let us consider what those stages may have been.

To begin with, the manuscripts themselves may have been nearly illegible, even inaccurate. Very busy masters, like Mozart and Haydn, often wrote at a rapid rate, using their own peculiar shorthand. Since they personally supervised rehearsal and performance, they could trust the players to read some abbreviations. But what happened when these sketchy scores were turned over to copyists? Copyright laws did not exist, and composers were quite without protection. They had to be very cautious when letting new works out of their sight. Mozart, we know, distributed his scores among several copyists, lest any one of them, possessing a complete score, sell it as his own. Thus, we should not be surprised if some of these scores, though made by professional copyists, were hurried and contained errors. As for the next stage, anyone familiar with the lengthy and laborious processes of engraving, printing, and publishing a piece, whether a simple letter to a newspaper or an intricate score with dozens of staves, knows what unforeseeable and often uncontrollable changes and mishaps can occur.

Because the earliest printed scores and even the manuscript copies of classical works contain ambiguities and downright errors, the modern editor who undertakes to establish a definitive edition faces many problems. Many modern editions are impressive works of scholarship, yet none is perfect. Scores are edited and printed by fallible human beings, not handed down on tablets of stone from Sinai. Editors are generally musicologists rather than performing musicians. In their preoccupation with documentary evidence they occasionally fail to consider how the music sounds. The examples of printed errors that follow simply demonstrate that responsibility for musical thought must not be shifted onto the shoulders of editors and publishers, with the bland assurance "I play what's printed." A conductor must learn to rely on his own critical intelligence in reading scores, not on the interpretations of scholars or other conductors.

In 1975 I was invited to be a part of a panel of four musical "experts." A recording of four unidentified interpretations was played for us to discuss and evaluate. The selection was the first movement of Mozart's Symphony in A, K. 201. After the music had been heard, my three fellow-panelists critically discussed the interpretations. I said nothing, feeling it inappropriate to participate in a critique on performances of a work that I myself had recorded years earlier. But when the erudition became too intense I mentioned my astonishment that nobody had noticed that version number three had recorded a bad printing error in the score. I found it impossible, with reference copies of the music in our hands, to make the three experts see the mistake in the score. Even after I pinpointed the two bars at issue, my neighbor on the right pushed his score at me with the comment that mine was an old edition and that I surely would find everything in order in Bärenreiter, the "last word" in Mozart scholarship.

From the drift of the discussion that followed, I had to assume that knowledge of the complete work was not part of the panelists' credentials. It is perhaps asking too much of three nonperformers to know both exposition and recapitulation of a Mozart symphony, but it is surely astonishing that a conductor eminent enough to be considered a Mozart "specialist" had included in his recording an error that required only a very simple correction. The bass note in bar 36 (example 2A) must be moved from the third to the fourth quarter. The correct version occurs 100 bars later (example 2B). It may be asked how we can be sure that bar 36 is in error and not bar 142. The answer is that if the bass note is played on the third quarter, the resulting interval is a tritone, a most unlikely occurrence even in Mozart's most daring moments. On encountering a Mozart symphony in which only one detail amid an otherwise identical pattern of recapitulation is different, it is not only permissible but mandatory to make the necessary adjustment.

Another type of error, fortunately of no particular importance to the performance level of the work, occurs when the main theme of the prelude to *Die Meistersinger* is quoted in act 2. The second half of bar 5 shows a harmony that is the first inversion of a seventh chord on the seventh step of C major. In all reappearances of this passage in the opera, the harmonization of this chord is the same, except in act 2, during the scene where Walther tells Eva of his adventures that morning in trying to qualify as a participant in the song contest. When he

Example 2A. Mozart, Sym. in A Flat, K. 201, 1st mvt., mm. 32–38

Example 2B. Mozart, Sym. in A Flat, K. 201, 1st mvt., mm. 138–44

quotes her father's words, the theme of the prelude is heard in light orchestration but is unchanged harmonically—or so I thought. One day, while browsing through a newly acquired, excellent piano-vocal score of *Die Meistersinger*, I played this scene. Suddenly I encountered an inverted ninth chord that I had never noticed before. To the four original notes of the prelude a fifth, G, had been added.

An apparent discrepancy such as this should be checked in the full score. Upon doing so I found that the fourth horn had a G in a transposing configuration, which means a printed E-flat on an instrument in E. Two other editions of the full score had it this way, too. This did not make sense, so I decided to explore the problem further. The facsimile of Wagner's autograph is easily obtainable. When I located a copy I turned quickly to the page where the questionable passage appears. What I found was not much of a surprise. In transcribing Wagner's manuscript, the copyist had misread one single note. In the fourth horn part, Wagner had made the loop ever so slightly higher than it should have been, making it appear as an E-flat to the copyist, whereas the note was intended as a D-flat. In actual sound, the D-flat would have been the usual F belonging to that chord. The lesson to be learned here is that whenever something found in the score of a great work does not make sense, one should pursue one's investigation to the earliest known source, if need be, the composer rarely having erred.

In these and some other cases there is more than one proof of error. The two

Example 3. Haydn, Sym. No. 96, 1st mvt., mm. 12–17

Example 4. Haydn, Sym. No. 96, 1st mvt., mm. 98–102

clues in the Mozart symphony have already been identified. In the Wagner example, the note G creates a chord not found before or afterward in the same
context. As a second proof of error, the third and fourth horns suddenly produce
the interval of a seventh in an otherwise unbroken line of octaves.

There are some much-touted "last-word" editions of Haydn that are accompanied by reams of learned notes; yet in the score of one of this master's greatest
London symphonies, No. 96, many egregious errors have been left standing
without a word from the editor.[9] In example 3 note how the bassoon and the
violas move in octaves in bars 12–17. If any doubt remains after bars 12 and 13,
we are convinced that this printing could not have been the composer's doing by
the time the bassoon crosses over the first violins. In example 4, bars 98–101,

9. H. C. Robbins Landon, ed., *Joseph Haydn: Critical Edition of the Complete Symphonies*, vol.
11 (Vienna: Universal Edition, 1966).

Example 5. Haydn, Sym. No. 96, 2nd mvt., mm. 78–79

why would the violas, in bar 100, play the G between the cellos and basses
instead of playing higher? As in practically all classical scoring, the basses and
cellos here form the fundament of the work. To assume that Haydn would suddenly, without any reason whatever, thrust the middle voice into the midst of the
bass voices implies either dotage or ignorance. In the second movement one
could find fault with nearly every passage where bassoons are involved, as in
bar 30, where the low D of the bassoon is out of place below the double basses.
Bar 78 (example 5) intrigues me even more. In this woodwind trio, flute and
two oboes play a sequence of harmonies for one and a half measures. This is
duplicated in a lower octave by the two violins and viola, except that the viola
plays in the same octave as the second oboe. Surely this was not intended by
the composer. In bars 41–46 in the third movement, the violas are consistently
in the octave above the bassoons and the cellos and, worse still, they hover like
mosquitoes around the violins, sometimes below, sometimes above, just close
enough to blur any lucid voice leading.

  What good is the beelike industry of the editor, who has compared so many
early copies and has so diligently listed in his report what comes from where, if
he does not deal with these far more important matters? We should question the
copyist, the first publisher, and the editor, but we should never imagine that

Haydn, or even a merely competent composer, would be sloppy about so basic a practice as voice leading.

As an indispensable part of his professional equipment, a conductor must study composition. Moreover, he must not seek out as his teacher some innovator who believes that the three great disciplines—harmony, counterpoint, and form—are dead. He must find an expert who will insist on a curriculum of choral harmonization. He must expect to have his work searchingly read and, where needed, corrected by an instructor to whom parallel fifths and octaves are anathema, as they were to the classical masters. The purpose of such practice is not to make the young conductor an original composer, but rather to give him enough technique in those three disciplines to recognize the difference between good and bad voice leading. Then he will be able to throw away the *Revisionsberichte* of the scholars. The conductor with proper musical training of his own need not consider the score a final authority, however scholarly the editing, if it conflicts with sound musical sense.

Two
Knowing the Composer

How to Understand the Composer's Art

If facility at score reading is a basic skill, then a knowledge of composers and their art is surely essential for anyone who wishes to perform their music faithfully. But this knowledge is far more elusive than is the straightforward mental discipline of reading music. Little is known about composers and about the act of composition. Most people outside the strictly professional world of music know nothing whatsoever about the way a musical score is produced, though they know a good deal about the working habits of painters and writers. There is no parallel in music composition to the person seen in a park or museum, on a campstool, with palette in one hand, brush in the other, and easel with canvas facing him. Most of us have produced drawings of our own, if only with crayons in elementary school. And all of us have written essays or other papers. But the average person has not had the comparable experience of composing music to stimulate his imagination.

Most people find it hard to believe, for example, that the majority of composers worked without a keyboard or other instrument. (Notable exceptions are Stravinsky and Wagner.) Yet for musicians it is of foremost significance that the process of writing music need not involve an instrument. Nor does the study of music by an interpreter. That the instrumentalist and the singer must "practice" on their instruments has bearing only on the training of the muscles involved in playing or singing, not on the process of learning the music. There are still musicians who sit at a desk or in a park, learning their score by reading it.

It is hardly necessary to say that popular operettas and films have done nothing to enhance our understanding of composers. Schubert, Mahler, Tchaikovsky, Schumann, and others have been so ludicrously depicted on stage and screen that one despairs of ever setting popular misconceptions aright. The fanciers of *Blossom Time* (called *Dreimäderlhaus* in culture-conscious Central Europe) are acquainted with a sentimental tenor rather than with the highly sophisticated and

20

complex Franz Schubert. One hundred fifty years after the composer's death, sketches are still being unearthed that show the labors he invested. The real Schubert did not dash to a linden tree and carve an immortal song into the bark so that an accidentally present chorus could sing it while an enthralled, blond-braided maiden dropped the steins of beer she was serving in order to embrace the darling composer. But of course no one turns to popular writers for real insight into the nature of composition.

What then can the serious biographers of musicians tell us? A good many facts of greater or lesser interest about their daily lives—the course of their careers; anecdotes of their dealings with their families, other musicians, and the public; a few useful tidbits about their working habits—but very little about the creative process. Many biographers are well grounded in music, but the temptation this field holds for the dilettante seems peculiarly powerful. In 1972, after performances of Mahler's *Das Klagende Lied*, I met a man who was then at work on a biography of the composer. He wanted a recording of the unpublished first portion, "Waldmärchen," which I could not provide. I offered him my score and the piano-vocal arrangement of that section to help him with his work. He refused with the comment, made without blushing, that he could use only records, because he was unable to read scores. I asked myself what a professional could possibly learn about the music of Mahler from a biographer who needed someone else's interpretation to know what was going on in a composition.

Poor Mahler seems to exert a special magnetism for the dilettante. In New York I once found myself in a private home listening to a talk on Mahler's death motive, given by a psychiatrist to a group of his peers—and myself—using phonograph records to support his claims. For ninety minutes we listened to a series of obvious and unoriginal conclusions that any person familiar with the outlines of Mahler's life and personality might arrive at. It was from what the doctor did *not* say that I gathered how little he knew. If one speaks of death, it is quite extraordinary to overlook the ending of *Das Lied von der Erde*. The unresolved chord accompanying the words "Ewig, Ewig" expresses a most desperate longing to come to terms with eternity. This conclusion is as moving, though in a different sense, as the "love-death" of Isolde or the last movement of the *German Requiem*. To end a work without a resolution, leaving everything to unending time, was an original invention never mentioned by the learned doctor.

Even more within the realm of psychological association is an omission in the second part of the Eighth Symphony, which has as its text the concluding scene of Goethe's *Faust*. The composer ostensibly planned to set the entire scene of 267 verses to music. He skipped a block of thirty-six lines that starts with those of Pater Seraphicus, who never appears in the symphony. This cannot have been an oversight or the fault of a poor edition (though there are also bad editions of Goethe), nor is it likely that Mahler shortened anything to avoid longueurs. The words of Pater Seraphicus tell the story: "Knaben, Mitternachts-Geborne" refers to a belief, first recorded in 1551 and known to Goethe, that children who die unbaptized soon after birth are relatively free of sin, except for the general condition of human guilt. They have not been subjected to the corruption of living and hold a middle position between mortals and angels. They are *selige Knaben* ("blessed boys"). It does not take much psychological training to understand why Mahler would wish to avoid reference in his composition to dead children. He had composed *Kindertotenlieder* before tragedy struck his family. The anxiety aroused by considering this work a self-made omen of dreadful events would explain the composer's horror of dealing again with such a motive. Thus, the thirty-six missing lines reveal a tragically moving story.

I am quite certain that the doctor and his guests would have agreed with the conclusions I suggest, so the doctor's failure to mention such an important fact lay simply in his ignorance of the full text. He had his phonograph and had surely heard the Eighth Symphony. Even if he had read the score, however, only the words sung would have been printed there. To spot the missing lines one has to read Goethe and ask oneself why these verses were omitted from the score. That presupposes a reading in depth that is too uncommon in our world of music. It should be reestablished, at least by conductors who want to understand the composer.

The Composer's Mind

It would be foolish to blame biographers for failing to illuminate a process so complex and mysterious as the act of composition. Yet, even without hope of fully comprehending it, a serious performer must never tire of the attempt to reach understanding through his own musical intelligence. It is my personal conviction that great music is made of a fusion of grace with intellect. I use the term *grace* in much the same sense as do Catholic believers when they say that a person is in a state of grace. Composers who left works of vastly diverse quality seem to allow us no other explanation than that they were in a state of grace when writing one work and not in a state of grace when writing another. Toscanini, speaking of musicians, used to say, "Nobody is a genius twenty-four hours of the day." The same inconsistency is found in composition. Even the greatest composers have produced uninspired works now and then. Lesser artists, most of whose work remains earthbound however masterly their technique, have occasionally transcended their limitations. A very few others, like Moussorgsky and Bruckner, show unmistakable genius in spite of never having fully mastered the craft of composition. It is necessary, then, to distinguish between craft and the inspiration that gives wings to the written symbols.

This grace, or inspiration, cannot be explained; it can only be marveled at. Intellect too can be marveled at, but its workings can be closely traced through a careful study of a composer's music—a task that richly repays the effort. There are many people, even among serious musicians, who believe that composition is possible without great intellectual power. It is unfortunate that intellect has been made into an antipode of the emotion and inspiration necessary to create great works. Inspiration and intellect are not incompatible; they must complement each other if a composition is to be a masterpiece. We can feel awe at the unfathomable and at the same time recognize the importance of conscious thought and effort. Perhaps the emphasis on systems of composition, so much publicized since atonality, polytonality, dodecaphony, aleatory music, and the like came into being, has created the impression that intellectual concepts have recently appeared in music for the first time. Quite the contrary is true.

For a conductor to study the operation of a composer's intellect through his music is no mere exercise in piety. The regular application of a conductor's own intellect to the problems of music, from a fresh and unbiased perspective, is crucially important. Music has too long suffered from inertia. In human affairs, as in physics, inertia can be overcome only by energy. A concentration of intellectual energy is desperately needed to counteract our uncritical reliance on accumulated beliefs and customs, many of which are based on fallacies. For example, we are told that Beethoven was too deaf to mark valid metronome figures, yet no one bothers to ask why the first notes of his Fifth Symphony are often mistakenly made to sound like the hooves of a buffalo herd. There is also an unwritten assumption that in revised works the version that came last is ipso facto the best. There are literally hundreds of such clichés and standard answers that require reevaluation. Every generation must consider anew the issues and ideas it has inherited, including those of music and the other arts. It behooves young conductors, then, to devote their highest mental abilities to investigating precisely how the great composers applied their minds to solving musical problems. I will try, through a few examples, to demonstrate how this may be done.

There are several approaches by which one can enter into the mental processes of a composer. One is through representational music, in which words make explicit the ideas that the composer has tried to express in his music. Striking examples of this can be found in Bach's B-minor Mass.

The "Crucifixus" of the Mass is written in the form of a passacaglia. The bass, a four-bar descending line of halftone steps, is repeated thirteen times. Can we doubt that Bach chose this number to represent Jesus and the twelve disciples, one of whom had betrayed him? Playing with numbers was a common practice long before Bach's day. There is no dearth of such examples, especially in sacred music, where many numerals have firmly established meanings. That the "Crucifixus" is among the most deeply moving and stirring pieces in all of music is due to Bach's genius. The thirteenth and final sequence of the basso ostinato gives us a chromatic figure in the voices that may seem nothing less than the image of laying the body into the earth. At the same time, the people singing, now without the instruments that were present in the preceding parts of the piece, appear to be so totally desolate over what is before them that, in the short space of four bars, a narrative is turned into a deeply personal outpouring of emotion. This transformation represents the lowering of the body into the ground and at the same time causes our hearts to sink in our breasts. This is a classic case in which an intellectual concept is transformed by genius into a transcendental experience.

A few pages before the "Crucifixus" comes a duet for soprano and alto to the words "Et in unum Dominum Jesum Christum." The first entrance of violins, foreshadowing the same play of the two voices, is set in canonic form. In the first bar the canon is in unison, making it appear as if one voice steps out of the other when the parts separate, just as in a film we may see a person stepping out of his own image to stand before us in two identical versions (example 6). Here in the unison measure the unity of Father and Son is made manifest. After estab-

Example 6. Bach, B-Minor Mass No. 14, mm. 9–11

Example 7. Bach, B-Minor Mass No. 14, mm. 59–61 (Eulenburg)

lishing this in the shortest possible time, the composer leads the continuation at an interval of a fourth. Thus he represents the two persons and, at the same time, allows for different voice ranges and a perfect canon.

In bar 59 (example 7) something new and startling happens. From the A above the treble stave the string instruments descend in a seventh-chord passage of twelve notes to the low G on the first stave of the F clef, a traversal of more than three octaves. This is particularly striking because the intervals in the rest of the piece are for the most part smaller, and nothing else is as pointed as this descent. There is no doubt that the music is meant to represent the words "descendit de coelis." But where are these words? Still eight measures away, which in this piece is quite a long distance. When I first noticed this curious displacement I had more confidence in the composer than to believe that it resulted from an error or oversight on his part. I turned to the appendix of the Breitkopf and

Example 8. Bach, B-Minor Mass No. 14, mm. 59–61 (Bärenreiter)

Härtel score. There I found, to my joy, that in another version of the duet the voices sing in bar 60 "descendit de coelis," after the descent of the strings has been heard long enough to make its meaning clear.

Why then is the version that places the words where Bach evidently had them in the first place merely an appendix? Turning to the Bärenreiter Bach edition, I found that there the two versions were reversed. What Breitkopf and Härtel considered the appendix was presented as the main text (example 8), while the other version was relegated to the status of a "variant." What can we make of this? The version presented in the Bärenreiter score appears to have been the earlier of the two, because it contains the words "Et incarnatus est," which later became a separate piece. It seems to me that a conductor is here faced with the task of making a new sequence combining the essential features of the two versions.[1]

The question naturally arises as to why Bach made this change. A conductor's reading must be broadly based to solve, or even to recognize, the curious puzzles that present him with some of his greatest difficulties. This example alone demonstrates that whenever two versions of a piece exist, it is essential for the conductor to digest both of them. Here the differences are easily discerned: the text and the sense of the symbolic musical passage fit together in one version and not in the other. A clue is the oddity of having in the Bärenreiter version two separate ideas—"Et in unum Dominum" and "Et incarnatus est"—in one movement, whereas in most masses they are separate pieces; and, because of the central significance of these words, the two pieces would be especially important ones. One need only recall the masses by Haydn, the Mass in C minor by Mozart, and the *Missa Solemnis* of Beethoven to realize how deeply composers felt the meaning of incarnation. This must be the reason Bach discarded the words from the duet and wrote a new piece. I surmise that in the probable haste of rewriting the text of the duet the "descendit de coelis" was dislocated from its foreordained place.

Another striking example of how composers represent dramatic ideas musically can be found in Mozart's *Così fan tutte*. It came to my attention this way: For its final night in the old Metropolitan Opera House, the company planned a gala farewell concert in which every available member of the Met, past and present, was asked to take part. I was invited to conduct the terzettino "Soave sia il vento" from *Così*, a farewell sung by the sisters, Fiordiligi and Dorabella, and Don Alfonso to the two gentlemen who have departed by boat, presumably to perform heroic deeds. Nine years had passed since I last conducted the opera, so to refresh my memory I borrowed a score from the library. My habit is to look at a well-known piece after a lapse of time as if I had never seen it before. I started by examining the orchestration, since Mozart used different instrumentation in different parts of his operas. On the first page of the terzettino, aside from the strings, only clarinets and bassoons support the voice parts. I said to myself, "I wonder where the flutes and horns come in?"

Turning the page I saw that they entered only to join in a harmony of wicked strangeness and dissonance. It was clear at once why the composer had reserved these instruments. At just this point the voices sing the word *desir*, which in the dramatic context means, "Please return our lovers to satisfy our desires." Quite

1. The commentary that was issued together with Bärenreiter's 1954 edition of the Bach B-minor Mass does, in fact, discuss this problem clearly. See the critical commentary by Friedrich Smend, *Johann Sebastian Bach: Neue Ausgabe Sämtlicher Werke* (Kassel: Bärenreiter Verlag, 1956), pp. 152ff.

obviously, however, these desires cannot be fulfilled for some time to come. The harmony yearns for fulfillment in a resolution, but instead we find in the next chord another dissonance. Thus we are told in no uncertain terms that the *desir* is far from fulfillment.

Musicians commonly exclaim in wonder when such "modern" harmonies turn up in Mozart, as they are wont to do. But their wonder seldom engenders more than admiration; many fail to realize the profound depth of psychological perception and sheer invention that every such moment represents. If we are astonished today, what must have been the effect in 1787?

There is always danger that the overheated imagination of a score-studying musician will find more in a score than the composer put there. But in fact we can usually find more evidence of genius in great music the more we search. Although the discoveries a diligent conductor makes may pass by audiences unnoticed in performance, they inevitably deepen his understanding. Moreover, the satisfactions of the search make his lot an enviable one.

A second useful approach to understanding a composer's intellectual processes is to study the ways in which he learned from earlier composers. Before we begin, however, it is necessary for us to realize that the currently popular notion that originality is a sine qua non of creativity was not shared in the days of Bach or Beethoven. In order to see this idea in historical perspective we need only recall that very few of Shakespeare's works could measure up to the standard of novelty that we demand of an original screenplay. This comparison should aid us in determining where creativity really lies. Shakespeare's practice of reworking familiar plays or episodes is very similar to what Bach did in his pieces after Vivaldi. The large works of the Viennese classical composers made widespread use of what might be called nuclear themes. In many cases it appears that these themes were similar to the topics instructors assign to students in writing classes, asking them to develop their themes in three thousand words. A musical theme might be treated in ever so many ways, according to the creative fancy and ability of the individual who used it.

That contemporary notions of originality are so much more restrictive may be due in part to the musical poverty of popular composers, whose total contribution can be a tune picked out on a keyboard with one finger. These tunes may deserve their enormous popularity, but they distort our concept of what constitutes creativity. The relative importance of the "tune" and its treatment was put into perspective in the volumes of Beethoven's *Variations*. There one finds the names of Mozart, Diabelli, Righini, Dressler, Dittersdorf, Haibel, Süssmayr, Paisiello, Salieri, Winter, Wranitzky, and others. Except for the first-named, how many would be known today if later and greater composers had not immortalized them?

A remarkable, though not surprising, phenomenon is the appeal that works of Bach held for composers of the Romantic era. Of the many examples of his influence I will mention only a few. Schumann wrote piano accompaniments to Bach's solo partitas. (That this was a musical misconception does not invalidate my point.) Gounod did exactly the opposite when he floated his familiar "Ave Maria" over the harmonic foundation of a Bach prelude. Brahms made piano arrangements of Bach's violin works. Moreover, as I will show later, he often adopted the symbolic musical formulas that Bach had, in many cases, absorbed from his own musical heritage. In fact, we need only turn to the opening of "Et resurrexit tertia die" of his B-Minor Mass to find formulas that persisted throughout the nineteenth century. Beethoven borrowed from both Bach and Mozart in a way that shows an intimate acquaintance with their works. It would be absurd, of course, to regard these borrowings as plagiarism. This was merely a way to give a quotation from an admired work a new dimension of meaning in the context of one's own composition.

A great work does not exist in splendid isolation. It is the result of a composer's development and of music's continuing history. Later works are syntheses, refined products of earlier ones. The whole of Beethoven's music would be different without the event of Mozart; the works of Brahms and Wagner would not be as we know them without the event of Beethoven. A notable break with the past occurred as a result of World War I, which seems to have caused as much upheaval in the world of music as it did in the world of affairs. For example, the careers of Richard Strauss, Arnold Schönberg, and Igor Stravinsky changed dramatically at that time. Strauss withdrew into a cocoon of the past, while the others broke radically with their past to explore new avenues. Up to that historic watershed, great composers always summed up the achievements of their predecessors by creating their own singular accomplishments, as it were, crowning the past. One has only to follow Wagner's development from *Rienzi* (or his two earlier works) to the *Ring* tetralogy to realize that he represents the end of an era. If more evidence is needed, consider those who tried to pattern their compositions after Wagner's. Not one true follower survived.

In Bach's day the prevailing system was to use the same music for more than one text. In literature and drama, as well as in painting, the same subject matter can validly be treated by many writers and artists. The story of Joan of Arc can be dramatized by Schiller, Shaw, Anouilh, and others without eliciting any question of plagiarism. The same principle once held true for music. That it no longer does can be seen from the disappearance of the variation form. This form was almost always present in the great classical works, even as late as Brahms. But the devising of variations, particularly over a theme by another composer, is no longer the main artery of musical creativity. It seems to me that the chief obstacle to the wide acceptance of the works of Arnold Schönberg is that, in the guise of very "modern" sounds, they are totally classical in form, always based on variation.

For the performer who approaches the repertoire of great works, it is of utmost importance to look for the connections both within a composer's total oeuvre and with the works of other masters. Merely spotting a theme that has been used before is of little interest. Stravinsky is a splendid throwback to earlier centuries; he hardly ever "invented" motives or melodies. Yet he demonstrated his originality, and indeed his genius, in the way he developed what he borrowed from Russian folk music and from other composers. By the same token, spotting in Mozart's *Les Petits Riens* the opening theme of Beethoven's *Eroica* Symphony is insignificant, since the theme does not make that symphony great any more than Schubert's lied "Der Tod und das Mädchen" does his string quartet of that name. The triad that opens the first movement of the *Eroica* could have been written by anyone, but who else could have composed such a gigantic, epoch-making work? A student will gain a better comprehension of the background and precursors of this work by comparing it with Mozart's Symphony in E-flat, K.543. Despite the lack of thematic or melodic resemblance, the earlier work must have been used as a model by Beethoven. The points of departure in both works are too much alike to be attributed to coincidence. E-flat is the key for both. The main section of the sonata movement in both pieces is in 3/4; the slow movement is in 4/8 (or 2/4); the third movement is here a minuet, there a scherzo, but in both cases wind instruments are playfully featured in the trio; and, to no one's surprise, the finale in both works is in 2/4.

Beethoven treated the themes of the final movement three times before introducing them into his great symphony: in a dance; in the finale of the ballet Opus 43; and in an essay in variation form for piano, Opus 35. It is of course indispensable for any would-be conductor of the *Eroica* to have an intimate acquaintance with these variations; but a little further off the main road lies another path to the *Eroica*, specifically to the slow movement. Just before the *"Eroica* Variations" for piano, Beethoven wrote Opus 34, another set of six variations, a piece not much played in public, yet one of considerable importance. The fifth variation is in C minor and is called "Marcia." It lacks the profundity that we find in Opus 55, but it is one of the slender tributary streams that ultimately flowed down to the sea of the *Eroica*. Opus 34 has an unorthodox sequence of tonalities, with each variation in a different key. The theme and the sixth variation are in F, and the sections in between are in D, B-flat, G, E-flat, and C minor, respectively.

Brahms had a special affinity for descending thirds, whether in key relationships or in actual thematic material. If we transpose the sequence of keys in Beethoven's Opus 34—F–D–B-flat–G–E-flat–C—one whole tone down, we get the theme of the slow movement from Brahms's Piano Sonata in F Minor, Opus 5. Brahms uses this theme of descending thirds at diverse points and invariably when a deeply reminiscent meaning is the message of the music.

Among my favorite discoveries is the origin of Klärchen's second lied in Beethoven's music to Goethe's drama *Egmont*. The poem opens with the lines,

Example 9. Beethoven, *Egmont* No. 4, mm. 1–9

Example 10. Mozart, Quintet K. 516, Adagio, mm. 1–8

"Freudvoll und leidvoll, gedankenvoll sein" (Joyful, sorrowful, or thoughtful to be . . ."), the setting of which is harmonically and melodically an exact quotation of the slow movement from Mozart's Quintet K. 516 (examples 9 and 10). If such a total resemblance occurred today, our views of property rights over original invention would produce at least raised eyebrows, if not a lawsuit for damages by the earlier composer. I see in this adoption the most beautiful of tributes, as well as an example of true inspiration. My joy at having found this connection is not the satisfaction of the sleuth, but rather comes from a keener understanding of what Beethoven heard in K. 516. How wonderful for five string players to start rehearsing Mozart's quintet with an awareness of what it meant to Beethoven. The sound and setting of the adagio's opening in the Mozart work surely reappears also as the introduction of the first movement in Beethoven's late Quartet Opus 127. The connection goes farther. In bars 5–8 of K. 516 there first appears a four-note motive which is woven throughout the instrumentation. That same motive plays a major role, accompanying and pulsating, in Beethoven's Sonata Opus 106 (slow movement).

In musical history classes we learn that Beethoven disapproved of the levity in Mozart's opera librettos. What we do not learn—and what would improve our understanding of musical history—is the evidence of how closely Beethoven studied Mozart, including the Mozart operas he "disapproved" of. It can hardly be a coincidence that Fiordiligi's second aria in *Così fan tutte* is in E major and features two obbligato horn parts of bravura writing, when E major is the key of Leonore's great aria, which has an accompaniment of three difficult and brilliant horn parts. That *Così fan tutte* impressed Beethoven can also be conclusively determined from the first five vocal numbers of the opera, which have exactly the same key relationships as the Variations Opus 34, with the difference that in *Così* the progression goes from G to E to C to A to F minor, while Opus 34 goes one third farther. This progression in thirds is then a link from Mozart via Beethoven to Brahms. Another rather odd link connects *Così fan tutte* with Beethoven and Brahms, with an extra stop chez Schubert. In the second finale of *Così*, when the two couples sit down for their wedding celebration, a beautiful eight-bar melody is sung in canon by three of the four voices. It is in A-flat major and closes with an enharmonic transition, startling for 1787, in which the A-flat of the bass becomes G-sharp for an E-major passage announcing the appearance of Despina, the maid, disguised as a notary.

In Beethoven's Quartet Opus 127, the second movement, variations in the key of A-flat, contains a center piece in E major that starts on an identical enharmonic basis, returning via the same route to A-flat. Was Brahms giving an admiring nod when in his First Symphony he chose to follow a slow movement in E major by an intermezzo in A-flat? I always feel that the final G-sharp of the solo violin should be followed without much pause by the opening of the next movement. Toward the close of the second movement of the *Unfinished* Symphony Schubert too chose to use the relationship of E major and A-flat to demonstrate his preference for that same enharmonic play. The keys with four flats or sharps, A-flat major and E major, were not frequently used in orchestral music of the time. Their rarity makes their appearance an event in itself, and this enharmonic combination reveals much about the interconnections in the work of the great masters. That Beethoven and Schubert liked the A-flat and E keys is quite evident in the piano music. The mood and color of C-sharp minor

in the *Moonlight* Sonata returns in otherwise totally original form in the B-flat
Sonata of Schubert, as its slow movement. A-flat appears so often in the course
of Beethoven's thirty-two sonatas that its rarity in his orchestral works must
have been due to technical shortcomings of his musical forces. Only in the Fifth
Symphony did he give in to his fondness for this mellow and warm tonality. In
all likelihood the tutti players of that era were only trusted into A and E-flat—
the three-accidental keys with their parallel minors. It was due to the expanded
technical resources of wind instruments that the keys with four and five flats
became favorites of Wagner and Bruckner and all the later orchestral masters.

Connections and affinities embrace the music of many generations. Bruckner,
in the slow movement of his Eighth Symphony—surely one of the finest of his
many moving adagios—pays special homage to two musical ancestors without
any loss of originality. The basic pulse of the first theme's accompaniment resembles that of the love duet from the second act of *Tristan*, "Oh sink hernieder
Nacht der Liebe," while the choice of the key of D-flat is surely a link to Beethoven's last quartet, Opus 135. That Bruckner tried to emulate Beethoven is
evident from several characteristic choices. Many of his openings, most certainly those of the Third and Ninth symphonies, were composed under the very
long shadow of Beethoven's Ninth. The slow movement of Bruckner's Seventh
Symphony is patterned after that of Beethoven's Ninth. What is missing is Beethoven's art of variation. As interpreters, we should try to absorb fully all the
connections, as well as the radical differences, between works. If that kind of
understanding is achieved, one will not perform the Ninth of Beethoven as if it
were written by Bruckner. In the heavenly lilt of the second subject (in 3/4),
Bruckner comes as close to Beethoven as anyone ever has. In the first subject,
however, there is no way to conceal what the younger master lacks. The themes
of the 3/4 portions are played twice, in both symphonies, between the three
appearances of the principal sections. Since this 3/4 melody is not subject to
variation, the heavenly Bruckner melody makes its impact and disappears, exactly like the melody in Beethoven's adagio. But the principal subjects are totally different: in Beethoven we have a moving melody with the potential of
variation, while in Bruckner we find a great theme of such keen harmonic bent
that in its self-sufficiency no variation can possibly be derived from it. As a
result of this thematic construction, the best we get is the grafting on of figura-
tions that merely avoid a problem that cannot be solved.

The conductor of symphonic repertoire will find that many of the popular and
successful works in the second half of the nineteenth century replace variation
by simple unvaried repetition. It is inappropriate to sneer at Tchaikovsky and
Dvořák; their impact lies in their melodic and emotional messages, just as
Bruckner's lies in his harmonic and melodic singularity.

With the death of Beethoven one mode of composition ended. There is the
unique case of Brahms, who was to Beethoven what Thomas Mann wanted to

be to Goethe—with the musician achieving more success than the novelist. Wagner recognized that Beethoven represented the end of a long road; fully conscious of the singular apex reached by the Ninth Symphony and the last quartets and sonatas, he traveled other avenues. Yet he too could not escape Beethoven's long shadow for some time. The opening of *Der fliegende Holländer* is another case of the Ninth reincarnated. Fifty-seven years later the gigantic shadow of Wagner helped produce *Gurrelieder* by Arnold Schönberg, whose sextet *Verklärte Nacht* still reflects the Ninth somewhere near the surface. Schönberg, as masterful a composer as there ever was, recognized as fully as did Wagner that his predecessor had put a definitive end to a certain kind of music; and, like Wagner, Schönberg chose a different road. That he did not become the third of the great finalists is part of that unanswered question, What is genius? For our purposes it is important only to recognize the continuity of music, which is comparable to legacies handed down in families from generation to generation.

For us the fountainhead of this great stream is J. S. Bach, who used expressive musical symbols that tell us more about nineteenth-century music than we would guess without knowing Bach's ways. These symbols are still valid two hundred ninety-five years after his birth. It is rewarding and revealing to go through Bach's cantatas singling out all the small motives and formulas that express the meaning of the text. I have already mentioned the graphic symbolism of intervals, such as the descending chromaticism in the "Crucifixus" of the mass to represent the burial of Jesus. It seems to me a most natural intellectual and emotional association to consider the graphic symbolism found there as indicative of what the composer meant. "Et resurrexit" arises on a perfect fourth, then continues for six step-progressions before leaping up another fourth. It is no exaggeration to speak of dozens of well-known themes that, through such intervals, create the spirit of a movement.

As simple a device as an upward leap can represent a great variety of images or ideas: the silent rise of the moon (in Brahms's *Mainacht*); the emergence of Achilles' mother from the waves (in Brahms's *Nänie*); the heroic resolve of Leonore ("Ich folg' dem innern Triebe"); the oncoming madness of the imprisoned Florestan ("Und fühl ich nicht: linde, sanft säuselnde Luft"); or the magic of something far away, which to the human imagination somehow always appears in the air ("Im fernen Land, unnahbar euren Schritten"). If anyone with a bit of imagination and romantic feeling delves into the musical interpretations of these words he may, by looking at the second movement of Beethoven's Second Symphony, or the third movement of Brahms's Third Symphony, or any theme with a memorable melodic strain, gain access to another dimension—the composer's inner state at the moment of his creative process.

But not only the actual tunes and themes are thus revealing; even secondary motives attain a new importance. In Bach's music the sequences of tied seconds mostly express sorrow, often seeming to suggest flowing tears. Perhaps the two best-known examples are found in nos. 33 and 35 of the *St. Matthew Passion*. The sorrow over Jesus' arrest in the first piece and the all-embracing choral text "O Mensch bewein dein Sünde gross" in the second are so piercingly expressive that this type of motive has become the musical symbol for tears. It will be a revelation for any musician to look for and find these tears, often in the most unexpected places, throughout nineteenth-century music. A concert pianist with a decade of deserved success behind him was pleased and surprised when I pointed out that the Brahms First Piano Concerto contained in the opening and in the slow movement the Bachian tears, though they are rarely, if ever, played with awareness of their significance.

The basis for these musical symbols is fascinatingly simple. "Et ascendit in coelis" can be found as an upward scale in masses by several composers. Beethoven used it in the *Missa Solemnis* by no means for the first time in vocal music. In Leonore's great aria, her confidence "sie wird's erreichen" is sung on that same upward scale, with the slow steady rise portraying the gradual accomplishment of her aim and purpose; and again in the allegro section the "drive," the "innere Trieb," at first fires her through instruments playing rapid scales, and then she herself takes the scales to affirm her confidence that she will succeed in freeing Florestan. Semantically, too, the phrase "scaling the heights" represents achievement of goals.

The depth of meaning these symbols hold for the great composers is made manifest in various types of compositions. The solo piano's opening in Beethoven's Third Piano Concerto is a case in point, for the scale is not even part of the theme itself; in this section it stands like a forceful ascent. Because scales are sometimes used to show off technique in piano and violin playing, it is important that we distinguish those scales that serve some purpose other than virtuoso display. For example, consider the profound difference between bravura vocal embellishment and the scales in *Fidelio*. By establishing the connection between the scales of "Et ascendit" in Beethoven's mass and then going back in time from Opus 123 (*Missa Solemnis*) to Opus 72 (*Fidelio*) and Opus 37 (the Third Piano Concerto), we can see that ideas with symbolic or poetic meaning are present in a composer's work sometimes years before they reach their full expressive fruition.

A violinist once discussed with me the middle sections of the finale of Mozart's G-Major Concerto K. 216 and wanted my opinion of the principal tempo for the 3/8 section. I advised a good look at such scores as the *German Dances*, K.509, and for the Allegretto I suggested consulting Papageno. It was at first a shock to the violinist to consider that works written much later could reveal a great deal about earlier ones. Yet the mind of a creative genius plays with some themes for many years, and a number of essays are required before the supreme accomplishment emerges in full glory. The spirit of Papageno was with Mozart in many a concerto movement and most certainly was present in K. 216. But I further suggested to the violinist that the relation of the short G-minor section to the G major in K. 216 is comparable to the change of mood of the birdcatcher when he contemplates hanging himself.

Such subtle interrelations as these represent in great music certain simple verities that, if unrecognized, can cause grave misinterpretations, especially in works of an earlier time. Remaining uncontradicted, errors are not only imitated but staunchly defended against the adventurous orthodoxy that I advocate (as in the case of the totally wrong tempos habitually chosen for the K. 216 finale). Most musicians study their special repertoire as if it had been created in a vacuum. The singer knows only vocal music; the violinist, only string literature; and the conductor, only orchestral composition. On such narrow specialization one can, if skillful enough, base a splendid career, but it will not allow for the most searching kind of interpretation. The broadest possible exposure to music, on the other hand, can undergird and inform the conscious knowledge of the specialized performer. In particular, instrumentalists and conductors need, if not actual singing experience, at least the curiosity to dig into the vast vocal literature. The connection between vocal and instrumental music is so intimate that I hesitate to call them two different kinds of music. Up to some indeterminate point in the nineteenth century, instrumental music was an elaboration of vocal music. Mozart was preeminently an opera composer. Let no one forget that fact when playing his concertos or conducting his symphonies.

To absorb fully the infinite connections between musical works, it is therefore useful to become familiar with the vocal music of those composers whose purely instrumental and orchestral works one wishes to perform. That the classical composers never abandoned the vocal style is proved many times when Beethoven insists in piano and string music on using terms such as *recitative, arioso, cavatina*, and the admonition *cantabile* ("singing," "singable"). Was it lack of inventiveness that made the inexhaustible Schubert turn lieder into chamber music? If we glance at the themes of many of Beethoven's variations we find little airs from long-forgotten operettas, as well as tunes from *Die Zauberflöte*.

The eventual polarization of instrument and voice was a reflection of several trends. The principal impetus, the one most pertinent to our topic, came from a few wizards of keyboard and violin who composed music primarily—if not solely—for display of dexterity on an instrument. Liszt and Paganini are the leading figures in a parade of flamboyant virtuosos who doubled as arrangers and composers to make their recitals ever more stunning.

It is symptomatic that the cello, a cantabile instrument par excellence, was left far behind in the enrichment of its repertoire, because it remained a singing instrument whose virtuoso possibilities were amazing but nonetheless never became the instrument's natural domain. Instrumentalists should regularly remind

themselves that the grand display of skill for its own sake cannot be made ret-
roactive. The music of the classical composers, despite its manifold technical
problems, is rooted in the glorification of singing. Although many movements
of concertos, especially the final ones, are not primarily cantabile, the opening
sections in sonata form suffer when played in an anachronistic virtuoso style.
There have been attempts—without success—to write original virtuoso pieces
for orchestra.

In seeking to understand a composer's mental processes, a significant exercise
is to examine the precise ways in which he emulated or transformed his models.
A fascinating example involves Beethoven and Brahms. Beethoven's famous 32
Variations for Piano in C Minor is in the form of a passacaglia. The theme is in
the bass: seven descending notes in six bars, followed by a simple cadence in
the seventh and eighth bars. (There are five eight-bar variations in C major,
where the fifth bar features not the A-flat but only the F-sharp; some earlier
variations in the minor key have A-flat and F-natural.) Essentially the same bass
line is treated to thirty-one variations of eight bars each. The thirty-second variation is extended and free, forming a grand coda and finale.

Can anyone seriously doubt that Brahms intentionally used this same plan
almost exactly in the finale of his Fourth Symphony? This piece, like Beethoven's, is in the form of a passacaglia, with an eight-bar theme. Here the line
ascends for six bars, followed by a simple cadence in the seventh and eighth.
This is followed by thirty-one variations of eight bars each (with a four-bar
addition between variation thirty and thirty-one). A final, extended thirty-second
variation is free and forms a coda, bringing the movement to a climactic ending.
In addition, both works are in a minor key (with a few variations in a major
key), and in both a radical change of mood takes place, starting with the twelfth
variation. Brahms starts with a game (repeating the formal pattern of another
composer's work exactly) and in the end creates a masterpiece all his own. Not
one note in the finale of the Fourth Symphony is anything but pure Brahms.

It is very important for conductors (as well as for pianists and other performers) to recognize such connections, because in gaining insight into the composer's thinking they also gain a clear idea of the way a work should be performed. Too many interpreters of the Fourth Symphony feel that for each group
of variations that has a different character the tempo must change, particularly
in the 3/2 section where the flute solo begins. In the chapters on tempo I will
say a great deal about the vagaries to which this movement has been subjected.
Here it should suffice to mention that an interpreter who understands the relation
of the Fourth Symphony to Beethoven's thirty-two variations will try to treat the
Brahms passacaglia as a gallery of vignettes, each placed in a frame of the same
size. Variations of eight bars in the same tempo are comparable to similarly
framed prints of a single subject, seen from different viewpoints. Imagine for an
instant what discomfort the same set of prints in frames of slightly varying sizes

would give the beholder. The same irritation accompanies the constant slight change of tempo in such a set of variations. There is a distinguished company of such works, which includes the chaconne for solo violin by Bach, his organ passacaglias in C minor, some piano variations by Brahms himself, and others by Beethoven.

Not all sets of variations belong to this category. The variations on a waltz by Diabelli are entirely different, with few variations resembling each other in shape and size. The fullest understanding of this form of composition is essential for interpreters, since the single most important skill that separates composers of the first rank is a command of the art of variation. To vary means far more than to compose formal variations over a theme or a tune. With Mozart, Beethoven, and Brahms it was second nature to turn themes around, elaborate them, and avoid literal repetition. One example is the main subject and its recapitulation in Beethoven's First Symphony. This is a showpiece for the twin forces of inspiration and intellect. At the beginning of the exposition, multiple statements of the opening theme serve as a transition to the first forte section, but in the recapitulation the return to the first theme is already fortissimo, and therefore just two statements of it suffice.

A third and very revealing way to understand the mind of a genius is to explore in depth works that he has revised. We have a considerable list, including works by Mozart (Symphony K. 297), Beethoven (*Fidelio*), Schumann (Fourth Symphony), Wagner (*Tannhäuser*), Moussorgsky (*Boris*), and Webern (*Six Pieces*, Opus 6). There are also composers' transcriptions for other groupings or solo instruments: for example, Ravel's *Le Tombeau de Couperin* was originally written for piano, and later four movements were set for orchestra. Extensive retouchings, such as those by Debussy in his orchestral masterpieces *La Mer* and *Nocturnes*, are also revealing. By studying only this small number of scores, with all their variants, we can learn a great deal.

In all our musical reading we should seek out the ideas and aims of the composer. Why was he dissatisfied with version X, and what did the changes in Y do to improve the message, the content, the expressiveness, or the clarity? Of all the revisions of the great composers, the most important, without much doubt, occurs between the overtures Opus 72 and Opus 72a by Beethoven, better known as *Leonora* No. 2 and *Leonora* No. 3 (examples 11 and 12). Let us look at the opening bars of both. In the third, Beethoven compressed the first three bars of the second overture into two, holding the first note, G, for five quarters. Thus he avoided the stop in bar 2, which, at the slow tempo indicated, was of considerable duration for a theater overture. These are the surface changes that would be duly noted in a composition class; but the real question is why the composer made them.

Leonora No. 3 now opens with four measures that depict the steps leading down into the dungeon, a descent impatiently awaited by our heroine, who,

Example 11. Beethoven, *Leonora* Overture No. 2, Opus 72, mm. 1–6

disguised as a boy, has taken employment as a jailer's servant for the purpose of finding her husband, jailed for political reasons. As this great passage was written in the earlier version, the descent was preceded by two bars that, when compared with the third overture's beginning, now seem conventional. Beethoven must have realized that the first G should be neither stopped nor repeated. In the revised concept this first note seems like a door flung open, so that we stare down a dark flight of stairs without seeing the bottom. Only when the strings enter in the second bar do we begin tentatively to go slowly down, down,

Example 12. Beethoven, *Leonora* Overture No. 3, Opus 72A, mm. 1–5

down, until the dampness and darkness of the jail envelop us, with the sound of the F-sharp.[2]

Beethoven's extensive rewriting of the overture is staggering. The improve-

2. In addition to these changes in the notes it is worthwhile to contemplate the revisions in instrumentation that Beethoven made. There is, for instance, the setting of basses and cellos starting in bar 2 with the upper G, which gives everyone the constantly descending line instead of having some instruments turn up a seventh, as they do in the earlier edition. For similar reasons the second woodwinds are omitted (except for the clarinet). The trumpets and timpani play only one note, which is more startling than the eight notes played in the earlier version. Furthermore we find that the

ments make *Leonora* No. 3 perhaps the single greatest piece in the classical sonata-symphonic poem form. They also have made musicians believe that all revisions are, ipso facto, improvements. This is decidedly not so. One need only compare Webern's *Six Pieces* or Stravinsky's early ballet scores of *The Fire Bird* and *Petrouchka* with their revised versions to see that there is no standard rule about works and their variants. It would be convenient to assume that later versions are always preferable, but even intensive study does not make it easy to decide which version is best. Argument over the *Tannhäuser* overtures defies a truly satisfactory arbitration. The Dresden version is the unified one; the later Paris edition contains music of such surpassing power and beauty that we do not wish to forgo it. Yet the new pages are so much in the language of *Tristan* and so alien to the style of the original *Tannhäuser* that the opera can be compared to a magnificent but cracked window with a replacement section that does not match.

Perhaps the simplest rule of thumb for deciding whether later versions are superior is to determine how much time has elapsed between original and revision. *Leonora* No. 3 was written in the spring of 1806, less than six months after the premiere of the second overture. On the other hand, Stravinsky's *Petrouchka* came thirty years after the original, and Wagner's Parisian *Tannhäuser* succeeded the Dresden version by fifteen years. Those years saw both men move into quite different musical realms, which they could not forget while reworking an earlier score. The only arbiter for the performer should be personal preference, because in most cases the composer made revisions for pragmatic reasons and was sometimes even compelled to do so. The Parisian demand for a ballet in *Tannhäuser*, the lack of copyright protection (which resulted in huge losses of revenue for Stravinsky from his early successes), and the absence of sufficient instruments in most orchestras to do the Webern pieces justice were among the practical arguments that have persuaded composers to make revisions not dictated by artistic considerations. Perhaps the most satisfactory explanation for the existence of great works in more than one version is that genius never stops its metamorphosis and is quite different after a decade or two.

How to Recognize Genius

While we will hear little argument about the stature of Bach, Mozart, Beethoven, and a handful of others, criteria for recognizing genius beyond the level

---

unbroken legato of the *Leonora* No. 2 in bars 3 to 5 has been changed and that a new articulation is called for between bars 2 and 3, again adding to the drama, as if the hesitancy of the first steps down has finally been overcome. The bar modulating toward the key of A-flat shows that the original matching of second violins and bassoons for the passing sixteenth notes did not work; by the same token, the lack of a full triad of A-flat was felt. These examples show that the orchestration and meaning of music are closely related and that instrumentation is no simple matter.

of the masterly composer are by no means absolute or universally agreed upon. If the yardstick is to be how music traverses the boundaries of time and space, if a work of genius must survive for a century and appeal to all ethnic groups within the realm of Western music, we will have few likely candidates. It is vitally important for the interpreter to recognize the relativity of musical values in order to broaden his own musical range. Reading a composer's works with a general background of cultural knowledge should help a conductor transcend his native limitations. There are still very important capital cities where music education is provincial, and I would not hesitate to place my hometown of Vienna at the head of this list. Although it is a major center of opera and concert life, its teaching community remains fully convinced that music outside the German-Austrian main line (from Bach to Schönberg) does not really "matter."[3]

Every place has a local spirit that wishes to elevate minor talent to major heights. That is the very essence of parochialism. It can become less endearing and more dangerous if serious critics persist in extolling Havergal Brian in the same breath as Anton Bruckner. Yet a performer who wants to acquire a catholic taste—which I consider a sine qua non, at least for an international career in music—must also be able to place Bruckner in the proper perspective. There are a number of very significant composers who are geniuses—but not everywhere. The claims for Sibelius, Elgar, Bruckner, and others must be considered. In the Germanic part of Central Europe (which includes a part of the Swiss population but not the Suisse Romande), Bruckner reigns supreme, along with Beethoven and Brahms. But perform his symphonies in Geneva and you encounter some wondrously different responses. There the non-Catholic, non-German strain is worse than indifferent; Bruckner's music produces an allergic reaction. The same response occurs if one forces Sibelius on the Viennese. Similarly, when a conductor of great personal appeal brought one of the most excellent orchestras to New York, he was taken aback that the house was only half-filled. Reluctantly his manager informed him that the fifty-minute symphony by Elgar, announced as the major work, was responsible for the lack of attendance.

There are no conspiracies or Mafias working to form these local prejudices:

---

3. *Plus ça change, plus c'est la même chose* came to my mind when I went to my alma mater, the State Academy for Music and Drama in Vienna, in April 1978, to give a seminar. I had been invited by the rector, who is a theater man. From the beginning of our preparatory discussions I noted that the director of the Music Division was not quite as enthusiastic about my visit as was the rector. I inquired what the director thought the students would particularly want to hear about. He replied that I should tell them something about Debussy, since they really did not know anything about him, while they knew a lot about Beethoven and Schubert. (Of course this was not so; one does not know a lot about Beethoven and nothing much about Debussy.) I was amused to find that in the forty-five years since my graduation nothing had changed. Then I had been asked to play the triple transposition from the score of Bruckner's Seventh Symphony (end of the second movement), which was one of Professor Schuetz's tests for a "good mark." Whether I knew anything about French or Russian music had interested no one. Now in 1978, I realized that the Danube must have stood still all these forty-five years, since the director admitted that nothing yet was taught about Debussy.

these are great national or regional composers whose appeal is not universal. It is important to know what to expect, particularly for Americans, who have been accustomed to the most liberal and catholic programming the music world has ever witnessed. Recognizing local tastes may be essential to self-preservation. At the same time, one must not allow one's own judgment to be swayed by factionalism among musicologists. Although there are no conspiracies, there are party lines, and they can be as fiercely antagonistic as any political philosophy. Theodor Adorno's essay on Sibelius shows the lengths to which such disdain can go.[4] The Schönberg circle has experts who know not only how the music of the Second Viennese School must be performed but also who may perform it. It also has an Index of unacceptables as severe as the list of books forbidden by the Vatican. These are the brainwashers of whom we must beware. An embattled composer, such as Schönberg was throughout his life, has every right to utter outrageous opinions. If Stravinsky said he preferred Gounod to Beethoven, why not? No one, no matter how much he admires *Sacre du printemps* or *Oedipus Rex*, need pay attention to quips that make a modest headline but are intended solely *pour épater le bourgeois*.

An interpreter, on the other hand, must be free of prejudices that are understandable in a composer. A musical performer is like a talented actor, whose greatest accomplishment is to achieve such a degree of identification with a character in a play that his own personality disappears. The musician should "become" Brahms or Debussy or whoever is on his program. A very good tenor once asked me whether I thought it proper for him, a pious Jew, to accept an engagement for the tenor part in Beethoven's *Missa Solemnis*. He had never been able to transcend his own persona when entering the opera house either; in the role of Don Carlo he refused to make the sign of the cross onstage. It would be unfair to accuse this tenor of narrow-mindedness and let Professor Adorno off more indulgently. Both were parochial in the most pejorative sense of the term. Nobody afflicted with that degree of prejudice—be it political, religious, stylistic, dodecaphonic, polyphonic, or what not—can hope to appreciate fully all the genius that is in great music.

The boundaries of time are more easily dealt with. Life expectancy of compositions is, like that of humans, not subject to much extension. If a score is dead we can bring the entire Red Cross of music to its aid and it will not revive. How quickly music ages is apparent when we browse through old programs. A season's repertoire of ten concerts under Nikisch in Berlin included Unger's suite called *The Seasons*, Moritz's *Burleske*, Duvosel's symphonic sketch for tenor and orchestra, and a piano concerto by Sgambati. This was in 1919. I can barely recall the name of the last composer, from catalogs of secondhand music stores, but have never even heard of the others. In the selections of 1918 I noticed three names—Reznicek, d'Albert, and Götz—that were familiar to me, but I have never heard a note of their music during all my years of listening. I did, as a very young lad, coach singers for their roles in d'Albert's *Tiefland*. In my late teens Respighi was modern, Honegger was radical, and Schreker loomed as a force on the opera circuit. Yet for Schreker's centennial it was quite difficult for me to find excerpts strong enough to justify performing a half hour of his music. In my youth I proofread scores for a Viennese publishing house, among them *Leben des Orest*, by Krenek; *Maschinist Hopkins* by Max Brand; and *Der Schmied von Gent* by Schreker—titles one would not submit today to the most demanding quiz game of operatic lore.

My most puzzling encounter with this vexing problem of musical life expectancy came in 1954, when I visited an exhibition of Richard Strauss memorabilia in Munich. I stood in front of a showcase that held two autographed full scores: on the left was *Elektra*; on the right, *Friedenstag*. I knew that one was a true masterpiece, while the other could not arouse even the composer's greatest devotees to more than a token acknowledgment. Yet there was no difference in appearance: the hand slightly less firm in the later score but still beautiful and neat, the same way of writing the notes and drawing the bar lines, the identical signature—and yet, what a difference! But how could one find out for certain if one were not able to read music in the deeper sense of recognizing what it says? We would become totally subservient to the record companies, admitting that their selections determine the music that will survive, while their omissions indicate a priori weak or dead works. Their decisions cannot substitute for the artistic judgment of a conductor. Dead music cannot be resurrected, but revival is possible if any musical life is left. Moreover, temporary declines in fashion can be reversed, if the right moment is caught. But the conductor must recognize the differences without having to rely upon tape or disc.

A particularly artificial criterion for recognizing genius is technical proficiency. Some musical theorists insist that mastery of composition is all that counts. If this were true the works of Schönberg would be more important than those of Dvořák and Tchaikovsky, who were not nearly so masterful technically. Yet these two composers had not only the gift of melodic invention but also their own brand of intellect—a kind that, unfortunately, goes unnoticed by those who declare that polyphony is of foremost importance. For example, H. L. de La-Grange, in his massive biography of Mahler, maintains that "later Mahler regretted his neglect of technical studies, saying that it had done him considerable harm, yet it would be absurd to accuse the composer of the first movement of Mahler's Eighth of lacking contrapuntal mastery."[5] Whatever one thinks of de LaGrange's opinion of Mahler's counterpoint, the implication that great composers must show contrapuntal mastery is disturbing. Schubert was not a master contrapuntist, yet his music has a uniquely transcendent quality. His chamber

5. Henry Louis de LaGrange, *Mahler* (New York: Doubleday and Co., Inc., 1973), p. 39.

music, piano sonatas, lieder, and several symphonies will live with the music of Mozart and Beethoven; he wrote a few wondrously beautiful masses in which only the fugues are inferior. Schubert, to whom Mahler owed a great debt, showed how absurd it is to consider contrapuntal expertise an indispensable element in the creation of great music. One might perhaps identify two types of intellect in music. One produces enormous technical proficiency, but of a sort that is often wanting in profound emotional qualities. The other, which manifests itself through the emotional responses it evokes, is less easily measured and is consequently not well appreciated, though it is a bosom companion of invention, inspiration, and indeed genius.

If one must play the game of assigning places on the scale between the genius and the academic composer, perhaps the most intriguing cases are those that fall on the borderline. Certain works of these composers seem to place them in the first category, but in others their severe shortcomings are readily apparent. Partisan judgment and excessive loyalty tend to press us into wholesale acceptance of composers who have produced two or three works of superior quality among many other works that are academic, mediocre, or simply innocuous. Such uneven talent is readily apparent in the vast repertoire of opera. There the grading is done automatically, because only a few works succeed with the public in the long run. The economics of opera usually prevent companies from producing anything but popular works. This is less true for instrumental music, yet the talents of a number of orchestral composers are just as inconsistent as those of operatic composers.

How many admirers of Alban Berg can determine which of his works are great and which are ordinary? Here brainwashing threatens objectivity. If we read the biographers of the Second Viennese School—Schönberg, Berg, and Webern—we are likely to conclude that the three great men of that school never composed a weak line of music.

This is not true. Nor is it true of Mozart, Beethoven, or Brahms. No one in his right mind would insist that *La clemenza di Tito* attains the same level of inspiration as *Die Zauberflöte*, though they were composed in the same year. I cannot be convinced that *Lulu* is on the level of *Wozzeck*, even though Berg's mastery of composition seems greater and more assured in the later opera. The vocal style of *Wozzeck* is wholly in keeping with the demands of the drama, while that of *Lulu* is somewhat stilted and artificial. In both works the organization of scenes into traditional forms—suite, variation, and symphony—is an essential part of the composer's plan. In the earlier work this intellectual determination disappears from the surface, and, though it serves to unify and hold the work together, it never intrudes or disturbs the dramatic impact. In *Lulu* it often sounds contrived.

One of the most striking characteristics of genius is the Spartan economy with which the greatest masters use startling devices, never repeating shock effects. In Schumann's lied "Mondnacht," a piece of sixty-odd measures, relatively simple in structure, the composer uses an augmented triad just once, in bar 50. He uses every other imaginable harmony and chromaticism but only a single bar of two major thirds. The poem at this point tells us, "And my soul spreads its wings wide." Schumann creates the image of extending wings with this one extension of the triad, in the basic key in which the lied is written.

When these inspired moments occur in vocal music, as settings for poetry, it is easy to pinpoint them and verbalize their meaning. But equally impressive examples of economy occur in the use of striking instrumental effects. In the hour-long second act of *Siegfried*, Wagner uses one stroke of two cymbals and one note on a triangle as the only percussion effects. The cymbals clash when the sword of Siegfried penetrates the vitals of the dragon, and the triangle sounds when the forest bird flies ahead of the young lad to show him "the world's most wonderful woman." Economy alone does not make genius, but overindulgence in empty effects and gimmickry strongly indicates the absence of genius.

Often economy is forced upon composers by the restricted forces at their disposal or by the limitations of the instruments themselves. An example of the way in which a creative intellect can employ great economy without damaging the music itself can be found in Beethoven's Third Symphony. Before bar 412 in the first movement appears the direction "Horn in F" and, after a passage of nine bars, another direction, "in E-flat."[6] To modern eyes, accustomed to the scoring of Wagner and Strauss, such signs are commonplace, and most contemporary musicians, including many conductors, never consider the problems that composers faced before valves were added to horns and trumpets. Horn players had to keep next to them cases containing several pieces of tubing, each producing a different key when inserted into the instrument. To extend the notes of the natural horn was impossible without changing these "crooks." This took time. At the point in the *Eroica* mentioned above, the first horn had last played in bar 370. Beethoven allowed forty-one bars for the horn to make the change and eighty-nine bars for the return of the E-flat crook. In the symphony's final movement, at bar 272, a similar change was made to allow for a four-bar phrase in the key of F.

The concert orchestras rarely boasted more than two horns, as is proved by the scoring of the works of Haydn, Mozart, and Beethoven himself. It must have bothered Beethoven to be limited to one horn for so many bars of the outer movements.

6. In the first edition of the *Eroica* symphony, there is this comment: "La parte del Corno terzo e aggiustata della sorte, che possa eseguirsi ugualmente sul Corno primario ossia secondario" (the part of the third horn is arranged so that it can be performed on the principal or the second horn). In orchestras all over the world there are "high" and "low" horn players, according to the way in which their lips and breath control have been developed and, I assume, favoring personal inclination and aptitude. The composer's comment indicates that he intended the third horn as a deputy for the stretches when the first needed time for a changeover to the other crook.

What was Beethoven's original intention? Did he write a third horn into the score in order to have an extra instrument to cover the long pauses while the principal player changed his crook, or because he had the idea of using the trio of hunting horns in the scherzo movement? However the great solution may have come about, the finished work exhibits the hand of genius. Puzzling and intriguing as this particular sequence may be, it is more important for composers to ponder than for conductors. Beethoven made do in seven great symphonies with only two horns without valves; Wagner used percussion instruments as sparingly as indicated above. Compare this frugality with the demands made by contemporary composers for dozens of percussion instruments, which rattle on with little pause, aided and abetted by "folk music" ensembles: accordions, banjos, guitars, Indian chiefs who slap their thighs, bullhorns, and electrical amplification to make sure that the noise is deafening. Is this not good cause to stop and think? Genius cannot be created by quantity.

In 1956 two anniversaries were celebrated: the bicentennial of Mozart's birth and the centennial of Sigmund Freud's. The latter was climaxed in New York with a lecture by Ernest Jones, Freud's disciple and biographer. It was entitled "The Nature of Genius." Upon discovering this, another eminent Freudian, Heinz Hartmann, commented, "We won't find out tonight either." No, we will never "find out," but for the performer the search is what counts. In the process of trying to apprehend the true nature of genius with both the intellect, through the careful study of scores, and the spirit, through the exercise of imagination, the conductor will enrich himself and enlarge his ability to interpret composers' works on their terms.

Elusive as musical genius is and will remain, it has one quality beyond debate: the ability to exhilarate the mind and the heart. While hearing a great piece of music everyone has felt at times a lift of the spirit, an elation, an all-encompassing euphoria, especially when it is shared by others present. In 1972, as part of the "Proms" at London's Royal Albert Hall, I conducted a performance of Beethoven's Choral Symphony (the proper title given to his Ninth Symphony in England). The oval downstairs was jammed with standees; the boxes were full to overflowing. The final reception was everything one expects from the jubilant conclusion of this score. The traditionally demonstrative Proms crowd called the participants to the front of the stage again and again, but the clamor did not abate. One of the officials backstage informed me that I would have to break up the gathering by taking the orchestra offstage with me. The audience dispersed by the time we arrived at the dressing rooms; but now instead of applause we heard singing. Some people in the audience had started to chant as they filed slowly out of the overcrowded hall. As others gradually joined in we heard strains of the great hymn "Freude schöner Götterfunken!" from listeners who had been uplifted by a direct encounter with genius.

Three
Knowing What Composers Wanted

What the Composers Said

There is a large and influential school of thought whose adherents believe that compositions are merely vehicles for performers. It has existed at least since the days of Franz Liszt. Some critics subscribe to this philosophy, while others deplore it. My own conviction is that composers have very clear ideas about how they want their works performed, and they are more likely than anyone else to be correct. At first glance the documentary evidence of the views of some composers seems ambiguous, if not downright contradictory. What they have said or written may be misleading if taken out of context. Anyone browsing through the files of the late Serge Koussevitzky would find a telegram from Igor Stravinsky: "Thank you for a perceptive rendition of my ode." This reads like a clear stamp of approval for the performance. In fact, as Robert Craft once explained, the message was sent as a courtesy to a staunch supporter whom Stravinsky privately resented for his idiosyncratic ways of interpreting compositions entrusted to him.

In the early 1920s I heard a story about Richard Strauss that would seem to contradict what I intend to show. During the Weimar Republic all sorts of experimental enterprises arose in Germany, among them a democratically organized touring opera troupe, called Wanderbühne, which in English might be "Strolling Opera Players." The troupe's principal innovation was a casting system that placed Tuesday's Countess Almaviva in the role of the First Bridesmaid in Wednesday's performance, while the reverse process gave Tuesday's comprimaria the lead on Wednesday. This worked for a while and then had to be abandoned, as must all schemes that are based on a fictitious equality of talent and drive. Rehearsal headquarters were on a mountaintop in Bavaria, near Strauss's home in Garmisch. One day, when Wanderbühne was ready with the composer's

Intermezzo, he was invited to hear a run-through rehearsal. The score contains some of Strauss's most intricate declamatory recitative passages since *Der Rosenkavalier*. To do full justice to these sophisticated parlando passages is difficult even for the most musical singers. The chief conductor of the troupe, proud of his company's meticulous preparation, spoke to the composer during the interval with considerable pride, claiming that every syllable, every small note, was sung just as written, 100 percent exact. To which Strauss retorted, "Why do you want it so exact?"

When I first heard this story as a teenager I took it at face value, thinking that scores were only an approximate mapping of the musical region, to be filled in with all sorts of detail by the performer. As time went on and I learned a bit more about placing the remarks of composers in proper context, I came to see the scene in a different light. The chief conductor had coached and drilled his cast in the best manner of a Beckmesser, demanding pedantic accuracy while missing the spark and spirit of the dialogue. When, after half a run-through, he told the composer with self-serving pride that every note was exact, the composer, a wit and a keen psychologist, wanted to administer a rebuff without being overtly offensive. How else could he have conveyed that the most exact solfège does not make a good recitative? How else suggest to the peacock vanity of the conductor that he had ignored the essence of the music while concentrating on the notes?

An anecdote about Maurice Ravel appears to contradict Strauss's point. The pianist Marguerite Long once wrote that Ravel wanted the notes to be played and nothing else—another of those ambiguous statements that can throw the unwary off course. It is impossible to play only the notes, especially in music of folk origin. Some of Ravel's works involve traditional dance rhythms that cannot even be written down accurately. A note-perfect rendition of the basic *Bolero* beat is as impossible as a literal performance of the Viennese lilt in *La Valse*. It would actually destroy the quintessence of those pieces, their authenticity and their flavor, be that Spanish or Viennese. What Ravel intended, I am sure, was (like Strauss's comment to the Wanderbühne conductor) a rebuff to self-important performers who believe they know what the composer wants without a closer examination of *both* the *spirit* and the *letter* of the score.

This problem is reflected in a letter written in 1890 by Richard Strauss to his parents, in which he laments that the first Berlin performance of *Don Juan* under Hans von Bülow, though a critical success, left him highly unsatisfied:

> Of what use to me is a success, which is based on a misunderstanding? Bülow took the tempos and everything else in my work all wrong. He has no idea about poetic content and handled the piece like any other agreeable, novelly constructed and harmonized, well-orchestrated work. Indeed, he rehearsed it with great diligence, utmost energy and in fear and trembling of a failure (which he cannot bear any more, since he is frightfully vain . . .) and presented the public with a very interesting piece of music; but not my Don Juan.

Strauss concludes, "I believe no one can do it the way one imagines it oneself, not even Bülow, this is clear to me now."[1]

Strauss's dissatisfaction echoes a letter from Beethoven to Czerny, in which Beethoven writes, "Tomorrow I will call on you to have a talk with you. I burst forth so yesterday that I was sorry after it had happened, but you must pardon that in an author who would have preferred to hear his work exactly as he wrote it, no matter how beautifully you played in general."[2] More recent composers, Stravinsky and others, have bitterly complained about their patron saint conductors. Bartók was torn between gratitude for financial support and rage over misunderstandings of interpretation. Like Strauss in 1890, latter-day composers have found it difficult to remonstrate and protest when they feel violated, lest they lose the support and opportunities offered by star conductors and performers.[3]

Strauss attributes Bülow's unsatisfactory interpretation of *Don Juan* at least in part to the conductor's fear of failure, which was rooted in his vanity. Vanity is indeed the archenemy of the interpreter, because it interferes with his ability to receive messages from other minds. *Freischwebende Aufmerksamkeit* ("free-floating attention"), a technique that is the sine qua non of dream analysis, is in my view the essential quality for a great interpreter. Unfortunately, the consensus has been that those performers who exhibit the oddest, most flamboyant, or most eccentric personalities have the greatest talent. This may seem true, as long as we do not know the composers they perform too intimately. If we do, the performer's idiosyncrasies and vanities rise to the surface like oil in water.

The conductor's obligation to the composer is not a concept of recent origin. We can read, for instance, in Johann Mattheson's *Der Vollkommene Capellmeister* ("The Compleat Music Director") of 1739 a passage which provides an admirable summary of the composer/interpreter dilemma:

> The greatest difficulty in performing the work of someone else consists indeed in the need for a sharp forceful judgment to meet head on the sense and individuality of a stranger's thoughts. He who has never learned how the originator himself would like to have it done will hardly do it well but will take away the vitality and charm,

1. Richard Strauss's letter to his parents, 3 February 1890, as quoted in Erich H. Müller von Asow, *Richard Strauss Thematisches Verzeichnis*, 3 vols. (Vienna: Doblinger, 1955), 1:94–96 (translation by Christopher Hailey).

2. Alexander Thayer, *The Life of Ludwig van Beethoven*, ed. Henry E. Krehbiel, 3 vols. (New York: G. Schirmer, Inc., 1921), 3:316.

3. This reminds me of a well-known story, though I doubt its authenticity. Rossini's years in Paris were partly spent in organizing musicales for parties given by very rich people. The composer would secure the artists, choose the programs, and see that everybody was at the right place on the right date. Occasionally he himself would participate. On one such occasion he accompanied Adelina Patti, who sang one of his famous arias, albeit with many roulades, cadenzas, and other embellishments such as those with which we are familiar from the usual operatic renditions. At the end of her performance, amid the applause, Rossini complimented Madame Patti on her beautiful voice—and asked the name of the composer whose piece she had just sung.

often in such manner that an author, were he to hear it, might be hard put to recognize his own work.[4]

In those documents that tell us what composers felt and what they rejected, the exhortations of composer-conductors are especially strong. This is to be expected: a composer with professional credentials as a conductor will be a more severe judge of other conductors than one who seldom or never directs. Thus, a statement of Gustav Mahler seems to me the best way to complete this dossier: "How long it takes, what total experience and maturity must be added, until one gets to do everything quite simply and really in such a way as it has been written down; not to add and not to overlay what isn't there, because more turns into less." Mahler continues, "As a young conductor I too was in my performances of the great works artificial and erratic and added too much of my own, albeit with comprehension and spirit. Only much later did I arrive at the full truth, simplicity and recognition that real artistry can be found only through a total lack of artificiality."[5] From a musician who was as much a composer as he was a conductor, the words "too much of my own" carry special weight. Here Mahler quite specifically speaks of the great works, probably referring to those of Beethoven, among others. This is as much as saying, "Before I heard what others did to *my* music I may have done the same in bending older masters toward my own compositional ideals."

I myself witnessed a comparable change of attitude a generation later. When I first heard performances of Bruno Walter, he quite often applied a type of *Luftpause* (a short wait before an especially important accent) in works of Mozart, Haydn, and Beethoven. The luftpause appears with regularity in Mahler's scores, for it is part of his typical phrasing. It is indicated by the comma and buttressed by shortening the note before it and delaying the downbeat of the next measure ever so slightly. This is perhaps best explained by imagining one's arm swinging a hammer, pausing above one's head just long enough to strike with extra strength the next time it comes down. This nuance was noticeable in Walter's performances of the classics to such a degree that it appeared to be a mannerism, an artificiality of the kind Mahler eschewed in his more mature years. Walter too became more straightforward as he aged, revising his technique from a somewhat nervous overuse of nuance toward ever greater simplicity.

Mahler's words "as it has been written down" may seem the clearest guides for achieving such simplicity. In fact, their meaning is enormously complex. For instance, the question remains, "How much has been written down?" The performer must distinguish music written during a period of strong and generally accepted traditions from that written at times of little or no traditions. (I shall devote the next chapter to a discussion of musical traditions, without which the

4. Johann Mattheson, *Der vollkommene Capellmeister* (Hamburg: C. Herold, 1739, fac. ed. by M. Reimann; Kassel: Bärenreiter, 1954), p. 484.

5. Natalie Bauer-Lechner, *Erinnerungen an Gustav Mahler*, ed. J. Killian (Leipzig: E. P. Tal & Co., 1923), p. 40 (from a conversation in the summer of 1896).

intentions of composers of the classical period and earlier cannot be properly comprehended.)

Nevertheless, however well a conductor observes a composer's stated desires and the traditions of his time, there are still areas in which he must fall back upon his own judgment. For this reason it is essential to understand where interpretation begins and where it ends.

The Risks of Interpretation

If we look at any score by Bach we find that he trusts almost entirely to the sufficiency of the notes, adding on rare occasions a *piano* or a tempo marking. In this he resembles Shakespeare, who gave few stage directions. But compare a Bach score to one by Schönberg. The modern composer insisted on specifying even the fingering for harmonics on the string instruments, having no confidence whatever in the performance tradition of his time. Schönberg too has a literary parallel: George Bernard Shaw, unlike Shakespeare, left nothing to the imagination but wrote reams of instructions to the actors and the scenic designer. In both theater and music we thus have the problem of how much authors specify and, in earlier times, how much they took for granted. Other things being equal (which, of course, they never are), the score with the fewest directives is usually the most resilient, because the text itself, free of extra comments, allows for the changes that decades and centuries bring about. These changes are comparable to the changes that take place in the human organism from birth to death. It is not accidental that the passing centuries have brought renewed youth and relevance to the works of Bach and Shakespeare. The architectonic quality of Bach's music in particular reminds us of great buildings and bridges that must sway with the winds and yield to the elements, lest they crack under the strain of too rigid a resistance. Ships and airplanes also must be flexible; and scores that are to survive the ages have some of these same qualities.

One of the interpreter's chief tasks is to perform works of earlier times in ways that make them most meaningful to audiences of his own generation, without in any way distorting the intrinsic nature of the works or violating the intentions of the composer or playwright. This requires an ability to distinguish between the essential character of a work—its structure, tone, and meaning—and its time-bound externals. The differences can be recognized more easily in theatrical productions, where there is more leeway for interpretation. For this reason alone it would be worthwhile for us to venture a short way into the labyrinth of contemporary operatic interpretation. In the years since the end of the Second World War the whole issue of interpretation in opera has drastically changed. Its guiding force is no longer the conductor but the stage director, or producer, as he is called in Europe. Since the two aspects of opera, drama and music, are inseparable, this shift of emphasis inevitably affects musical interpretation, and for this reason it is of crucial concern to the conductor.

This change is not necessarily for the worse. A few true creative artists of operatic staging have been as sensitive to the music as to the drama. How admirably one of these artists sensed the passage of time and fashion struck me with full force when I reread some of the Wagner librettos at the time when the first storms broke out over the new Bayreuth style devised by Wieland Wagner, the master's grandson. Wieland Wagner's public image was that of a wild reformer, attempting to do away with all the excess paraphernalia and the old Teutonic spirit, using only the essential minimum of external embellishments while concentrating on psychological, sociological, and other human factors in these dramas. Some of the credit for Wieland's success should have been given to his grandfather, who never asked in his texts for helmets with horns, mailed armor, or shields. Theatrical designers and directors had failed to notice the scarcity of directions in these librettos. Decades of seeing the same papier-mâché rocks and props had led people to conclude that these were what Wagner wanted. In fact, the second act of *Die Walküre* is introduced by the author as follows: "Wotan, in warlike armor, with the spear; before him Brünhilde, as Valkyrie, also in full battle dress." This is quite different from the minutely detailed directions on costuming given by some theatrical authors. The spear is specifically mentioned only because it is a part of the drama itself. Wagner, like all great creative minds, wrote for more than his generation. His description of Wotan in "warlike armor" leaves to the imagination every liberty and, if used wisely, allows for constant renewal.

If used foolishly and irresponsibly, however, such liberty may lead to absurdity and a waste of effort and money. (It cannot destroy works that are, as Strauss once called the great scores, "invulnerable.") An incident that occurred during the 1976–77 season of the Paris Opera demonstrates how essential is the ability to distinguish between external trappings and dramatic essentials. The *Ring* tetralogy was being newly staged by German directors of the anti-Wagnerian school. For the production of *Die Walküre*, the soprano who was Sieglinde asked for the sword splinters that she must carry with her into the wilderness in the final act. This is the famous sword Nothung, which is thrust into the ash by Wotan as Wanderer, found by Siegmund, shattered on Wotan's spear, and reforged by Siegfried—in a word, an important property. The stage director, however, refused to let Sieglinde have the sword. When she protested that it played a central role in the next opera of the cycle, he declared that he was not concerned with *Siegfried*, for someone else was slated to stage it.

Such displays of arrogance and ignorance have become increasingly common. The idea that a performance should recreate its premiere is widely regarded as outmoded. Instead, new productions have become contests between stage directors and theater managers as to who can be more original and innovative. *La Traviata* was recently staged as if the play started with the deathbed scene and all the earlier acts of the opera were flashbacks. This was indeed a novel interpretation; but it had no connection with the music. A similar idea became the basis for a new production of Wagner's *Der Fliegende Holländer*. In that staging, the dream of the Steersman, who falls asleep at his post, constituted the frame for the action.

Such violations on the part of stage directors not only show unconcern for the fact that opera is a musical form of art; they also reveal insensitivity to, if not contempt for, the dramatic intelligence of the librettist. The director of the Parisian *Walküre* showed an unusually flagrant disregard for an essential element of the plot. But even a seemingly external element such as costume, though it may perform no specifically dramatic function, must not be tampered with thoughtlessly. The dress of a particular period inevitably carries with it implications of social attitudes and thought that are characteristic of its historical time. I sometimes think the first production of *Hamlet* in modern dress encouraged later reinterpretations of the classics. Because it was a gimmick rather than a true rereading, it attracted much attention. Operatic stage directors, a curious breed of intellectuals who often lack theatrical and musical experience but know a lot about sociology and psychology, began to search for operatic guinea pigs onto which "relevance" could be grafted. In recent years such self-serving indulgence has become a commonplace. Rudolf Hartmann, a German director and intendant (general manager) of several important opera companies, has expressed alarm in a well-reasoned article that is worth quoting at some length:

> Operas and music dramas were written for the sake of the music. . . . The recreators, conductor, and stage director are the responsible representatives of the authors or, after their deaths, the custodians of the works entrusted to them.
>
> That order sounds clear and normal. It was valid up to now as a philosophy for those performers who took the very large scope of their tasks as a stimulating artistic challenge. Listening to the heartbeat of a work, learning what the creative intelligence had in mind, and staging from the inside out, not the other way around, resulted in a constant stream of optimal solutions which had, with all the differences between them, still one common ground: the development of our precious theatrical heritage. During the recent decade certain changes have occurred which disrupt in a most disquieting manner the basic relationship between creation and recreation, between work and interpretation. The prima facie self-explanatory concept of loyalty to the work is smilingly dismissed as "totally old-fashioned," and replaced on stage, under the slogan of progress, by uninhibited anarchy. . . . Nobody professionally connected with the performing arts will wish our theatrical stages to become lifeless, rigid refrigeration preserves. Theater always breathed with the environment of its era and drew its vigor from social influences. Yet there is an immense chasm between an organically developing metamorphosis and brutal, self-indulgent altering of the works.
>
> Naturally the stage directors offer explanations and justifications of their conceptions. These are recited intelligently and in the best phraseology, many ending with the contention that all that is happening came out of the work and was conceived in

its spirit: because Wagner could not think beyond his time, since his mythological figures and actions were merely a pretext to a bitter critique of his own era, he being a well-known eternal revolutionary. To illuminate this concealment and adapt it for our own time should be the sense and ambition of any new production.[6]

Few works of the opera repertoire have suffered more from the trend to update, illuminate, and reinterpret than Mozart's *Zauberflöte*. Because it was composed shortly before Mozart's death and because the composer and librettist were involved with a Masonic lodge, it has been approached with a mixture of confusion, false reverence, and symbolic paraphernalia that at times has made an unattractive shambles of this radiant and humane masterpiece. For an appreciation of a recent experiment with *Die Zauberflöte*, consider this review of a Parisian production from the *Neue Zürcher Zeitung*:

Mozart's "Magic Flute" in a Psychoanalytical Interpretation
A New Production at the Paris Opera

The music accompanying the appearances of Sarastro and his retinue may sound ever so festive, lofty, and solemn: in reality his realm of light and reason is a vain delusion, a system of oppression, doomed to failure in the face of the demands of external life; and the story of Tamino and Pamina essentially has to be understood as a conflict with the "père castrateur." This is the quintessence of an "Essai de lecture psychoanalytique de l'oeuvre" printed in the program and—worse—the motto of Horst Zankl's and Arik Brauer's new production of *Die Zauberflöte*.

After having safely left the dark, mountainous realm of the Queen of the Night—a sinister creature with glittering, scaly snakeskin—after the repulsive bleeding halves of the slain dragon have been cleaned off the stage, Tamino and Pamina logically enter a nightmarish world. The magic flute attracts gruesome monsters rather than beasts: the slaves are fools miserably tied to chains, Monostatos appears as a weird man of the woods with a bushy beard and brown tights, Sarastro wears a crown of porcupine quills, while the priests remain totally anonymous under shapeless cloaks and hoods. And the props that designate Sarastro's realm make ugliness and morbidity quite truly the stylistic principle of this scenery: there are three doors of which one is decorated with a pair of human ears, the center one with eyes, and the third with lips; in addition to these, there are two emaciated hands with claws, a massive tree which appears to have been taken from a delirious dream, as well as sundry creations of a half vegetative, half ornamental nature which allude to Egyptian-Freemasonic symbolism—everything being clearly identifiable as plastic. The Israeli painter and sculptor Arik Brauer, who, seven years ago in Zurich, created the world of demons for Ginastera's opera *Bomarzo*, once again reveals himself as a representative of the Viennese school of Fantastic Realism. It is his inventions which give their imprint to the appearance of this production of *Die Zauberflöte* and which incite the audience to angry protest.

But wherein—aside from ideological underpinnings—lies the contribution of the director, Horst Zankl? His directing is limited to the devising of partly theatrical,

6. Rudolf Hartmann, "Grenzen der Interpretation auf der Operbühne. Persönliche Anmerkungen zu einem brennenden Thema," *Neue Zürcher Zeitung*, 5–6 March 1977 (my translation).

partly parodic gestures to which are added a few gags with stage machinery. But the facial expressions of the singers are mostly frozen or remain hidden behind masks. Thus, at least for the eye, almost everything which accounts for the uniquely human magic of this multilayered, universal work, the unburdened, naive serenity of the piece as well as the emotion of the love story and the sublimity of the mystery, freezes to a pose.[7]

Such absurd excesses on the part of stage directors might deserve no more than contemptuous laughter from musicians if it were not that in opera the dramatic action and the powerful implications of stage design cannot remain separate from the music. Hartmann's concern for the dangers of idiosyncratic and self-indulgent staging did not stop short of the orchestra pit:

> One asks with anxiety: how much longer? One day this discrepancy of the musical element and the dramatic presentation will be noticed by the zealous improvers of the original works and then the threatening catastrophe will be quickly completed.[8]

Hartmann imagined that the realization of this danger lay in the future, however imminent. In fact, at the time he was writing it had already begun. Perhaps Hartmann was not worried by the work of the late Walter Felsenstein because it was carried on at his theater in East Berlin, beyond the range of the Western free press. In these truly astounding and marvelous productions the musical scores were treated cavalierly. Since Felsenstein seldom chose works with music of the highest caliber, his treatment of the scores was not particularly offensive. If, for example, he reversed the sequence of two acts in *Tales of Hoffmann*, he violated no observable plan of Offenbach's, for the composer died before finishing the work. Felsenstein worked exclusively with obedient conductors and with singers whose vocal limitations made them willing to suffer through the meticulous but interminable preparation required for his productions. I believe that Felsenstein was as keen of mind and shrewd of choice as was, in a totally different way, Wieland Wagner. Yet few disciples of these two great directors are of similar caliber. The worst excesses have been perpetrated in their names.

At Bayreuth I had the greatest difficulty in reestablishing a practice that had been followed as a matter of course for ninety-six years: that of performing Wagner's works without cuts. Not only did no one, with the possible exception of the orchestra members, appreciate my efforts, but I encountered resistance from everyone, including the composer's grandson Wolfgang. Finally, after the stage director totally demolished *Tannhäuser* as Wagner had conceived it, I resigned after the dress rehearsal.

Unfortunately even the most gifted stage directors can do unintentional violence to great scores. Perhaps no production of *Die Zauberflöte* has more sensitively brought out every aspect of the work than Ingmar Bergman's film version, which is a wondrous fantasy. Yet the great Bergman had poor musical

7. "Mozarts 'Zauberflöte' in psychoanalytischer Deutung," *Neue Zürcher Zeitung*, 20 May 1977.
8. Hartmann, "Grenzen der Interpretation auf der Operbühne."

advice. In reordering sections of the finale of act 2 he destroyed Mozart's archi-
tectural scheme. From the start of the trio by the three Genii, this finale is built
like a pyramid. (See the diagram.) The first and last scenes are in E-flat major,
the key of the overture. At the apex is C major, the key that Mozart used for
every important reference to the magical instrument. C minor is the relative
minor key of the E-flat sections, and sections F and G are in the subdominant
and dominant of C, respectively. Any change in this planned ascent to the C
major of the magic flute and the subsequent descent to the conclusion will destroy Mozart's simple plan.

$$C$$
$$F \quad G$$
$$c \qquad c$$
$$E\flat \qquad\qquad E\flat$$

Although I understand Bergman's wish to get the comic couple, Papageno
and Papagena, settled first with their happy ending, leaving the tension of the
more serious, aristocratic pair for the end, this change to increase dramatic suspense ruins Mozart's musical plan. In Mozart's day, at least in the theatrical
tradition out of which Schikaneder's plot grew, it may have been an unwritten
rule to treat the scene with the comic couple like an encore in a recital: after the
serious business is done, we enjoy the merrier side of life.

If we look at the opera's score it is easy to see that the drama of Tamino,
Pamina, and their trial in fire and water ends in C major, with a short fanfare
after the successful completion of the second test. Then comes the entire scene
of Papageno's mock suicide and his duet with Papagena, in G, which was the
key signature at Papageno's first appearance and on other occasions, such as his
rout of Monostatos and his henchmen. Mozart uses the key of C minor for the
forces of adversity, first the men in armor and later the subversive group—the
Queen, Monostatos, and the Three Ladies.

It would be interesting to see how Bergman's rearrangement of the events of
the finale would fare in a live performance. I should think that after the delightful "Pa-pa-pa-pa" duet it would be difficult for the spectators to settle down to
the solemn fugato chorale of the armed guards. I find Bergman's rearrangement
most instructive in showing how the intimate interconnection between a composer's dramatic and musical conceptions can be damaged in even the most
sensitive attempts at reinterpretation.

But not only stage directors distort great works, intentionally or otherwise.
Performers too disregard composers' wishes, explicit as well as implicit, either
because of a conviction that they know better how a role should be performed
or because they are unable to perform it properly.

That irreparable changes can be grafted onto a masterwork was made clear to
me one day when Toscanini explained why he had never attempted a full pro-

duction of Rossini's *Barber of Seville*. Since its first performance in Rome in 1816, the score has enjoyed more than a century of world success, with singers and stage managers playing increasingly to the gallery, inventing new gags, doing anything for an easy laugh, adding high notes, holding final notes through tonic and dominant regardless of dissonance, omitting and adding pieces, transposing some into other keys, and indulging in flourishes, embellishments, roulades, and cadenzas. If one cleaned the score and the stage directions of the accumulated chaff, the total effect of the opera, Toscanini feared, might be jeopardized. After an overly salty herring, a finer fish would never satisfy the jaded palate. Thus, the pragmatic conductor diagnosed the results of a century and a half of cheapening a masterpiece. He found this thoroughly despicable but did not feel that a return to the original score would solve the problem, the cure being perhaps worse than the sickness. However justified it might have been, Toscanini refused to perform the operation.

One of the popular operas most prone to mistreatment is Richard Strauss's *Salome*. I discovered how difficult it is to counteract seventy years of accumulated waywardness and caprice one year when I restudied this opera at the Metropolitan. My first encounter was with a well-known singer who had been entrusted with the protagonist's role. After watching her antics in a stage rehearsal I paraphrased for her in private the composer's comment: "Salome, as a chaste virgin, as an Oriental princess, must be acted solely with the simplest and noblest gestures, lest she provoke shock and horror instead of compassion."[9] I tried to tone down her acting and to redirect her manner of singing the part toward a more youthful and touching inflection and away from the rather ugly and vindictive way in which she addressed the severed head of the prophet.

9. It may be instructive to translate the full text as it appears in Asow, *Them. Verzeichnis*, 1:368 (my translation):

During the blocking rehearsals, the dramatic soprano Frau Wittich, who had been entrusted with [the part of] the Isolde-voiced sixteen-year-old princess because of its taxing nature and because of the thick orchestra[tion]—one simply shouldn't write such things, Herr Strauss; you can't have it both ways—went on strike from time to time with the indignant protestations of a Saxon burgomaster's wife: "I shan't do that, I'm a decent woman!" She thus drove the stage director Wirk, oriented towards "perversion and total abandon," to distraction. And yet, Frau Wittich, obviously unfit for the part in physique, was actually right, though in a different sense, for the excesses which exotic snaky vamps (*Tingeltangeleusen*), swinging Jochanaan's head through the air, permitted themselves in later performances often exceeded all bounds of propriety and good taste. Whoever has visited the Orient and has observed the decency of the women will realize that Salome, a chaste virgin, an Oriental princess, must be acted only with the simplest and most aristocratic of gestures if in her downfall upon encountering the mystery of a sublime world she is not to arouse only disgust and horror rather than compassion. . . . In general, the acting of the performers must, in contrast to the all too exciting music, be limited to the greatest simplicity. Herod in particular, instead of neurotically dashing about, should remember that as an Oriental parvenu he is constantly concerned, even with all his momentary erotic lapses, with preserving his poise and dignity in the presence of his Roman guests, in emulation of the greater Caesar in Rome. Ranting and raving both on and below the stage—is too much. The orchestra can handle that by itself.

My efforts were of no avail because she was unable (and I suppose unwilling) to change accustomed ways. One of her comments shows the attitude of many "interpreters" when a fresh reading is suggested for a role already congealed into habit: "Perhaps if one explained your suggestion to the critics . . ." She left in the air the unlikely assumption that in such a case she might do things differently. Despite having learned the explicit intent of the composer, she evidently believed that the press, not the composer, was the final arbiter. In spite of my total disagreement with her belief that one must explain one's performance to the critics, I realized that it reflected the inanity of directors who brainwash the press through interviews in which they promulgate the new ideas of their own productions. The singer failed to realize that these are precisely the types who do disservice to both author and composer.

On another occasion a tenor who sang the role of Herod stopped in the middle of a full orchestral rehearsal. When I asked why, he replied curtly, "Too slow." A few months earlier I had heard this singer in the same role at New York's other opera house and knew that he tended to rush his part like mad, but I had ascribed the wrong tempo to the conductor. The tenor was so used to rushing that he could no longer control the speed of the words—which he had learned by rote in the first place.[10] Earlier in my career I would have been embarrassed and flustered by such a comment, made from stage with well over a hundred people around, but at age sixty-four I had become more certain in knowing what is correct. I simply said, "Perhaps for you."

The serious part of this story concerns the wayward tempos that are now customarily taken in *Salome*, as if the composer had been dead for centuries and the correct style lost and forgotten. Because Strauss held a number of powerful positions in the German musical world, he had greater control over the fate of his works than more retiring composers can exert. Yet thirty years after his death his major works are sadly distorted and misinterpreted.

Despite the deterioration of operatic staging, music—the scores, if not the interpretations—has remained relatively free from tampering. This is due in part to a certain orthodoxy of solfège that has kept scores less easily changeable than written words. In a superficial sense more people recognize words than notes. On an even more materialistic level, it is not unimportant that copying music is far more expensive than setting words into type. This seemingly irrelevant fact makes the introduction of radical changes into musical scores a major undertaking. This is fortunate. If it were easy for conductors, many of whom are frustrated composers, to alter scores at will, the majority of classical works might

10. The section of the score that caused my exchange with the tenor carries a metronome reading of 76 for the minim. In relation to the following passage this is not a great speed, and it allows every verbal inflection to come through. That is a major concern of interpretation—and it was totally lost when the singer's pace was a gallop. See Richard Strauss, *Salome* [orchestral score] (London: Boosey & Hawkes, 1905), pp. 188 ff., rehearsal no. 232; and Strauss, *Salome* [piano-vocal score] (Berlin: Adolph Furstner, 1905), pp. 128 ff., rehearsal no. 232.

by now have become unrecognizable to their authors. There are, in fact, well-known instances of changes made in major works. Mozart elaborated on Handel's *Messiah*, and both Rimsky-Korsakov and Shostakovich revised Moussorgsky's *Boris Godunov*. In the last case the alterations were made to correct real inadequacies in the original, as I shall explain later in my section on editing for performance. So far, however, the technical limitations mentioned above have for the most part confined revisions to interpretations of scores rather than to the scores themselves.

There may be as many conductors as stage directors who are eager to leave their personal imprint on musical works, at the expense of composers if necessary. On the other hand, many genuinely try to be faithful to composers' wishes, when they know how to discover them. More often than not the chief obstacle to their success is a lack of confidence based on knowledge in approaching the music of a past age. This leads them, however good their intentions, to substitute instant interpretation for understanding borne of study.

The Limits of Interpretation of Music

Today's younger performers seem to lack an intimate relationship with the classics, while they are apparently in their natural element with twentieth-century compositions. It is almost universally recognized that pianists fare better with Rachmaninoff and Prokofiev than with Mozart and Schubert, and conductors find Mahler and Bartók closer to their hearts and minds than Beethoven and Wagner. Most musicians would agree, at least in theory, that the ultimate purpose of a performance is to recreate each work as it sounded and was experienced when it was first heard. Yet it becomes increasingly difficult to do so. The practice of composition itself moves on in an inexorable process of change, and every new work of importance tends to push older works further into the past. With each new crop of scores, the eras of Wagner, Schumann, Beethoven, Mozart, and Bach recede into a dimmer past. A sense of what a performance was like in 1805 becomes harder for each generation to conceive. Yet, if modern programs are to continue to include works by earlier composers, conductors and performers must find a way to bridge the cultural and temperamental gap that separates them from such works.

An indication of the sensitivity to the past that must be acquired can be found by examining Mozart's Serenade K. 320. In the midst of a work apparently intended to provide light entertainment, the composer placed a tragic movement of searching spirit and great emotional tension. Since that time, two hundred years of increasing chromaticism—up to and including atonality and dodecaphonic composition—have vastly expanded our musical vocabulary. Yet familiarity with modern developments in technique, harmony, and attitude must not be allowed to destroy our appreciation of the newness and freshness in a classical composition. Unless conductor and players can respond to the extraordinary innovation that the andantino of Mozart's Serenade represented in its day, they cannot hope to reproduce its initial impact.

I do not wish to imply that one must become a musical archaeologist, digging up every old instrument or custom that is historically authentic. We do not need candlelight for a Shakespearean production, nor should we assign the role of Cleopatra to a boy. We must perform with every modern resource, not attempting to make documents of our masterpieces. Yet in order to communicate the original excitement or charm of a work to a modern audience, the interpreter must fully grasp what made it modern in its own day. To give Beethoven's Third Symphony compelling power today, a conductor must be completely familiar with the rhetoric of 1805. For this reason the plays of Grillparzer will serve as a better guide to the student of Beethoven than will Wagner's ideas about how to interpret the *Eroica*.

The limits of personal interpretation in conducting were interestingly discussed by the famous Viennese critic Eduard Hanslick in his review of a concert conducted by Wagner in Vienna in 1872. Included here almost in its entirety, this review shows that Hanslick was not the monster of philistinism that Wagner's zealous idolaters made him out to be.

> The concert conducted by Richard Wagner consisted of two parts, the first bringing us Beethoven's *Eroica* while the second contained only Wagner's own compositions. Since Beethoven's *Heroic Symphony* is one of the most overplayed compositions in the Viennese concert repertory, Wagner must have chosen it less for its own sake than to show how it must be conducted—as a practical example for his essay "On Conducting", as it were.
>
> In that tract, which contains very stimulating guidelines and intelligent observations, Wagner speaks repeatedly of Beethoven's *Eroica*, principally in order to prove his favorite thesis that our conductors have no concept of tempo and that the "true Beethoven" as we have come to know him from public performances is still a "mere chimera" for us.
>
> Wagner is recognized as a brilliant conductor; he has spirited intentions and, with his great authority over his musicians, he knows how to realize them. His energetic, fine and distinctively nuanced rendition of the *Eroica* provided us, by and large, with true delectation.
>
> This notwithstanding, it would be sad if we had come to know and understand this work only since last night, and solely by the grace of Wagner. . . .It would be unpardonable ingratitude if we did not declare that we heard quite first-rate performances of the *Eroica* from the same orchestra under Herbeck and Dessoff, performances which, even after that of Wagner, still appear excellent. One conductor takes a tempo somewhat faster, while another takes it more slowly; one colors the contrast between loud and soft more brilliantly, another less so.
>
> Such discrepancies will always exist, as long as living human beings conduct and not machines. With serious conductors of solid erudition and unquestioned talent these differences will usually be only slight; no one will do an adagio quickly and an allegro slowly, or will change a "forte" to a "piano". About deviations which lie within narrow, artistically incontestable confines one may argue; a final decision in

such an argument could be made by only one person: the composer himself. As long as Beethoven does not personally declare that Wagner's interpretation of the *Eroica* is the only correct one and that those traits which look Wagnerian are really genuinely Beethovenian, we cannot grant even the hero of the day the right to call every other conductor of the *Eroica* a jackass.

The novel element in Wagner's interpretation consists, in a word, in the frequent modification of the tempo within a movement. With this slogan and with a second, "correct grasp of the melodic element" (which supposedly gives the key to the right tempo) Wagner himself characterizes the reform of performances of Beethoven's symphonies which he has demanded and attempted. There are movements where the "dynamic monotony" that Wagner loathed can indeed be livened and broken without detriment [to the music]. The finale of the *Eroica* is such a movement; it is based in the main on an enlarged variation-form and thus undoubtedly permits a characteristic "tempo-modification" for each variation of the theme.[11] A set of variations all played in the same tempo can easily congeal into mindless formalism. . . . In other spots Wagner appears to us to go too far with his "modifications"; for instance where, after a very quick opening of the first movement, he slows the second motive (bar 45) so radically that the listener becomes confused as to the basic mood, which was barely established, and the "heroic" character of the piece is diverted into the sentimental. Wagner takes the scherzo unusually fast, in fact, presto, a daring act which can become dangerous even to a virtuoso orchestra. The Marcia Funebre sounded wonderfully beautiful, particularly the gradual fading away of the main subject. The whole performance was, as stated, of the greatest interest, full of stimulating fine traits and effects; nevertheless nobody could doubt that such modifications are of Wagnerian rather than Beethovenian origin.

A special and spirited personality will so convincingly bring off many a daring deviation from the letter of the law[12] that only philistine narrow-mindedness would take exception. But there is nothing more dangerous than to attempt to generalize a clever insight or to enlarge a purely personal sensation into a universal law. If Wagner's tenets [expressed in] "On Conducting" were generally adopted, the principle

---

11. The passage on variations requires more detailed debate, lest the impression be created that all variations call for varied tempos. This may be appropriate for Brahms's set on the Haydn Chorale Opus 56 a. There the composer stops after each piece and asks for a different tempo as the new variation starts. But the finale of Beethoven's Third Symphony is a set of variations within a symphonic movement. From bar 117 to the andante section it is basically in a single tempo. (Modifications to this rule will be discussed later in the chapters on tempo.) The three variations in the andante section are again in one tempo. It is incumbent on the conductor to find a basic allegro molto and a basic poco andante.

12. In January 1977, when I was preparing for a conductor's symposium that was the basis for this book, a review in the music section of an important newspaper caught my attention. A young pianist had performed one of the Chopin sonatas, which moved the critic to comment: "In the sonata Mr. —— ignored or flatly contradicted many dynamic markings in the score; . . . Rachmaninoff did similar things in this piece and got away with it, but lesser folk probably ought to do what the composer suggested." Essentially this reviewer expresses the same opinion that Hanslick voiced 105 years earlier.

There is one grievous error and one misunderstanding in this quoted comment. The pianist under scrutiny did badly in Chopin because he imitated a man whom he should not have imitated; he should

of changing tempos would open the door to an insupportable willfulness and we would soon no longer hear symphonies by Beethoven but rather symphonies "freely after Beethoven". . . . The wretched "tempo rubato," this musical seasickness, which ruins for us so many renditions by soloists and singers and against which up to now only orchestral performances offered a sufficient antidote and restorative, would then take hold of these as well and the last healthy core of our public music life would be lost. Wagner does the same thing with conducting that he does with composition: that which appeals to his singular personality and succeeds under his exceptional gifts must become general law in art, the only true and correct way. . . . As soon as all opera composers write in the manner of *Tristan and Isolde*, we listeners must without fail repair to the madhouse, and if Wagner's "tempo modification" achieves unbounded sovereignty in our orchestras, then our conductors, violinists, and windplayers will follow us into the same establishment.[13]

Hanslick recognized that if only people of Wagner's stature indulged in their interpretative fancies the result could be totally absorbing. But our fascination would be derived from hearing one great composer say of another great composer's work, "This is the way *I* would have done it." Unless a Wagner is on the podium, serious music lovers do not attend concerts to learn the conductor's notion of how Beethoven should have written music. They go to hear the music he did write performed the way he conceived it. Large pieces, such as symphonies, operas, oratorios, and quartets, are built, as all structures must be, on principles of proportion. No work of broad scope, whether created by an architect, a playwright, or a musician, can exist without such an underlying plan. No artistic edifice can last unless the basic laws of art have been made its foundation. Because the works of great composers are so solidly constructed, they have seemed invulnerable. A long history of error, misunderstanding, and outright violation has been unable to destroy them. Today special courage and energy

---

not have imitated anybody. Two different personalities cannot ever produce the same result, no matter how hard they try to mimic one another. (This is the misunderstanding.) To state that "lesser folk" should do what the composer suggested implies that *only* lesser folk should do so. The impression is given that only dullards follow the composer's directions and that cavaliers do what "comes naturally," be it ever so whimsical. This is the grievous error. To set up standards by which all interpreters should proceed is the raison d'être of this book. I agree with the indulgence Hanslick and the more recent reviewer extended to Wagner and Rachmaninoff, respectively, mainly because Wagner and Rachmaninoff were composers, and the creative mind is never as open to someone else's creative concept as to its own. *Getting away with* is a silly phrase. We have no laws requiring accurate musical performance, and the young pianist chided in the above review got away with his rendition too, except that a reviewer from a newspaper spotted the distortions. But Rachmaninoff's changes were also distortions, and we must suspect that the *Eroica* was distorted by Wagner as well. In criminal law *getting away with* means merely not being brought to justice. But in music, justice is in the mind, and I propose that we do our level best, using our imagination and knowledge, to do justice to the great composers.

13. Eduard Hanslick, *Concerte, Componisten und Virtuosen der letzten fünfzehn Jahre 1870–1885* (Berlin: Allgemeiner Verein für Deutsche Literatur, 1886), pp. 47–50 (my translation).

may be required to sweep away the detritus of misinterpretation and reveal a composer's work as he first constructed it. Ironically, faithful interpretation of a great master's wishes often seems not conservative but radical.[14] But to discover the composer's grand design for each work is both the conductor's mission and his reward.

14. An American music critic once told me that he had been particularly taken by my "unorthodox yet fully convincing" tempos in the middle movements in Beethoven's Second Symphony. I showed him that when Beethoven's metronome markings were taken to heart these tempos were interrelated both with one another and with the allegro section of the first movement. The critic agreed that my "unorthodox" approach was truly orthodox and came to see that what passed, through custom, for orthodox readings were instead accumulations of poor reading habits.

Four
Knowing Musical Tradition

What Is a Tradition?

On some occasion, though no one seems to know the exact date and circumstances, Gustav Mahler made the landmark statement, "Tradition ist Schlamperei." The last word is difficult to translate. *Schlamperei* is so intimately related to the Austro-Hungarian monarchy's style of muddling through that neither *sloth* nor *sloppiness* will capture the exact flavor of the word. We can only surmise that on this occasion the young, ambitious opera director had advanced some new ideas, only to have them turned down by the staid, aristocratic inertia of a civil servant, who believed that if something had always been done in one way it had to be good. At such a moment Mahler evidently burst forth with his incensed outcry.

Mahler's misuse of the word *tradition* must be set straight. A new talent rightly tries to sweep away inertia, ingrained habit, and accepted methods that have outlived their usefulness. Such deadwood is not tradition. Tradition consists of a great body of unwritten laws. These were indeed disregarded by the nineteenth century, at least as far as our musical heritage goes. But the decades before the French Revolution—one of the watersheds of our Western culture— knew about musical tradition. Our own era is fast relearning many musical traditions of the eighteenth, seventeenth, and even earlier centuries.

Those who wonder whether we have unwritten musical traditions today should consider the way jazz music is written, compared to the way it sounds. Few musicians play both "classical" and "popular" music today, because all classical musicians have been trained, and still are trained, to translate what they read literally into sound. Maurice André would not be able to decipher a sheet from which Louis Armstrong played—if indeed he played from a sheet at all.

One of our most difficult tasks in reading music is to know when we are looking at a traditional notation and when we are faced with an explicit one. There is no sharp demarcation line; we find the two intermixed throughout works of the nineteenth century. It would take a deep study of sociopsychological orientation to find out why musicians gradually became literal-minded and began to forget or simply disregard tradition. One of our present problems is that too many important musicians, including very prominent conductors, are sitting on the fence, not knowing what to make of traditional modes but hoping to conceal their ambivalence.

Appoggiaturas and Other Ornaments

The tradition was to write out everything for the instruments, while treating the voice parts to a different spelling of the same cadential phrases. In the days of Beethoven and earlier it could be assumed that singers knew the tradition and would amend the written parts accordingly in performance.

No such assumption can be made today. During an audition for me, a baritone sang the recitative passage from Beethoven's Ninth Symphony without the appoggiatura on the word *Töne* (example 13). When I inquired why he had omitted it, he said that this was, after all, a matter of personal taste and opinion. "Not so," I replied, pointing to the earlier appearance of the same passage in the parts of the cellos and basses, where the notes G–F are spelled out (example 14). The singer then put me in my place by reporting that he had sung the passage in his manner under a noted colleague of mine, who had liked it.

O   Freun -   -   - de, nicht die - se Tö-ne!

Example 13. Beethoven, Sym. No. 9, 4th mvt., bass recitative

Example 14. Beethoven, Sym. No. 9, 4th mvt., instrumental recitative

Beethoven, his contemporaries, and their predecessors would have been astonished at the notion that personal preference had any bearing on a tradition as long accepted as that of the appoggiatura. Yet the unimaginative rigidity of musical training during most of the nineteenth century so firmly inculcated the idea that music must be played or sung exactly as it is written that centuries of tradition were nearly washed down the drain. For example, when I was twenty years old I coached a number of singers, some of them full professionals. A soprano whom I prepared for performances of the *Missa Solemnis* warned me that the very prominent conductor of the concerts frowned on appoggiaturas.

In recent years our interest in tradition has revived and our knowledge of it is becoming more widespread, but many serious and dedicated musicians still resist adopting musical conventions that appear to be beyond dispute. Another convention, almost as common as the use of appoggiaturas, was the practice of improvising short ornamental phrases at points in operatic arias indicated by fermatas. Yet I can recall only one instance in which an opera singer not only consented to introduce such elaborations but actually wished to do so. The artist was Elisabeth Schwarzkopf and the year was 1957. When we met on one of her American visits nearly twenty years later, she told me that no other conductor had ever consented to let her use these ornaments, though they were indubitably traditional in 1787.

A still more elaborate kind of ornament is the cadenza, or *Eingang*, the appropriate place for which is also signalled by a hold. It has been obvious for some time to many artists that there are several spots in the piano concertos of Mozart where a cadenza is in order. That we are nevertheless far from a consensus on this question I discovered when rehearsing K. 467 with a soloist widely regarded as a Mozart expert. We launched into the final movement, and at the hold the soloist began at once to play the theme as printed. I stopped him and asked if perhaps he planned to play the eingang only at the concert. He proudly and somewhat patronizingly replied, "Not at all. I do not believe in that." If he had not been helping us out on short notice I would have been less tolerant of his argument. I wondered, however, how a musician could be considered a Mozart specialist if he did not believe in the traditions within which Mozart wrote his music.

This mortal fear instrumentalists, singers, and conductors have of playing anything that is not printed is understandable. Few of our conservatories give their students a thorough grounding in the performance traditions of earlier times. It is infinitely less taxing for these students to play only the printed notes than to undertake a close study of musical traditions on their own. Moreover, by ignoring tradition they can establish themselves, ostensibly at least, as composer-fearing musicians.

Fortunately not all musicians take this easy way out. How delightful the right approach to tradition can be was shown in a performance of Mozart's Concerto K. 503, in Zurich, by the pianist Malcolm Frager. At the appropriate spot he launched into a cadenza composed by himself. After the customary play of themes he gave the second subject a little push that developed it into Papageno's second aria. To witness, as Frager's partner in the performance, the utter delight the audience (a tradition-bound group of solid Zurich residents) derived from that flight of fancy was better proof of authenticity than any amount of cant about playing what is printed.

It would be vain and against my intention to spell out suggestions for the implementation of traditional practices. It is of little use to set out rules for the "proper" interpretation of Baroque ornaments. It seems to me that thorough understanding and, if possible, a personal acquaintance with harpsichord and organ will do more to enlighten performers about the proper use of ornaments than will memorizing particular formulas. It will help to read Carl Philipp Emanuel Bach's book, and Leopold Mozart's writings are also instructive.[1] Mattheson too has written a valuable volume that will extend horizons. In the end, the performer's imagination must determine what approach to take. The traditions contain sound, healthy sense that supersedes codes and rules. Too much elliptical thinking and prolonged debate over minutiae is always a danger.

Almost all ornaments are, in a sense, extensions of the appoggiatura, or *Vorhalt*. This device, with its momentary dissonance, introduces an instant of suspense that serves many expressive purposes. That it is far more than mere decoration can be seen if we look at the second movement of Mozart's Piano Concerto K. 467 (example 15). The use of the appoggiatura in bar 4 and its repetition in bars 7, 9, 12–16, 18, 19, and later, should make it evident that the appoggiatura is not merely a convention for cadences but a profoundly significant element of melody and harmony. An elementary grasp of the traditional way of performing appoggiaturas would preclude a common perversion of the melodic phrasing in bar 18 that has been perpetuated in the soundtrack of a popular motion picture. The first two notes in bar 18 are not to be considered a mere continuation of the descending scale of eighth notes in the previous measure, even though that passage consists of two appoggiaturas with their resolutions. Instead, the appoggiatura in bar 18 is a forerunner of the one in bar 19, which ends the long phrase. To play the first note in bar 18 as an eighth produces the effect of losing one's footing, as if one had missed the last step of a stairway and arrived too soon on the landing. By extending the duration of the *la* to a quarter note, we can avoid the sudden dropping sensation created by the customary phrasing and establish the broad sweep of the entire melody.

The importance of coming to terms with the tradition of the appoggiatura is thus far-reaching. In pieces with a lyrical bent many appoggiaturas are spelled out. I find that those musicians who refuse to acknowledge unwritten, though traditional, appoggiaturas also tend to overlook those that are explicitly marked in the text of a score. In the first four bars of the slow movement of Beethoven's *Pastoral* Symphony there are three appoggiaturas. In the slow movement of the Seventh the melodic line has two appoggiaturas between bars 102 and 110. The bucolic trio of the Ninth is built on the appoggiatura; in the slow movement, appoggiaturas are everywhere; and the hymn (which is introduced by the recitative discussed above) is also filled with descending seconds (not all of which, however, are true appoggiaturas).

1. Both the C. P. E. Bach and Leopold Mozart books are available in English translation: Carl Philipp Emanuel Bach, *Essay on the True Art of Playing Keyboard Instruments*, trans. and ed. William J. Mitchell (New York: W. W. Norton, 1949); and Leopold Mozart, *A Treatise on the Fundamental Principles of Violin Playing*, trans. Editha Knocker (London: Oxford University Press, 1948).

Example 15. Mozart, Piano Concerto, K. 467, 2nd mvt., mm. 1–22

Wherever appoggiaturas appear they deserve close attention. They provide the inner tension that is aroused by dissonance, or, more specifically, by suspense. Generally they signal a mood of mellow lyricism. When these rising or descending seconds are given their proper due they take on a special meaning

that eludes a casual reading. Not only the voice has the ability to exploit the appoggiatura; instrumental music too can make the most of this expressive device by adding an agogic accent on the first note, just as a fine singer produces the word *Töne* in the great recitative of the Ninth Symphony.

Triplets and Dotted Rhythms

Two unwritten methods of playing certain dotted rhythms are implicit in much music of the eighteenth century and earlier. The first tradition involved what appear to be dotted rhythms played against patterns of three notes. In triple meters, a pattern that would today be written as a quarter note followed by an eighth was written in Bach's day as if it were a dotted eighth note followed by a sixteenth. The last note, however, had half the value of the first; when played against a triplet it would sound with, not after, the third note. The second tradition was that in dotted rhythms the longer note was extended, cutting the final note shorter, as if the first note were double-dotted. That these conventions were observed over a long period of time has been widely recognized. Yet they are not universally accepted, nor are they taught in all conservatories.

A pianist once told me of his experience in collaborating with a venerable conductor in a performance of Bach's *Fifth Brandenburg Concerto*. Not an old man, but evidently still rooted firmly in the rigid ways of the nineteenth century, the conductor insisted on performing the final movement exactly as it was printed, despite the tradition that all dotted rhythms should be adjusted to coincide with the triplets. Several players, who knew better, tried to persuade the conductor, but without success. This was not mere stubbornness. It is very hard, if not impossible, to shake off one's entire orientation to musical spelling. I have had similar difficulties with orchestral players, some of whom simply cannot do anything that runs counter to their training—which has taught them to play only and precisely what appears in print.

However understandable this approach may be, there is danger in it. The considerable group of specialists who have emerged in the last few decades may come to constitute an elite, in whose care the works of the pre-1800 masters will be exclusively authentic. This is not an idle fear: I know of members of great orchestras freely admitting, "We have no technique for playing music written before 1800." If this unfortunate compartmentalization is to be avoided, it is essential that every serious musician learn to master the traditions of the time prior to 1800. Thus he will not only avoid confinement to a modern repertoire but will also discover how far into the nineteenth century the Baroque traditions extended. Beethoven, Schubert, and Schumann are often misread because it is assumed that they wrote their music exactly as it was to be played, with no dependence on traditional interpretation. If such misreading seems improbable, let us look at several examples.

In Beethoven's First Symphony there are three spots on just two pages where traditional notation is used. If we keep in mind that a primary purpose of both traditional methods of playing dotted rhythms was to ensure that changes of harmony occurred simultaneously in all instruments, these spots will be easy to find. In bar 44 of the second movement (example 16), the first violins should play the C as if it were double-dotted, bringing the C-sharp in line with the

Example 16. Beethoven, Sym. No. 1, 2nd mvt., mm. 43–54

harmonic changes in the other stringed instruments. In the next bar, the lower strings must play the dotted rhythm as a triplet—again in order to bring about a uniform change of harmonies in the entire string ensemble. Finally, from bar 53 on, the kettledrum must play in triplet rhythm throughout the violin and flute passage. (Unless the right tempo for this movement is found, these spots will become very awkward; the tempo must not be dragged out.)

The first signal that we will find traditional notation in this symphony has

Example 17. Schumann, Sym. No. 4, Romanze, mm.
7–10

already appeared at the close of the slow introduction to the opening movement.
The transition to allegro con brio sounds better, as well as being ever so much
simpler to play, if the long note, G, in bar 12, is double-dotted. In the introduction to his Second Symphony, Beethoven actually wrote in the double dot. Yet
this does not mean that henceforth in his music everything should be read literally. In the slow movement of the Fifth Symphony the second clarinet should
not play its thirty-second note in such a way that it hobbles after the flute triplets
in bars 14 and 19; likewise, the viola and bassoon in bar 18 should not lag
behind the violin triplets. Such a reading would be positively antimusical.

It would be useful for music teachers to have a music dictionary, comparable
to the *Oxford English Dictionary*, which would cite the date and occasion a new
formula of notation was first used. Such formulas are invented in music much
as words are in language, to accommodate new situations as they arise. It would
also be useful to know why traditions were abandoned in favor of literal readings. Such historic moments would be almost impossible to identify, however;
as we have seen, older forms of notation are occasionally found long after they
have been generally given up.

It should not be too surprising, then, to find that traditional notation survived as late as Schumann. He still resorted to Baroque notation, equating dotted rhythms with triplets. Whenever I bring up the example shown here (example 17), from the slow movement of his Fourth Symphony, I am asked how I can be certain that Schumann did not intend the pizzicato notes of violins and violas, as well as the notes of clarinet and bassoon, to be played *after* the triplet of the theme in the oboe and cello solo. A glance at the trio of the First Novelette for Piano should leave no doubt about the meaning of the composer's use of traditional notation (example 18). (I hope that this example will not only make my point about notation but will also demonstrate once more the importance of knowing the full range of a composer's works.) In the third movement of Schumann's Second Symphony, too, there are places where Baroque notation is evidently still used. In bar 35 (example 19), it seems absurd to squeeze the last sixteenth note into its exact mathematical place. It is far more musical and natural to await the final note of the triplet and sound the sixteenth with the C of the lead voice.

Example 18. Schumann, Novelette, Opus 21

Example 19. Schumann, Sym. No. 2, 3rd mvt., mm. 33–38

Whenever something appears artificial or unduly complex, it is useful to examine the surrounding fabric carefully. It will then often become clear that a traditional and generous approach is required. Composers were not mathematicians, nor were they intent on crossing every *t* and dotting every *i*. It is precisely because I believe that the works of composers should not be trifled with that I feel obliged to search for the extent to which, even in the Romantic period, composers continued to use old methods, traditional spellings, and Baroque ways. The great nineteenth-century masters, including Richard Wagner, still showed great confidence in the ability of interpreters to fathom their music. After Wagner the trust diminished, and more and more explicitness prevailed.

It is most important for conductors to study the music of periods when the traditions were taken for granted, immersing themselves in it until the meaning and the rightness of the conventions become self-evident. As a starting point, the conductor might examine Bach's aria for alto, with cello obbligato and continuo, from the Cantata No. 70. In this piece of ninety-two bars I find fifty-six separate confirmations of the need to coordinate dotted rhythms with triplets. But a conductor cannot assume that his orchestral players will have sufficient familiarity with tradition to grasp, or at least keep in mind, general directives to this effect. Before beginning Bach's Third Suite (example 20), the conductor cannot simply announce that all dotted quarter notes should be double-dotted. In each part he must have the double-dotting and the extra sixteenth flag marked, as if each occurrence were a new event. In bar 9 the oboes and the first violins must be so corrected; similar corrections must be marked in bar 10 for the second violins and violas and in bars 11 and 12 for all high instruments; and so on, throughout the piece.

Example 20. Bach, Overture No. 3, 1st mvt., mm. 9–13

One reason why otherwise expert orchestral players adhere so rigidly to printed orthodoxy became clearer to me recently when I heard a fine orchestra of one of the great American conservatories perform the entire introduction of this piece as if it were marked *grave*—as indeed a misguided German editor specified in one edition. The orchestra played the section in a heavy "eight beats to the bar," hammering out each note as if it had been written by Bruckner. Any musician who directs youngsters in such an outdated, discredited style commits a musical crime and should be given assignments of a less sensitive nature. Such a disregard for tradition makes it difficult for students to learn a crucial stylistic distinction and the proper way to realize it in performance.

A glance at the other three Bach suites (or overtures) shows that each opening movement follows a similar pattern—a richly dotted, festive 4/4 (not 8/8) followed by a fugal section.[2] One of the clearest proofs that double-dotting should be used in these movements appears in the Second Suite (example 21). The rests in the first bar make clear both how Bach wanted the movement played and his reason for not making his intention explicit. If bar 3 and all similar patterns thereafter are played as bar 1 is written, the proper rhythmic vitality will be achieved. Bach merely wrote the music in a shorthand that his players were expected to translate, in accordance with traditions all of them knew. As anyone who writes music will immediately understand, each of the traditional spellings saves considerable time.

Example 21. Bach, Overture No. 2, 1st mvt., mm. 1–3

In the passage shown here (example 22), from the first movement of Bach's Fourth Suite, both traditions, double-dotting and dotting against triple rhythms, are represented. In bar 22 the first and third oboes and the first violin must double-dot their long notes, so that they continue with the last sixteenth in the bass and the other middle voice. In the following 9/8 section we see how the composer sets the intended pattern in the first entrance of each voice, in bars 24, 25, 28, and 29, by printing the rests; afterward he reverts to the shorthand method of writing a two-note triplet. Bar 28 should convince us that it would be absurd to play the dotted eighth with a sixteenth, when the harmony obviously demands that the 6-chord sound on the sixth and ninth units of the bar.

2. The editor of Bärenreiter's New Bach edition, who marks this 2/2, has misread the sign of the tempo tagliato as alla breve. The tempo tagliato merely indicates that the tempo and phrasing are to be in the larger unit, that is, in four, not in eight. This common error will be discussed later.

Example 22. Bach, Overture No. 4, 1st mvt., mm. 22–29

Alla Breve

Ask almost any musician what *alla breve* means and you will be told it means
"in two." This is totally wrong. If this were true, it would follow that the opening andante of the overture to *Don Giovanni*, the comparable section of the *Così
fan tutte* overture, and the opening adagio of the overture to *Die Zauberflöte*
would all have to be played in two, which is obvious nonsense. I have nevertheless known eager, scholarly conductors to attempt it—with rather disastrous results. The correct tempo cannot be achieved in any of these sections if the con-

ductor insists on counting them in two. The fact is that alla breve merely refers to the *next higher unit* as the basis for the phrase and the tempo. One need only look at an alto aria from Bach's *St. John Passion*, "Es ist vollbracht." This piece, for voice and viola da gamba, begins quite clearly in a slow "eight." Later comes a triumphant and jubilant middle part, "Der Held aus Juda siegt mit Macht," which the composer has marked "alla breve." This section is in a 3/4 meter. To those who hold to the "in two" belief, something appears to be wrong. But the only thing wrong is the accepted association of alla breve with the numeral 2.

In the critical commentary that is a part of the subscription series of the New Bach edition the editor dutifully records that bar 20 of the *St. John* aria bears the marking "alla breve." The words do not, however, appear in the main text of the score. What prompted the editor to omit this directive from a new and authoritative publication? I can only surmise that he was misled by the usual misinterpretation of the term and thought that the marking was a mistake.

Folk and Regional Traditions

At the beginning of this chapter I pointed out that jazz is an obvious example of a type of music in which the manner of playing written notes is governed by unwritten traditions. The way in which printed jazz music is transformed in actual performance has its closest parallel in music of folk origin, particularly in dance music. The most familiar example is the Viennese waltz. Johann Strauss and his contemporaries were content to write "tempo di valse" over the first bar. Yet, though some eager musicians have invented ingeniously explicit spellings for intricate music, no one has ever mastered the problem of writing a proper waltz accompaniment just as it sounds. In the spring of 1975, a Johann Strauss festival was held in Vienna to commemorate his 150th anniversary. Every concert, no matter what the program, featured at least one piece by Strauss. As a result Vienna was regaled (as one wit put it) with Russian waltzes, Italian waltzes, English waltzes, American waltzes, German waltzes, and occasionally Viennese waltzes.

What was the essential difference? The tradition of authentic performance was achieved at the festival only when the leader had the courage to be very simple. One should conduct these pieces almost as straightforwardly as would a bandleader, pretending that the musicians are not a symphony orchestra but merely an enlarged ensemble gathered in a park pavilion or an outdoor restaurant. Note how the violinist-leader begins the first of the waltzes making up a set. He slows down the upbeat or the first bar—but only to prepare the ensemble for the proper attack of the main tempo. This effect must not be repeated, as many conductors are wont to do. It is generally dangerous to add nuances to these pieces in an attempt to make them "worthy" of a symphony concert. Many are already masterpieces of their own genre. Adding ritards, accelerandos, or instrumental changes to a waltz will lower its vitality without producing a symphony.

When Mozart wrote reams of minuets, German dances, and country dances (a source of steady, though small, income from the Viennese court), he did not need to mark tempos or specific nuances beyond the barest outlines. Ravel was not so fortunate when he composed his *Bolero*, which has a rhythm that also defies accurate transcription. Spanish dances always present a problem to musicians unacquainted with national traditions, particularly if castanets are called for. Percussionists, no matter how excellent in other respects, are untrained in the playing of hand castanets. They rest the instrument on the knee, with the result that the intended effect is lost, and what emerges sounds stiff and inflexible.

Spanish dance rhythms are matched in intricacy by those of many other nationalities, and the problem is not even confined to dances. Rhythms built on peculiarities of language are equally hard to transcribe. In recent times the efforts of "nationalistic" composers to revive their countries' folk music have encountered many difficulties. In collecting Hungarian folk songs, Kodály and Bartók found that the accents and inflections of the language could be sung and played but not precisely notated. When I prepared the music for a performance of Kodály's *Háry János* Suite with a famous Dutch orchestra, the principal violist was quite unable to grasp that the solo could not be played in the classic solfège. I went so far as to learn the Hungarian words of the song, imagining that if I pronounced them with the proper accent the player would perceive that his literal reading was inadequate. All was in vain. The solo in performance sounded exactly as it is written—that is, wooden and totally unidiomatic.

Staccato

We have discussed traditions that are not written down (ornaments) and those that appear to be written incorrectly (various dotted rhythms). A third kind of tradition, which is at least as likely to cause misunderstanding and lead to argument, involves signs that seem to be explicit but in fact have variable meanings. A prime example of such signs is the dot that is placed under or over a note, instead of after it. Because of rigid and unimaginative teaching, most players believe that this "staccato" sign means simply that a note is to be played as short as possible. Nothing could be further from the truth. No greater diversity can be found in music than in the possible interpretations of this little mark. Tradition may not specify a proper style of staccato playing for a particular piece, but it does imply the range of appropriate interpretations of staccato in each era. Moreover, understanding the original meaning of the term should help to clear up a basic misconception.

Staccato simply means "detached." It was first used to indicate that notes should be separately articulated, rather than tied together. Apparently the dot began as a vertical dash, indicating that a note should be separated from the next by a new attack (on a keyboard), an articulation (in wind instruments), or a new

Example 23. Beethoven, Sym. No. 3, 1st mvt., mm. 27–34

stroke of the bow (on strings). Detaching one note from the next inevitably makes the first note slightly shorter. But shortness was not the basic idea, as should be proved beyond doubt by the fact that in a number of Bach cantatas the word *staccato* is written side by side with *lento*. An equally telling proof is the presence of the dots in bar 182 of the funeral march of the *Eroica* Symphony. Given the character of the music, a scale of short notes would bring a spirit of levity into this most tragic peroration. In fact, this symphony is an ideal subject for a study of the many meanings of staccato and it will be worthwhile to examine it closely.

Let us begin with the third movement, because it makes the greatest use of the light, short sound that is commonly taught today as the *only* kind of staccato. It is significant that on the first page of the scherzo the word *staccato* is spelled out twice, as if the dots themselves might not be a sufficient signal to the players to make the notes very short. Also, on the first three pages of the third movement, the words *pp sempre* (or *sempre pp*) are printed four times. We may guess that the composer did not have great confidence in the memory or the discipline of his players. Most important, we should suspect that, even in Beethoven's time, dots over notes did not necessarily imply extreme shortness.

If the dots in the scherzo have one meaning, those over the first movement's two opening chords have another: "Do not sustain these notes, making them pompous or solemn, but tear into the full tempo with two hammer-blows." Any note can be ended either abruptly or with a mellow rounding. The dots here signify that the composer wants a forceful, unsustained ending.

Example 24. Beethoven, Sym. No. 3, 1st mvt., mm. 13–17

In bars 29, 33, and 34 (example 23) the dots have another function: they call for rhythmic awareness and precision. At the third quarter of bar 28 the composer changes from 3/4 to 2/4 (clearly indicated by the sforzato marks) while continuing to spell out his intentions in triple meter. In bars 32–33 the rhythm shifts back into 3/4. Here the unaccented quarter note should be shorter, or the effect of the dramatic change will be partially obliterated. It is here that the composer begins to set the stage for the six chords in bars 128–31. At bar 254, the climax of the whole movement, we again find the six 2/4 chords, and at bar 258 a dot is placed under the low C of the cellos and basses, to emphasize that this last note is not to be accented. (It is always hard to convince the respective sections of an orchestra that this note, and its four successors, must be unstressed so as to avoid interrupting the constant 2/4. Only in bar 284 does the triple meter return—and with terrifying effect, because of the dissonance produced by the E/F.)

Still another meaning of the little dots can be seen in bars 15–17 (example 24). Here a pattern for accompaniments appears in the middle voices of the string ensemble; this pattern should be observed in all similar contexts. In bars 3, 4, and others Beethoven felt that no dots were needed. Because there had been no legato passage it was taken for granted that the second violins and violas would continue with separate strokes. But in bar 15 Beethoven felt it necessary to establish that the accompaniment was to be performed not on the string, but off the string. The cellos in bar 14 must match the legato character of woodwinds and horns and should not indulge in a short-note pattern. Here the dots

Example 25. Beethoven, Sym. No. 3, 1st mvt.,
mm. 46–49

mean merely that one note should not be run into another; they are an admonition to articulate the two B-flat quarter notes.

In bars 47–48 (example 25), a pattern is set in the bass strings that is nearly always interpreted as if it were a scherzo movement. Oblivious to the nature of the motive played by woodwinds soli and violins from bar 45 on, the low strings bounce happily through their triads. No matter how expressively the oboe, clarinet, and flute sigh, no matter how elegantly the violins respond, the bass strings insist on playing their jig. Why? Because there are dots under or above their notes. In this case a simple corrective device can be applied by drawing an arc over all six quarter notes. This compels the low strings to play these six notes on one up-bow. (Starting with bar 83, we find a type of marking that will be helpful to the basses and cellos from bar 47 on, and in all similar passages.) We find another important signal in bars 55–56 (example 26). The force desired in the three notes of bar 56 will be much stronger if the notes in bar 55 are held for their full value. Once again, bar 56 is not meant to be very short, for a real *ff* cannot be developed in excessively short notes. It takes some time to bring forth a fortissimo. Beethoven's intention, then, is to detach and strongly articulate the quarter notes.

Musicians are wont to shorten almost every note that is not tied to the following note by a legato arc.[3] This is the basic misunderstanding of th: whole staccato-legato question. In bars 59 and 60 (example 26), a very short staccato in the cello and viola parts can only cause distress. Violins and winds have an arc over their repeated notes that makes them broaden their phrasing ever so slightly.

---

3. There is a universal tendency to rush or drag certain kinds of phrases. This tendency is not a poor habit but is somehow based on a natural musical instinct for the character of a passage. The

Example 26. Beethoven, Sym. No. 3, 1st mvt., mm. 55–60

Unless this is matched by a rather heavy stroke in the lower strings, albeit always played piano, the synchronization is bound to suffer, with the lower strings galloping ahead, while the upper instruments try to sing lyrically. Bars 99–102 (example 27) are frequently played exactly like the following six, though the first group consists of quarter notes, the second of eighth notes. This produces a feeling of scherzando alien to the passage in question, which is misterioso, hushed, and intensely serious. Short staccato phrasing is nearly always gay, jocose, flippant, and dancing. Such a mood is totally out of place in this section, which leads, within a space of two dozen bars, to one of the most awe-inspiring outbursts in symphonic-dramatic music.

From bar 136 on (example 28) we find two different kinds of staccato. One group is formed by the eighth notes of the second violins, violas, and cellos (but only the eighth notes), while the other group is once more the six times 2/4 rhythm, as begun in bar 136 in an interplay between lower strings and winds. Here is one of the most sophisticated and intricate ensemble problems in classical music. The middle string voices change roles constantly, alternately participating in the relay of eighth notes and the 2/4 pattern. Over the whole mixture

conductor should always try to attain a perfect ensemble without straitjacketing either the lyric or the running instinct. It is of prime importance to adjust the type of bowstroke used, in order to lengthen or shorten notes, thereby achieving better ensemble and a higher quality of musical representation.

Example 27. Beethoven, Sym. No. 3, 1st mvt., mm. 99–108

Example 28. Beethoven, Sym. No. 3, 1st mvt., mm. 135–38

floats the melody of the first violins and flute in a grand legato. In bars 627–30 one can find the final clear statement of these six 2/4 patterns, with a legato melodic motive spanning it.

By such conscious grading of staccato realization we can underline and emphasize one aspect of this gigantic movement that is generally glossed over: the interplay between 3/4 and 2/4. The following phrases are directly involved:

Example 29. Beethoven, Sym. No. 3, 1st mvt., mm. 686–95

25–26, 28–32, 119–21, 128–31, 136–39, 254–83 passim; all parallel spots in the recapitulation; and bars 627–30 and 687–89 in the coda. In this final appearance of 2/4 (example 29), in the coda, it is worth directing the reader's attention to the startling fact that no *f* is marked on the first beat of bar 689. This makes it doubly certain that this quarter should be felt as the second beat of the last 2/4. There are two long 3/4 chords, followed by two 2/4 chords; and this last 2/4 in two strokes prepares for the following bars, which mix both elements, with the first violins phrasing 2/4 (as in bars 29–30) while the rest of the orchestra insists that the piece closes in 3/4.

Performances of the funeral march of the *Eroica* Symphony are often prime examples of the misinterpretation of staccato. Beginning with the first bar in the double basses, and from bar 8 onward in the whole string ensemble, we have an accompaniment that is intended to sound like a glorified funeral drum, such as the one found in any solemn cortege escorting a great person to burial (example 30). This accompaniment appears in the first section of the movement forty-two times. If the tempo is too slow, a string section cannot possibly play this drum motive with the appropriate sound. The figure must be very short, resembling a *free* drumroll; this in turn necessitates a speed at which sixty players can produce such an effect confidently and naturally. It is very important to dissuade the strings from playing this motive at the point of the bow. If the tempo is too slow there can be no ensemble in the drumming passage. This deficiency is then masked by nondescript playing on the string. For the strings to play the drum-rolls with the proper effect in mind, the tempo must be the one indicated by Beethoven's own metronome marking.

The dots under the eighth notes of the basses in bars 1, 2, and 3 have a different significance. This type of dot is a warning not to linger on the note,

Contrabasso

Example 30. Beethoven, Sym. No. 3, 2nd mvt., mm. 1–3

lest it become a lower octave for the bass of the string quartet, which in this case is the cello range. Except for the eighth bar, the composer set the opening theme for string quartet without the sub-bass notes; by the same token, the wind phrase from bars 9 to 16 also has a narrow setting. Thus, any indulgence by the bass players, any holding of the note C, would create a lower octave bass doubling, which Beethoven took pains to avoid. Hence these dots. The drum effect is all the basses are asked to produce, with the final note as much a part of the drum effect as the first three.

In bar 18 (example 31) the dot is given yet another meaning. Here it simply indicates that the notes are détaché. Composers not only write signs indicating

 Example 31. Beethoven, Sym. No. 3, 2nd mvt., mm. 17–18

what to do but also signs warning what not to do. This sequence of dots seems to be of the latter variety. The message is, "Do not slur this passage."

The C-major section of this movement has suffered even more injury from the wrong type of staccato playing than the first part of the march. It is not uncommon for conductors to inject a good deal of jollity into this section, especially from bar 84 onward, particularly when they wish to make up for an overly slow beginning by investing the major key with a più mosso. This mood is often established as early on as the three notes of the string bass (bar 68), when these are made to sound in a short staccato, as if we are readying for a jig. This entire section, with its masses of dots, must be articulated clearly, but without ever slipping into a trot of a jolly mood. It is a transcendental piece, containing in bars 84 and 85 strong reminders of the "lacrimosa" motive of Mozart's Requiem. Even though there are no dots, habit has invested this brief phrase with a short last note, which gives the lacrimosa "the character of a mincing dance step."[4]

The trouble goes beyond this one movement: it arises whenever an accompaniment or countervoice has a rest on a strong beat. No matter what notes follow, the players are so eager to give the rest ample time that they shortchange the end of each group. The result is that such passages necessarily terminate with inordinately short last notes. Decades of practicing such habits have so dulled our ears and our sensitivity to expressive meaning that jollity in the midst of the funeral march is accepted as proper Beethoven.

It is a revealing and rewarding experience to go over the entire movement, looking for those places where the staccato dots are marked and those where they are not. In all classical music (indeed, in all music from an age when composers followed generally known traditions in writing their music), what was taken to be self-evident was not specifically marked. Thus, when we find detailed instructions for the performance of nuances it often—and in Bach, nearly always—means that we are encountering an exceptional case. In the coda of the funeral march it has always been fully understood that the dots over the notes in bar 209 and following (example 32) merely indicate a distinct separation, not anything approaching a short sound. When this passage is performed

4. This custom never fails to remind me of the story of a well-to-do man who haggles with a clergyman over the cost of a burial with oration for a distant relative, who died a pauper. The clergyman describes his selection of eulogies, along with their prices. The choicest, he promises, will make the women faint with emotion. "Too expensive," the rich relation says. The next eulogy will leave no handkerchief dry. This also is too expensive. There is the very serious eulogy without tears. Still too expensive. "I do have one for a very modest price," the clergyman admits. "But I must warn you that it is slightly on the hilarious side."

Example 32. Beethoven, Sym. No. 3, 2nd mvt., mm. 208–13

properly (Hanslick favorably mentions Wagner's interpretation of it in his *Eroica* performance in 1872), it is deeply moving, as if the funeral train has halted and now everyone is free to pray or to feel the pain and sadness in a personal way. There is no doubt that the fullest expression of such intense music can be attained only by adding to the overall concept consideration of the minutest details, such as these variable signs.

After taking into consideration these many interpretations of staccato dots in three movements of the symphony, the finale will pose few mysteries. In general, such nuances as staccato are far easier to interpret in light, fast movements than in tragic, slow pieces. The original dance tune that became the theme of the finale of the *Eroica* is, like most dances, built on a strong rhythmic pulse. This demands a decisive beat and short, accented notes. One particular spot is worthy of detailed explication. The fifth bar of the theme (bar 88) should be the model for the entire development in the finale (example 33). The winds have an arc over the two quarter notes and their dots (bar 80); the strings have no arc. Later on, in the poco andante section, this pattern is repeated. The ultimate and thoroughly transformed version of these two notes appears in the sequence beginning with bar 410. To produce the great climax of bar 420 (which recalls powerfully the G-minor episode in the funeral march, bar 145), the two quarter notes and the other bar with the half note must be performed with ever-increasing intensity, which in this case means an increasingly long sound. Bar 410 is still playful, emerging from the previous phrase, which is very light and quite Viennese in character; but over the following sequences these notes assume a terrifying power. Yet the same two dots remain our only indication of how to phrase this section. The principle of the variable meanings of the staccato dot, illustrated in these examples from the *Eroica*, could be applied to almost any other work of the great repertoire.

The question is often raised whether the whole approach to such matters as staccato playing is not dependent on a so-called classical, as distinct from romantic, approach. We should always bear in mind that some interpreters tend to

Example 33. Beethoven, Sym. No. 3, 4th mvt., mm. 86–93

adopt the same approach to all music. I recall one very gifted conductor who, like most artists, went through a period of intense experimentation. This took the form of a tendency to play everything more slowly than marked. His finale of Mahler's Third Symphony lasted several minutes longer than the slowest on record. Perhaps this made some sense, for it is a very slow movement. But he also applied this monolithic slowness to Strauss's *Der Rosenkavalier*, a glorified operetta and farce that must be quicksilver light. The fact is that applying one approach to all musical works is ridiculous. The same is true of most particulars of music, such as staccato. One school plays nearly everything long; there is also an opposite style of playing that makes everything secco. A musician once told me that a certain famous and splendid orchestra had not been asked to play a single short note in Stravinsky at anytime during the past half century.

To play everything short or everything long is simply wrong. This is not a matter of personal choice. If the C-major section of the *Eroica* sounds as gay as the "jolly gathering of country folk" in the third movement of the *Pastoral* Symphony, then a mistake is being made—and my guess would be that the staccato playing is too short. If the scherzo of the Sixth Symphony is played with notes that are longer than a very short staccato, the jolly gathering will be positively drab. To call one approach romantic and the other classical merely dignifies poor interpretation with two words of dubious meaning.

As with tempos and nearly all other elements that make up a musical performance, there are variables, especially of acoustics, that determine whether certain notes should be short or less so. Short notes will be most effective (as will all great music of the past) in the old type of concert hall that has a lengthy sound decay (a good reverberation). In "dry" halls with a quick decay, the music will be better served if the musicians do not favor a very short staccato style. This would produce the sterile sound characteristic of lecture halls. For speaking, the lack of reflected sound is essential; for music, reflected sound is essential. If music must be played in a lecture hall, the whole approach determining the length of notes must be adjusted. Aside from such practical matters, however, the spirit of the music is never served well by a uniform approach.

The accepted practice of playing short staccatos almost everywhere must be revised. It is not classical, nor is it romantic. Neither is this practice Baroque, although it has recently spilled over into the vast field of Baroque music. Newly formed chamber groups demonstrate their classicism by making all their music very jolly, very bright, and most of the time very short. For a while this was a welcome antidote to the customary heavy-handed approach to Bach. But having performed the *Brandenburg Concertos* and the overtures with enormous kudos, expert ensembles seem to have decided that this is proper Baroque style. Consequently, they apply it to all compositions of the period. When the final chorus of the *St. Matthew Passion* is performed in this manner, and the most deeply moving ariosos are gaily speeded up, all sense of the music is sacrificed to a simplistic notion of period style. The same holds for the symphonies of Beethoven and others. Every great work is first and last a meaningful musical utterance unlike any other. If it did not have its own unique meaning it would have come and gone and would not be part of our living repertoire.

Wagner, perhaps as a result of hearing many performances of uncertain delivery, was quite explicit in his directives on staccato playing. Just as the *Eroica* is a good example of the variability of the staccato in the symphony repertoire, so is *Die Meistersinger* a prime example in an opera of the later nineteenth century. In the prelude we find very precise comments, such as *Sehr gehalten* (at the very beginning of the score). When the violin run commences in bar 33, the word *stacc.* is added to the dots over the violin notes. At the entry of the march theme we find *Sehr gehalten* once more, cautioning the brasses and winds not to play short notes. At the entrance of Beckmesser's music we find the admonitions *Sehr kurz* ("very short") and *Immer stacc.* ("always staccato"). In view of the foregoing, it is easy to conclude that the dots alone, as they appear after bar 151 in the transition to the three-theme combination marked in trombones, violas, and cellos, do not call for short notes at all. The additional word *marcato* tells us that this main theme is to be well articulated and the eighth notes are to be separate from one another but not particularly short. At the confluence of the three themes we find that the woodwinds and middle strings have dots for one bar with the word *scherzando* written out. Throughout this music Wagner uses the term *stacc.* instead of continuing the dots ad infinitum. In bar 160 we find the comment *Immer gleichmässig leicht* ("always equally lightly").

This brief illustration shows first of all that the composer uses short notes for the "light" characters. They suggest sarcasm and irony when applied to Beckmesser, scherzando when applied to the apprentices. When the latter have their dance at the festival meadow in the last scene, Wagner is once more quite specific. In the violin passage *stacc.* is used without accompanying dots. When the actual dance music begins, the first bar is carefully marked with three dots over the three quarter notes in the violins and one over the third quarter in violas and cellos. This pattern must then be continued; violas and cellos are thus reminded that the half note is to be held full value and the quarter shortened, thereby giving the right lilt to the dance; when the woodwinds take up the theme, *stacc.* is again written out rather than represented by dots. During the entrance of the Masters, the *stacc.* is a necessary reminder, since this particular passage could conceivably be grand détaché. On the following page, without specific mention, the bowing becomes broad as the tempo slows down for the introduction to the chorale. In the last measure of this chorale we find dots under the strings' sixteenth notes that have nothing to do with short staccato, being simply directions to articulate and use more bowstrokes while the winds play in strict legato. Large portions of the *Meistersinger* score contain excellent documentation of the great variety the word *staccato* can have.

Accents

Accents belong to the same category as staccato dots. They serve as signs for many nuances and are frequently misunderstood. There are various theories about the difference between a $\wedge$ and a $>$, just as there are learned disagreements over the difference between the raindrop and the dot as staccato signs. Organs and harpsichords must play accents by adding notes—trills or other embellishments—since these instruments do not allow any dynamic gradation within a set registration pattern. Thus the reading of accents began after the end of the Baroque period. Within the category of accents are the dynamic signs *sf*, *sfz*, *fp*, *sfp*, *fpp*, and so forth. All of these are intended to emphasize a note or a chord.

Let us look at the first movement of Mendelssohn's Violin Concerto, bar 418. This is one of the rare cases where a composer is explicit in such matters. After four bars of *pp* orchestral accompaniment, Mendelssohn takes no chances on an uncertain approach by players, marking his score *forte sforzato*, literally an "effort" within forte range attacking the note. At bars 173 and 175 (example 34), the intention is not as explicitly stated, yet it seems obvious that the phrase *si-la-sol-mi-sol-re* when first played, by the solo instrument (bar 171), is slightly nudged by an accent in the orchestra. Then the melody itself has an accent, this time within the piano range, as if to reaffirm the validity of the statement. At the third occurrence of the phrase, when it appears with a fuller arabesque in the solo part, there is no accent but rather a general crescendo. To translate this into a dramatic dialogue, imagine a statement set forth casually at first, then with a little more emphasis, as one accentuates a key word when repeating a sentence one wishes to drive home. Finally, in its grandest form, the entire phrase becomes louder and more firmly restated. It is also worthwhile to look at the harmony, which changes after the third statement.

Example 34. Mendelssohn, Violin Concerto, mm. 168–76

In the adagio of Beethoven's Quartet Opus 127, amid a plethora of accents, there are only two spots, bars 9 and 111, where a $>$ appears. Beethoven used this particular sign of emphasis as an agogic rather than a dynamic accent. I find that each time I use the term *agogic* in rehearsal it is misconstrued. It seems that

Example 35. Beethoven, Opus 127, 2nd mvt., mm. 1–14

most musicians no longer understand what it means.[5] An agogic accent is exe-cuted by a slight lengthening or extension of a note. Here in the quartet move-ment this stretching of the marked notes comes after a uniform rhythmic pattern that goes on for ten units of rhythmic evenness (example 35). In bar 9 the theme in the cello has been counterpointed by the first violin, creating a uniformity of rhythm that is not apparent in the sequence, bars 3–5, because there the theme is played without counterpoint and the variance as shown in the second half of bar 4 is sufficient to avoid the appearance of rhythmic sameness. Hence there is no agogic accent in bar 5.

In bars 12, 15, and 16 we find another kind of accent, a delay of the main note through the addition of grace notes. To do justice to the composer's intent the grace notes must be performed with the understanding that rhythmic variety

5. I was brought up with the term and found only recently why many professional musicians do not know it. Grove's dictionary defines it as "a word not accepted by the O.E.D. as English but used by German and hence by American and some English musical scholars to denote quantitative as distinct from stress accent in musical phrasing (from Greek carrying away or off, leading towards, directing; more specifically, a rhythmic movement)."

is their function. Of course, before any of these fine points can bring about its proper effect, the tempo of the movement must be correct. Too often it is taken at a snail's pace, out of misguided "reverence." Although there are other cases where the > indicates an agogic accent, we must not extend this as a rule to the works of other composers.

This Beethoven quartet also demonstrates the general pattern of the sforzando accent. This accent appears in the motto of the first movement, bars 1–6 (example 36), again in bars 75–80, and later in the bars after 135. From bar 147 on the *sf* appears again (example 37). Both these marks— > and *sf*—signal a strong accent on the offbeat, but there is a difference. The motto puts the *sf on* a note to be held, whereas after bar 147 the accent is in a passing movement of notes. Here the *sf* should be followed by a lighter dynamic shading so as not to blot out the phrase of the first violin.

Example 36. Beethoven, Opus 127, 1st mvt., mm. 1–6

Example 37. Beethoven, Opus 127, 1st mvt., mm. 147–55

There are instances, as shown here from the first movement of Beethoven's Quartet Opus 130, where sforzando is written in shorthand; a mere *f* is used after the first spelling out. In bar 45 (example 38) and following, it is quite clear that fifteen sforzatos are desired, though only the first is marked. A few measures later, between bars 85 and 89 (example 39), every single sforzato is marked, since in this spot it is by no means self-evident that each half note in bars 87–89 is to be thus accentuated. It is quite conceivable that each might be held tenuto forte without the impact of the accentuation. In bar 137 (example 40) the additional sign *ten.* (for tenuto) indicates that a different approach is called for. The composer sets a pattern in the first appearance of the phrase, assuming that the next two quarter notes in the following bar, and also the final note of the phrase, are to be played in an identical manner.

In the next movement of the quartet we can see how carefully this great score has been marked. In bar 17 (example 41) of the presto the first violin has an *sf* while the other parts are invested with only an *f*. A skeptic may ask how we

Example 38. Beethoven, Opus 130, 1st mvt., mm. 44–48

Example 39. Beethoven, Opus 130, 1st mvt., mm. 85–89

Example 40. Beethoven, Opus 130, 1st mvt., mm. 137–39

Example 41. Beethoven, Opus 130, 2nd mvt., mm. 15–19

know that this is not the same abbreviated writing we discussed earlier. The answer is that the composer has already stressed the notes by placing a grace note in front of each, so that in this case the *sf* serves as an underlining of something already there. A twentieth-century composer given to using footnotes might have written, "Not an appoggiatura-like flourish, but a violent, devilish, quick stress."

Beethoven's Third Symphony is generously supplied with accents of all kinds. Since one of the most significant characteristics of the first movements is the 3/2 rhythm—or, if you will, 2/4—that crosses bar lines of the continuously written 3/4 meter, these sforzato marks signal to the musician that the weight is being shifted from the 3/4 to other rhythmic patterns. In the exposition, the first 150 bars of the opening movement, there are 44 sforzatos. The first > accents appear in the latter part of the funeral march, in bars 170–77 (example 42). There can be little doubt that the kind of stress intended by this accent is different from the *sf* signs mentioned before. We have here another agogic accent, which is best performed by an ever so slight anticipation of the marked note.

Example 42. Beethoven, Sym. No. 3, 2nd mvt., mm. 168–75

There are several more of these accents in the scherzo, from bar 49 on (example 43). Orchestras customarily attack these notes with a light tearing sound, as if they are quickly ripping sheets of paper along perforated lines, and they shorten the notes to perhaps half the value of a dotted half note. In these cases the accent sign means that the players should hold the note for its full value to

Example 43. Beethoven, Sym. No. 3, 3rd mvt., mm. 49–57

indicate that a new strain of music has begun. How we should read Beethoven's
sf is shown explicitly in another place. When we compare bars 383–85 with the
next phrase, bars 391–94, we realize that the first sequence is given three sforzatos in order to ensure that the syncopated character comes out strongly
stressed. On the other hand, when the dam bursts at bar 391, and the whole
musical fabric seems to explode, Beethoven uses here a double forte.

I suggest that a thorough examination of these two passages will do much to
clarify the way not only the sforzando but the entire movement should be taken.
In a tempo that is too rapid (compared to Beethoven's demand), the metric difference between the 3/4 and the 2/2, which ought to be quite noticeable, tends
to shrink. The sideways accent appears again, in the finale in bars 377–80 (example 44), where the oboe and the clarinet have these accent signs in their parts.
A brief perusal will once again show that these accents are meant to be agogic,
with a rhythmic stress and not a dynamic one.

In the famous trio the *sf* mark is misread more often than not. The entire first

Example 44. Beethoven, Sym. No. 3, 4th mvt., mm. 377–80

Example 45. Beethoven, Sym. No. 3, 3rd mvt., mm. 244–54

horn passage is piano, so the *sf* must be kept within the piano range. In bar 182 only the first horn has an accent, which is within a crescendo configuration. But the worst mistake usually occurs in bar 244 (example 45). Because there is a widespread habit of equating any sforzato with a very strong accent, the one here usually sounds, in the midst of the phrase in piano (bars 243–55), like a sudden and unexpected burp. I know of few grosser misreadings than this particular overstress. But in fact the general dynamic level of the entire trio has been subjected to whim and caprice for so long that the original now appears odd to experienced players who have every note "in their ears."

To digress for a moment to a more general question of dynamics, the first part of the trio is written out twice, while a double bar repeat sign is used for the second section. It is likely that the composer, indulging in a device quite in vogue at the time—the hunting motive with horn calls—was trying to forestall the arch practice of playing the repeat as an echo. The idea of the trio is of course the opposite; the horns are approaching, not going away.

In another era, the late nineteenth century, the meaning of some accent signs is different, at least insofar as they are used by some composers. Let us take Dvořák, for example. In his Ninth Symphony (*New World*) there are thousands of accents. The > sign in this symphony means tenuto. It is used instead of *ten.* or a horizontal line over the note. In Dvořák's scores the *sf* and the wedge accent often appear together, not as mutual reinforcement, but to discourage shortening of the notes thus marked. While the lack of the usual tenuto sign is characteristic of the Ninth Symphony, the Eighth Symphony employs this marking often and clearly. Thus a new approach to reading the Eighth must be found. This kind of flexibility is necessary if our interpretation is to represent the original concept of the composer. Blanket rules do not serve us.

Some composers wrote extra accentuation into their scores to make up for insufficient numbers of players. Wagner, on the other hand, wrote with complete confidence that he would have the right balance and the right number of musicians. Therefore we find, not surprisingly, fewer accents marked in Wagner's scores. When they do appear they are meant to be observed with panache. One of the best examples of this practice is the introduction to the dance of the apprentices, in the third act of *Die Meistersinger*.

Tradition versus Custom

It is essential that an interpreter of the music of past eras be able to distinguish between tradition and mere custom. Of course, tradition *is* custom—but not just any custom. With respect to a particular musical or dramatic work, the one authentic tradition is the custom of the composer's or playwright's own time— that is, the conventions of writing and performing that he and his contemporaries took for granted. The customs of the interpreter's day, or of any intervening period, are at best irrelevant, and at worst inimical, to realizing the author's intentions. The goal of the conductor should be to recreate as faithfully as possible the customary practices that came naturally to the composer and therefore influenced the act of composition. These are the true traditions, and the only ones that should be taken into account in interpretation.

An understanding of musical history is necessary not only to know true traditions but also to recognize false ones, which are accretions of customs from later times. While knowledge of the performance traditions of Bach's day is becoming more widespread, old habits die hard, especially when performers have a vested interest in perpetuating them. How difficult it is to reestablish lost traditions was made clear to me some years ago when I was invited to perform Bach's *St. Matthew Passion* in Holland. Long before rehearsing the work I had (I thought) settled with the chorus master that the double choir for all the dramatic utterances, the eight-part opening choral fantasia, and the final pieces would be sung by a maximum of forty-eight voices, or six voices to a part, and that the other two hundred members of the choral society would be placed around and above the stage, as if they were the community singing the chorales. Unexpectedly, this attempt to use a force appropriate to the needs of polyphonic writing was ill-received by the two hundred chorus members who had sung the entire work for many years and were sure that their method was the proper and traditional way to perform Bach. Indeed, when we read about the German revival of these works, starting with the famous performance under Felix Mendelssohn, we see pictures of masses of people, fairly piled on top of one another, and large orchestral doublings. This resulted from an effort to translate the grandeur of the work into what the nineteenth century thought was the embodiment of grandeur: a very large ensemble. Such massed forces of voices and instruments are inevitably unwieldy and lead to slow tempos and mushy counterpoint.

A far more complex antitradition is the customary division of Bach's B-Minor Mass into sections for full chorus and for soloists. For well over two hundred years it has been taken for granted that the solo voices sing only the arias and duets. Yet there is no indication whatever in the original score to justify the arbitrary divisions that have become almost universally accepted. Nowhere does the word *chorus* appear in our modern sense of a *ripieno* group. To anyone reading the score without preconceptions it appears quite clear that Bach assigned a considerably larger portion of the Mass to soloists. There are extended passages in which he gave the vocal lines no unison support from the instruments, though he provided such support in comparable passages elsewhere. It is reasonable to assume that he entrusted the lightly scored passages to his soloists. When the full chorus entered he helped the voices out with orchestral doubling.

The first example of a solo section that is commonly assigned to the chorus appears in the first "Kyrie," at bar 30. There the voices sing to an obbligato of only two oboes and continuo. From bar 45, after the entrance of the basses, the ripieno voices are supported by instruments up to bar 58. Then once again the solos sing, until in bar 65 everyone participates, continuing to bar 112; then the interlude, bars 112–18, is again given to solo voices. The upbeat ("eleison") to bar 119 is taken by the four upper voices in ripieno, and the basses join them from bar 119 to the end of the movement. Formally speaking, the interludes of the fugato appear to have been designed for solos, whereas the main subject, except for its first appearance, was intended for the chorus.

In "Et in terra pax" of the Gloria, Bach's intention to divide the voices is apparent from the fact that they are accompanied only by light harmonic interpolations from bar 23 to bar 34, and the identical music from bar 46 on is consistently supported by instrumental unison. At bar 57 Bach found it necessary to support the fifth voice with the trumpet in the octave of the second sopranos. In the "Cum sancto spirito," bars 37–64 appear to be intended for solo voices. In "Et resurrexit" this is true of bars 9–14 and also of the long phrase for bass voice, "Et iterum venturus est," in bars 74–86.

If Bach's evident wishes in the assignment of choral and solo sections were followed, another common practice that ignores his score—the use of only four soloists instead of five—would become impossible. This has become an almost universal custom, not only for obvious reasons of economy but also because it is not easy to find a second soprano with a vocal timbre sufficiently different from those of the first soprano and alto to provide a desirable contrast. The second voice in the "Christe eleison" duet is, in fact, very low for a soprano and is easier for a contralto to sing. The only other solo for second soprano is the "Laudamus te." This can also be sung by the alto. If, however, sections of the great five-part "choruses" are reassigned to the soloists, the practical advantages of hiring only four soloists will have to be relinquished in favor of carrying out the composer's intent.

Studying the way in which Bach used his chorus and soloists provides some interesting insights into their quality and number. In the first ripieno of the fugato section of the "Kyrie," the second sopranos sing the main subject from bar 48 on, supported by the second flute, second oboe, and second violin. At bar 50 the first sopranos take up the subject, supported by first flute, oboe, and violin. Yet the altos and tenors are not supported by instruments until later. The tenors, in fact, are given almost no instrumental support; they sing either unsupported or are helped by the continuo organ. Considering the normal dynamic balance for voices, it is apparent that Bach's altos and tenors were particularly able singers.

In general we should keep in mind that before music became institutionalized the assignment of parts took little account of numbers. Mozart's K. 525 (*Eine kleine Nachtmusik*) can be played with the same wonderful effect by four or forty string players. It can be done by a quartet or a quintet, depending on the conditions of performance. In a small room the double bass may be too weighty; in a concert hall or an outdoor park the lower octave in the bass line becomes essential. There is little doubt that Mozart would have adjusted his forces in accord with such pragmatic considerations. In a work of this kind there is no reason why a modern conductor should not do the same, if the performance will clearly benefit. This is a very different case from Bach's B-Minor Mass, where the arbitrary redeployment of singers defies the inner logic of the composer's scoring.

In rare instances it may also be advantageous to rearrange the sequence of sections in a work that has many movements. An example is Mozart's Serenade with the Posthorn, K. 320, which has seven movements. Two of the movements, both in G major, involve woodwind solos. They fall side by side as the third and fourth pieces. Since the other five movements are mostly in D, I have, for as many years as I have performed the work, reversed the order of movements 2 (minuet and trio) and 3 (concertante), in order to separate sections with identical key signatures. This changes the sequence of the first four movements from D–D(trio in A)–G–G to D–G–D(trio in A)–G.

The original arrangement probably resulted from the problem posed by the horn crooks, which had to be changed when passing from the movements in D to those in G. If the serenade was played under conditions that prevented the horn players from keeping their cases of crooks handy, the delay caused by fetching the G crooks and later the D crooks was quite enough to influence Mozart's arrangement, even if it happened only twice. In my version, natural horns would have been faced with four such intervals. I feel that Mozart's work has a better sequence in my version than as printed, and it seems justified, if it is true that the original arrangement was based mainly on the limitations of the natural horn rather than on purely musical considerations.

There are other cases in which it is wise to distinguish between traditions built upon musical intent and those that have come into being through expediency. One of the latter, which must be critically examined each time one encounters it, is the widespread use of three trombones to support the three lower voices in sacred music. In any mass written before 1830 we find trombones aiding altos, tenors, and basses. It is easy to imagine why. There were in most church ensembles a disproportionate number of boy sopranos, along with weak-voiced altos and a small group of men making up the vocal quartet. Also, the trombones were lighter in caliber than our present-day variety. The "Quam olim Abrahae" from Mozart's *Requiem* is a good illustration of why every page of sacred music must be weighed before a decision is made about whether to allow the trombones to play their parts as written. The balance of the chorus in present-day concert renditions is more or less taken for granted, and the balance within the orchestra will be unnecessarily strained if the director sticks to the "play what's printed" maxim. I shall not suggest specific solutions to this problem but merely insist that it must be handled with imagination and knowledge. Perhaps the best solution is to decide the particular places where a *tacet* is in order only after hearing the choir and wind instruments in the hall where the event will take place. Theoretical decisions have a tendency to boomerang.

Expediency is also the reason for certain modern practices that are occasionally mistaken for traditions. In some popular operas necessity has led to widely accepted transpositions of pieces that in their original key prove uncomfortable or unmanageable for some singers. Let us take as an example the aria of Rodolfo, "Che gelida manina," from the first act of Puccini's *La Bohème*. Here the music is printed in orchestra parts both in the original key and a halftone lower. In the latter version (G major) many tenors have an easier time. Next comes Mimi's aria, which is followed by a short duet. For this too the publisher has supplied a transposed version, which concludes the act in B major. These transpositions ruin the key relationships the composer had in mind. The note E, which opens Mimi's solo, produces a startling contrast when it follows the glowing and somewhat flamboyant conclusion of the tenor solo in A-flat. But if this moment occurs after a G-major conclusion it loses much of its poignancy. This one note must be in stark contrast to the preceding notes, or the feeling of the girl's shyness, modesty, and weak health cannot manifest itself. The duet in transposition is an even worse affront to the composition, for the act was designed to open and close in C. This practice, then, no matter how clearly it is sanctioned by the publishers, cannot be considered a tradition. It is perhaps an unavoidable adjustment for the paucity of singers who can sing high notes, but it will never be more than that.

Five
Knowing the
Right Tempo: I

The Importance of Tempos

No matter how diverse their views on every other topic, most musicians agree
that finding the right tempo is at least half the interpretation. Wagner went further, asserting that the right tempo *was* the interpretation. In his essay *On Conducting* he writes: "I am persistently returning to the question of tempo because,
as I said before, this is the point at which it becomes evident whether a conductor understands his business or not."[1] Tempo is also the principal feature singled
out by critics in commenting on performers. With all this consensus on the
crucial importance of tempo, it may seem curious that musicians hardly ever
agree on the *proper* choice of tempo. Accord in theory has never spread into
agreement in practice.

Perhaps the problem can be simplified: one should only speak of tempos, not
of tempo in the singular. This is not a semantic quibble but a musical problem
of the first order. Tempos involve balance and overall concept of interpretation
for most of the works musicians tackle have many movements interrelated to
form a unit. It seems unlikely that a musician performing a Beethoven sonata
could be wrong in one movement and above reproach in the others; if the adagio
in the *Waldstein* Sonata sounds too slow, chances are the first movement was
taken too fast. Each choice of tempo is implicitly linked with other sections of
the same work and, as will be shown, with the composer's overall ideas. Tempos
are a persistent source of conflict between conductors and instrumental soloists;
the more intransigent performers are known to each other and avoid appearing
together on the same stage.

It is, for example, very difficult for a conductor to execute a composer's in-

1. Richard Wagner, *On Conducting*, trans. Edward Dannreuther (London: William Reeves, 1897),
p. 34.

101

tention when a solo violinist has for many years practiced certain bowings that are not only different from what the score demands but compel, for their best execution, tempos that do not correspond either to the conductor's or the composer's ideas of the total work. In the slow movement of the Violin Concerto by Brahms, if the tempo of the oboe solo is slower or faster than that of the first entrance by the violin, the sense of the movement is at once vitiated. Many virtuosos have their own notions of phrasing, and one violinist may take the first bar of his solo entrance in one bow while another takes it in two bows. This seemingly minor choice can materially affect the tempo of the solo and hence the tempo that the wind instruments ought to take for the introduction. I cite this concerto because its solo part was edited by a leading virtuoso and friend of Brahms, Joseph Joachim. We are not discussing, therefore, a composer's vague notions of bowing, which a performer may treat as the merest blueprint; we have here an authorized set of directions to the soloist. Yet one encounters every possible vagary and deviation from the text of the score, affecting the tempos of the work.

This type of disagreement is relatively simple compared to an opera, which has not three tempos for a forty-five-minute piece but twenty, thirty, or fifty—involving many singers—for compositions lasting three or four hours.

Singers are not nearly as fussy about tempos as dancers are. True, both singing and dancing depend for their success on the responsiveness of the body, in the same sense as athletics. Singers and dancers are, at their best, artists, yet few ever can believe that the public clamors for them because of their superlative musicianship. They know very well that it is the vocal feats or the leaps and extensions that bring down the house, no matter whether the tempos taken were the composer's choice. In my early days at the Metropolitan Opera I had ample conflict with a few very accomplished singers, one of whom confided after a number of drinks, "Maybe your tempos are right, but if I sang those tempos I couldn't possibly take home three checks each week for such strenuous performances. To do them that often I need some relief by taking easier tempos." This frank admission of the problem of strain and stamina brought home to me early in my life that concept is one thing and realization of concept another. When the twain meet it is a most fortunate and happy event, but it does not happen often.

Dancers are so rigidly trained in their movements that conductors who accept the task of directing the music for a dance company should remember the inscription on the gates to Dante's Hell: "Lasciate ogni speranza voi ch'entrate."

The clear concept of tempo is the first necessity for a conductor or any other musical leader. In a large and many-faceted work, that concept implies an awareness of the high and low points. When the first downbeat is given, a conductor ought to be fully in command of the entire range of tempos demanded by the work at hand. The tempo of the overture to *The Marriage of Figaro*, for example, is not an isolated incident, but is related to approximately fifty other tempos that will be played and sung within the coming three and a half hours.

This score—one of the supreme masterpieces of all time—is a good example of the interrelation of tempos and its effect on interpretation. After meeting with only a fair reception in Vienna the opera made an instant sensation in Prague. Yet even in Vienna the organ grinders had the best tunes of the opera in their repertoire after a few days, and the Emperor Joseph had to limit the number of permitted encores, lest an already long show should become interminable.[2]

Customs have changed in the 190 years since the premiere of *Figaro*; and so have some of the ways in which it is performed. Fortunately we can still ascertain with much assurance what must have been added or taken away from the original impact of the work in these nineteen decades. We may take relative comfort from the fact that *The Marriage of Figaro* has not suffered the fate of its first cousin, Rossini's *The Barber of Seville*. It is probably because Mozart has been held in more awe than Rossini that less vulgarization and false liberty has been allowed. Nevertheless, enough strange practices have entered the habitual production scheme and musical rendition that it may be high time to take a close look at the score. If the *Barber* is the ne plus ultra of opera buffa, *Figaro* is the olympian achievement in comic opera. A comedy is a play of mores, never very far from slipping over into tragedy, while a buffoonery is a farce meant for laughs only. A beguiling paradox concerning these two operas set to Beaumarchais's Figaro plays is that *The Marriage of Figaro*, based on the second play, was composed in 1786, thirty years before *The Barber of Seville*, based on the first.

Tempos in "The Marriage of Figaro"

I could have chosen for this basic demonstration of tempos and their interrelation any large-scale work by Mozart or Haydn. *Figaro* happens to be the most perfect of Mozart's great operas. It does not have two versions, like *Don Giovanni*; it does not need the dramaturgic face-lifting of *Die Entführung aus dem Serail*; and it has a great libretto, which *Così fan tutte* lacks. It also does not pose the singular problems of *Die Zauberflöte*. Thus, it seems to me the peerless masterpiece that can open the way to Mozart's entire repertoire. Like every other great master, Mozart expressed himself in forms and patterns that grew in complexity with the passing years and yet remained unmistakably his. It was thus with Beethoven and with Brahms. This continuity helps us to get a clear idea of tempos when we are able to recognize that piece *D* has been designed according

---

2. This, at least to me, and despite much available testimony, indicates a great success in Vienna too, but it may have been not enough by the standards of the day. We must not forget that a contemporary Broadway show is a success only after it begins to pay its angels a profit, and that takes a longer run than even moderately successful plays can anticipate. Thus, any and all historic reports need to be understood in the context of their own time, not that of a later age and its standards. We also should understand that customs in the opera house were looser and less stuffy than they are today—when no emperor limits encores, but the overtime payment to the unionized participants puts a lid on freewheeling response to public enthusiasm.

to a characteristic pattern that we know from pieces *A*, *B*, and *C*, not necessarily from the same work.

To ascertain relationships between pieces through their tempos, one must separate different metric designs. There would be no point in comparing two allegro molto sections if one were in 3/4 and the other in 2/2. Therefore, in the discussion of the tempos of *Figaro* we separate the metric patterns into four groups: C (4/4 and 2/2, which are frequently interchangeable or alternate with one another in the same piece, according to phrasing); 2/4 and 4/8; 3/4 and 3/8; and 6/8.

For the following discussion, the reader should have a full study score of the opera before him. All references will be to the number of a piece and its bar count. Any of three editions—pocket score Eulenburg EE 4446, Broude Brothers 146, and Peters 4504a—will do, since all have the same numerals for the pieces and for the bar count. The last two are reprints of the excellent Schünemann-Soldan labors. Eulenburg, which is not quite as readily available as Broude (at least in the United States), is the least expensive of the three. Anyone who uses the Bärenreiter score must be aware that the chorus no. 8 is numbered 9 when repeated. This moves all the rest of the pieces one figure higher for the balance of the work. Bar counts in Bärenreiter are not the same either. While in the other editions accompagnato recitative and aria have bar counts running through, in Bärenreiter the count starts again when an aria begins.

The Finale of Act II In a seminar for conductors, where I demonstrated tempo relationships using the score of *Figaro*, a violinist with several decades' service as a section leader in a prominent opera company's orchestra asked, "Why does one always seem to arrive at the final prestissimo of the second-act finale [no. 15, bar 907] in a tempo so fast that nobody is able to play the notes?" I replied that her experience, which was probably identical with that of many other orchestral players all over the globe, was sufficient proof that the passage mentioned was not only taken at a wrong tempo, but much of what came before must have been overdriven as well. This finale, no. 15, is unique in all operatic repertoire: for a classic work it is unusually long, 939 bars compared to *Così fan tutte*'s 697 and *Don Giovanni*'s 653. It consists of ten sections, which means that without any interruption the conductor has to build one long, continuous line over these 900-odd measures.

There are four separate sections in 2/2: the opening allegro to Susanna's unexpected appearance; the second allegro from bar 167; the allegro molto, commencing with Antonio's loud entrance at bar 467; and the arrival of the three "conspirators"—Marcellina, Basilio, and Bartolo—at bar 697. This last section has two further changes in tempo, a più allegro at 783 and the aforementioned prestissimo. If we compare these four sections, it will be clear after a quick perusal that one of the plans is for each allegro in 2/2 to sound more pressed and more dramatic, faster and larger, than the previous one. The section from bar 1 to 125 is a duet; from bar 167 to 327, a trio; from bar 467 into the next andante section, a quintet; and the allegro assai stretta is a septet.

The first and second allegro (bars 1 and 167) are marked alike, and after relating them to other sections, we find that they are to be performed in the same tempo. Yet the section from bar 167 will and should sound faster, because it is so composed; the phrasing in the orchestra, a sequence of two slurred and two articulated notes on one beat, bespeaks the extreme nervousness of both the Countess and Susanna. The Gardener's entrance is definitely faster than these two allegro sections; if there should be a question whether the allegro molto is faster or slower than the section allegro assai (at 697), the answer can be found by taking a good look at the last symphonies of Mozart. For a start let us consider the Symphony in G Minor, K. 550. The first movement is allegro molto; the last movement is allegro assai. Should a comparison between these two movements be insufficient evidence, we might take the finale of K. 551, the *Jupiter* Symphony, which is molto allegro, and see if that tempo is more akin to the first or the last movement of the Symphony in G Minor. (It is always presumed that such comparisons are not made by consulting only the first page. There are in every sizable piece passages that tell us in no uncertain terms at which speed they come off best. It is not a matter of playability only—modern technicians can play a lot of music faster than it can be heard. The message from a passage to a performer, "I like to be presented thus," goes far deeper; it conveys the idea of how the total fabric of the music will come across best.) If this comparison of K. 550 to K. 551 is still not enough, put the finale of K. 385, the *Haffner* Symphony, next to that of the G-minor and consider that assai allegro and presto are very close in speed; indeed, at times they were interchangeable in different Mozart editions.

Assuming that the result of this little investigation is to place molto allegro somewhat below assai allegro in speed, we have the mechanical and mathematical relation of these four tempos. (It is taken for granted that the allegro assai must be started at a pace that still leaves room for the più allegro and the final prestissimo; these are basic musical demands and need no underlining.)

The first two allegros together with the interlude in 3/8, a molto andante, form the opening part of the finale. From the intensely temperamental, furious, and somewhat violent opening, it moves to a soft ending after the Count, reluctantly convinced that he has been mistaken in accusing his wife, kneels and is graciously—with many coquettish runs in thirds by the ladies—forgiven. The unity of this three-part section is enhanced by the simple equation that the eighth beat in the 3/8 passage equals the half-bar beat in the two allegros. If Susanna from bar 161 onward does not indulge in musical whims and makes no ritard, the sixteenth notes flow directly into the eighth notes. In a score written in a later era the composer would have marked that the half note equals the eighth note.

To establish this equation on firm ground we have to know that many cognoscenti have debated what the "molto" before andante means: Does the molto mean it is a fast andante or does it mean it is a slow andante? I think that such debates are unproductive, just as is the theory that poco andante in the finale of the *Eroica* Symphony is a very slow andante because the "poco" refers to a slow tempo. There is no accounting for different logical notions, and I am persuaded that the whole question of tempo at this point in the second-act finale of *Figaro* can be resolved by looking at the meaning of the music. What do the first phrases (in the rhythm ♪♫♫ | ♪♩) of the 3/8 mean? They are the fast and somewhat anxious heartbeats of the two ladies, who cannot be sure how the trick will work with the Count. Therefore, if the molto andante is quite deliberate, the heartbeats of the culpable women would be amazingly phlegmatic, almost comatose. Without a nervous pulse, the scene makes little sense dramatically. How can we be sure? For about a dozen measures nervousness is noticeable; then Susanna gets the upper hand (bar 138) and ironically taunts the Count with her own presence. A deceptive calm underlies the short trio (bars 145–55). As soon as the Count shows that he is not yet satisfied with the situation, the pulsation of the beginning is heard again (bar 155), alternating between the two horns and the strings. If this is still insufficiently clear we can turn to *Don Giovanni* and find Zerlina's second aria, "Vedrai, carino" (act 2, no. 5). This piece is in 3/8 and has as distinct a heartbeat, which even the gauche Masetto can feel when he is so charmingly invited to put his hand where the heart is.[3] The rhythm is slightly different from the one at the 3/8 in *Figaro*, but the family resemblance is too close to be ignored.

In finding the right tempos for these opening pieces, it will help to notice several wonderful stage actions that the music clearly mirrors. The Count was presumed to be hunting (recitative after no. 10, bar 81, "Ito e il conte alla caccia"). He still has on his riding costume and, surely, carries a whip. This he swishes furiously up and down, perhaps even at his own boots as irate people are wont to do, with each sforzato of the opening. From the fifth bar on we can see the Countess wringing her hands, as the octave jump of the violins quite humorously depicts. In bars 14 and 16 we hear the Count's attempts to control himself, after having started to shout (the forte in bars 13 and 15), lest he be overheard. He tries to curb his terrible temper, to restore his good behavior. Hence the alternating forte and piano. At bar 31 the violins and violas play sixteenth notes for the first time in this piece. Why? The Count begins to tremble with rage and jealousy when his wife admits Cherubino's dishabille and describes it just before we feel the Count's control finally shatter.

Every one of these nuances needs time to be heard. We must keep always in

3. Musical (and general) illiteracy has established a gag, of Masetto placing his hand on Zerlina's heart in bar 52 (with horseplay added for laughs). The libretto indicates that action in bar 58 to start slowly, since the heartbeat is clearly written into the score in the winds but not before the middle of bar 63. In the current fashion we get the thumping of double basses in bar 53, as soon as Masetto feels Zerlina's heart—a fine sound for a young elephant's heartbeat, but not for Zerlina's, to be sure.

mind that the total effect is paramount, not the technical ability to play a section faster or slower. The innumerable subtleties of this comedy need time to be heard and appreciated, or they will pass unnoticed. Moreover, in purely musical terms, there are syncopated rhythmic figures with a small inner voice that demands a certain restraint in speed to be heard. (These figures can be found in bars 11, 12, and 15 in the violas, 13 in the first violins, 68 and 69 in all upper strings, and again in 113 and 115.) Such rhythmic movement is meaningful and must not be blurred, as it is sure to be at too rapid a speed. In the second allegro we find once again the tremendous dynamic contrasts in the Count's music, who returns torn between suppressed fury (bars 175–77 and 179) and profuse apology (176, 178, and 180).

If one identifies each emotional and dramatic strand of the music that makes up this allegro section, one finds first the nervousness of the Countess (bar 167), four bars later the reassurance of Susanna that all has been resolved, then the conflicting reactions of the Count, with the somewhat ironic running comments of the two women (bar 191). Each of these is introduced in sequence and then interwoven to make a most artful trio which, in a span of approximately three minutes, emerges in a structure as intricate as if it were chamber music. For the conductor the main problem is to bring every one of these strands under one tempo without slighting any.[4]

The second large section of the great finale consists of a short passage of entrance music for Figaro (bar 328) and three contrasting pieces, in 4/8, in 2/2, and in 6/8 (bars 398–696). Figaro appears to the sound of a German dance. It is the plebeian's tune, just as the minuet is the music of the upper classes. The tempo of this piece can be easily ascertained, for Mozart wrote some forty-nine German dances, mostly in sets of six, twelve, or four. (K. 509 would be the closest in time to the Figaro score.)

After Figaro has appeared, the Count prevents his leaving by an investigation set in a 2/4 movement in C major (398). It is a type of piece that we find most prominently used by Haydn in many of his symphonies. Numbers 94 and 101 reveal a pattern that Haydn seems to have appreciated: two hammered notes repeated in groups. It is useful to browse through some of Haydn's andante movements in order to get a better sense of the best tempo for this C-major section of the *Figaro* finale. It is rare for Mozart to use such a pattern, though the lyric effusion in bars 425 and 449 is echoed in a somewhat similar phrase in Zerlina's first aria, "Batti, batti" (*Don Giovanni*, no. 12, the opening phrases).

4. Here lies perhaps the greatest difference between a Mozart and a Rossini ensemble. In the latter's immensely effective finale sections, each portion is a unit featuring a single expression. In nearly all of Mozart's music, instrumental as well as dramatic, there is the contrast between worlds. In my youth I listened to some very prominent conductors who invariably slowed down the second subject of a Mozart symphony—sometimes having already slowed down the contrasting element in the main subject. They were aware of the two worlds without heeding the classic concept that both had to exist under the same sky.

The inner relationship between these two pieces is that the singers in both pretend innocence. The seeming naïveté of Susanna, the Countess, and Figaro is quite hypocritical when they plead, "Deh Signor, nol contrastate," in bar 449, as is Zerlina's when she asks, "Batti, batti, oh bel Masetto." Up to that moment Zerlina has not struck us as being masochistically inclined. Neither are the three characters under scrutiny by the Count as pure as the deceptively bland phrase sounds. All these motives of deception, slyness, and devious pretense point to a fluent tempo, lest some phrases become seriously sentimental, which they are assuredly not intended to be. From bar 457 on the parlando of the men is in counterpoint to the renewed pleading of the women. Here is the moment when a bad choice of tempo would make either one or the other of these two strands unnatural. A slow andante will affect the parlando phrases adversely, making them sound stilted and artificial, while too speedy a tempo will damage the nice cantabile phrase of the sopranos. It is a good general rule that the key in matters of tempo is to be found in passages where several themes sound together. (We need only remember the prelude to *Die Meistersinger* at the meeting of the three themes.)

In relating tempos of the same metric pattern we have established that the molto allegro (467) is faster than the two opening allegros and less fast than the allegro assai (697). It has to accommodate the stomping rhythm of the boorish Gardener's entrance and the rapid triplet passages in forte, which must make their telling effect by being clear and furious-sounding. If there has been an ever so slight error in the tempo it will show beyond any doubt in bar 483. There begins a type of violin passage (triplets, alternately slurred and detached) that needs the one right tempo to become effective. If it is too fast, the second and fourth triplets will not work in spiccato and must be slurred, which ruins the whirring effect of this theme. There are further the parlando phrases of the three men. They must be intelligible, yet the repartee should be in the quickest sequence possible.[5] To round out the second section of the finale, there remains a

---

5. Study of such works by conductors should always be from the full score. The piano-vocal score, which serves for many musicians in preparation, is totally insufficient, and many wrong tempos come from the limited outlook provided by these scores. Singers are prepared by coaches who rarely have the full score, but for conductors to limit themselves to the keyboard arrangement means ignorance of many factors, such as the technical limitations of instruments mentioned above. A Mozart score is much more difficult to represent on a piano and in a piano arrangement than is any Wagner or Strauss opera. Since the Mozart orchestra is transparent to a degree where every smallest inner voice can be clearly heard—if the music is played as it should be—full awareness of the orchestral texture must be part of a conductor's preparation. Antonio, Figaro, and the Count could take scene 11 far faster than the right tempo; it is in the triplets of this section that the tempo becomes compellingly clear. The pattern of the Antonio scene reappears in the finale to the first act of *Don Giovanni*. The rapid triplet figure that in *Figaro* (bar 498) goes down, in *Don Giovanni* (no. 13, bar 577) goes up; otherwise it is the same. The tempo indication over this section in *Don Giovanni* is merely allegro, though it has the same pattern as the scene at Antonio's entrance. It is possible that Mozart felt after his experience with *Figaro* that perhaps the molto allegro could drive the speed beyond the sensible. More likely is the assumption that every tempo marking is a purely relative one

movement in 6/8, starting at bar 605, which will be discussed below in the section on 6/8 meter.

With the entrance of the trio—Marcellina, Basilio, and Bartolo (bar 697)—the stretta of the finale begins with a brisk and aggressive motive, strongly colored by the trumpets and timpani (their first appearance since no. 9, Figaro's aria at the close of the first act). Here, as well as in no. 28, the last-act finale, an allegro assai follows an andante in 6/8. It is fairly obvious that these two pairs of tempos were meant to be alike. In the first allegro assai (no. 15, bar 697) there should be the keenest awareness of what is still in store for singers and players over the next 242 bars. It is all too easy to start here at a fast gallop and end at unplayable and unsingable speeds.[6] Five of the seven participants have some of the fastest parlando chatter in this section—an additional hint for a perfect tempo. It will be most illuminating to compare the two allegro assai movements of the last-act finale of *Figaro* (bars 335 and 448) with all 2/2 ensemble sections in *Don Giovanni* and in *Così fan tutte*; a clear picture will emerge of the tempo headings Mozart typically assigned to particular tasks that he gave to singers and orchestra players. These problems should be considered only after expressive content and dramatic situation have been thoroughly understood.

The last allegro assai in *Figaro* is as ornate and undramatic as the final presto in *Don Giovanni*. The comedy is over and we go to supper. We return to the 2/2 and 4/4 patterns aside from the sections already discussed.

2/2 and 4/4 Meter Among the pieces marked very fast is the terzetto no. 7 in the first act. The fury and flurry of the opening belong to the Count; from bar 16, the smooth sliding legato phrase belongs to the intriguer Don Basilio; and the nervous running eighth notes belong to Susanna (bar 23). It will be illuminating to compare the short burst between bars 6 and 11 in this piece with the passages in no. 15, bars 737 and 753. In both cases these are motives given to the Count, who is angry each time. Mozart must have meant these little runs to be clearly heard and understood not as mere piquant effects but as music, since he never writes sixteenth notes after we get to più allegro in the finale no. 15. Here in no. 7 the nudging little phrases go on and on, throughout the piece.

---

to be weighed in balance with those sections that precede or follow it. One can conclude that the words indicating tempos are always secondary to the notes when a conflict is apparent.

6. I should like to recall a letter by Mozart to his father concerning Osmin's second act aria in *Die Entführung aus dem Serail*, in which he writes (though in a different context):

Passions, whether violent or not, must never be expressed in such a way as to excite disgust, and music, even in the most terrible situations, must never offend the ear, but must please the hearer, or in other words *must never cease to be music* [italics mine] (Emily Anderson, ed. and trans., *The Letters of Mozart and His Family*, 2nd ed., 3 vols. [London: Macmillan and Co.; New York: St. Martin's Press, 1966], 3:1144).

This warning applies perfectly to the final section of the second act of *Figaro*, though it made no impression on the producer of the aforementioned *Zauberflöte*.

Susanna's constant alertness is depicted here in two ways: her indignation comes out in a lively parlando (bar 92), insisting on, rather loudly repeating, the note F, like a youthful Xantippe scolding someone; her fake fainting spell is brought into the music gradually as the scheme develops in her clever brain. The first inkling is in bar 30 in the first violins; the same note in that syncopated rhythm that bespeaks a short breath returns an octave higher (hence more noticeably) in bars 34 and 36, to become fully thematic in 47. If all three strands—the Count's ire, Basilio's hypocritical smoothness, and Susanna's little comedy—are all brought under one arc, without pushing or pulling back, then we have the one right tempo. This same tempo will be right for the entrance of the three characters in no. 15 at bar 697, and for the Count's wild shouting "Gente, gente" in no. 28, bar 335 and again at 448. I can guarantee that, if all these considerations are observed, the final prestissimo in no. 15 will be playable.

Having noticed the relationships between several movements marked allegro assai, in *Figaro* or elsewhere, we must turn to one more allegro assai (always in duple meter), the last section of the Count's third-act aria, no. 17. It will be very quickly apparent that any equation between this and other tempos marked with the same words would be an empty exercise, a theoretical toying without musical sense. It will be the same with other arias, specifically no. 19 of the Countess, no. 24 of Marcellina, and no. 25 of Don Basilio. These four pieces share several features: they are divided into parts or sections, and each was composed to fit one individual singer. In the case of the Count's aria, the "assai" follows a section marked "allegro maestoso." In each of the other three pieces mentioned, the (final) allegro section also follows a slower tempo. In no. 17, the assai is part of the "stage direction" belonging to the Count. Whatever he does is "assai"—his fury, his repentance, his sense of lost rights (droit du seigneur), and his tempos.

There is Cherubino's first-act aria no. 6, "Non so più cosa son," marked allegro vivace. The term *vivace* pertains more to expression than to speed, and here it is quite clear that a truly romantic delivery of this singular piece is not possible in an overdriven tempo. *Vivace* refers to the feeling of breathless eagerness, in the constantly exciting accompaniment a true portrait of an adolescent youth swarming all over the estate to sample the girls. (As an aside, it is perhaps necessary to point out that the adagio in bar 92 has nothing to do with a slow movement of a symphony or even the slow early part of an aria; it is merely the composer's way of saying that these bars are to be taken freely.) In the first act there are three pieces in C meter marked simply "allegro": the opening duet between Susanna and Figaro, the aria no. 4 of Don Bartolo, and the duet no. 5 of Susanna and Marcellina. (No. 9, Figaro's aria, will be discussed later, since the tempo marking is not original.) There is a very simple equation among these three pieces. If one compares bars 73–80 of no. 1, bars 56–65 of no. 4, and the passages from bar 29 on of no. 5, the general idea will be apparent at once.

The chatter of the instruments in nos. 1 and 5 is the same as the rapid parlando of the good doctor in no. 4.

The opening duet has in recent years been performed as an attacca to the overture, particularly in Europe. Perhaps some stage director or conductor felt that the so-called dramatic continuity would be ruined by waiting after the overture for applause of the audience. If so, it was one of those apparently fine ideas that are counterproductive, especially in matters of tempos. In this manner of performance the opening duet is usually taken at a speed that throws the whole scheme out of balance. The overture is a cousin of the final movement of the *Haffner* Symphony, K. 385, and to the last ensemble in *Don Giovanni*. All three are presto, in D major, and very light in character. The duet no. 1 should be in complete contrast. It begins tenderly, with the bass line in the low strings representing Figaro in a fine humor, measuring the space for the double bed. (The repeated note in the violins could be translated into Figaro's mutely counting, "One, two, three, four," then singing aloud, "five.") The woodwinds tell us how Susanna primps in front of the mirror. All of this is crystal clear in the music. But the new stage business opens the curtain sooner than asked for in the libretto. Susanna is not on stage but enters later. Thus, the music becomes, if not senseless, far less meaningful than composer and librettist meant. On top of this, the practice of not pausing after the overture pushes the tempo of the duet too much, for, in immediate proximity to the brilliant presto, the mellow and comfortable opening of the G-major piece does not come off as it should.[7]

This short excursion may show why tempos become clear only when the spirit, expression, and meaning of the entire work and of each piece are fully understood. The fact is that the overture *should* be followed by applause, after which brief acknowledgment the gentle sounds of the G-major section commence, without being weakened by the attacca. Mozart must have liked this sequence very much, for he repeated it almost immediately in the *Prague* Symphony, K. 504. After a most festive closing of the first movement in D major, with trumpets and timpani, the second movement of the symphony has the same key and same instrumentation as the duet of Susanna and Figaro. (The only

7. How Mozart relates every element of the music to the dramatic plan and to psychological characterization is shown here at the very beginning of the work. The choice of G major for the Susanna–Figaro duet establishes that key for the servants of the Alamaviva establishment: the chorus of the villagers, no. 8; Susanna's ariette while she dresses Cherubino as a girl; Figaro's entrance, no. 15 (the German dance); the flower offering of the village girls to the Countess, no. 21; the start of the procession for the wedding of two servants, no. 22; and Marcellina's aria, no. 24—all are in G. The Count's jealous rage when he believes that his servant has cuckolded him is also in G, because the nobleman is reduced to a plebeian outburst, in no. 28. The section in which the Count tries to seduce Susanna (it is of course the Countess) is again in the plebeian key of G major, as if even the noble gentleman turned to that key when making love to a chambermaid. A little later in the act Figaro sings in E-flat: thus, when Susanna (disguised as the Countess) calls out to him, we are in the key in which we first encountered the Countess, in her cavatina "Porgi amor."

minor difference is the presence of clarinets in the overture to the opera, where they have only a tutti role.) Bartolo's aria no. 4 shows us how the composition of the *Prague* Symphony was greatly influenced by *The Marriage of Figaro*, which was produced in that city in December 1786, the period of the symphony's creation. From the relation of the 4/4 pieces in the first act of *Figaro*, one can conclude with great assurance that this is the classic allegro (giusto) of Mozart's 4/4 pattern and would apply to the sonata movement of K. 504 as well.

Earlier I have explained why the simple allegro marking in last sections of arias need not be fitted into any pattern. It is in such instances that the flexibility of terms becomes evident. It is the same with practically all musical signs and symbols. They mean something here and something else there. The entire question of how to read music is illuminated in such moments. Although there are definite relationships among tempos, these are not dogmatic. There are no rules to reading; there are no systems that can serve as Figaro's yardstick to measure the bed. From the fabric of the two allegros in nos. 19 and 24 we can conclude that the singer of Marcellina had a flexible voice that could negotiate the florid passages or they would not have been in the aria, while the singer of the Countess had fine breath control, necessary not only in the two sections of no. 19 but especially in no. 10, her opening aria of act 2. Since singers change in two hundred years, so will their possible best tempos, always—we hope—within the frame of good taste.

In the editions suggested for study, Figaro's aria no. 9, "Non più andrai," is marked vivace. In Breitkopf and Härtel it is marked allegro vivace; and in the new Mozart edition of the Bärenreiter publication, the "vivace" is in brackets. The editor states in the preface to the volume that the tempo marking in the autograph score is not by Mozart, as is the case with several other tempos in this opera. The notation is *Von fremder Hand* ("in someone else's handwriting"). It makes complete sense that originally there should not have been any special marking. By bar 43 it is abundantly clear that we have here a march, which is used to poke fun at the impending change of life for the little page, who will be compelled by the ukase of the Count to serve in uniform far from all the pretty girls. When the piece is understood as a march it needs no more indication of speed than does no. 22, the wedding march of Figaro and Susanna at the end of act 3, which is called only "Marcia." That waltzes, minuets, German dances, and marches all had their own proper tempos was taken for granted in Mozart's day. Tempo elaborations were added only when the character of a piece resembled one of those pieces, not when it actually was one. In Beethoven's Sonata for Piano, Opus 101, the second movement is marked "Lebhaft marschmässig" or "Vivace alla marcia." Such an indication is unnecessary for "Non più andrai": the piece *is* a march and will make its proper effect only if performed that way.

As for the marking added later, one may imagine that in rehearsal the often impatient composer admonished a basso, eager to show off his grand voice by dragging the tempo, to sing it "più vivace." A bystander later added this ad hoc remark to the score. We must not forget that the language in rehearsals in Italian opera troupes of the time was Italian. They probably spoke nothing else while preparing the production. Words such as *vivace, più vivace, allegro,* and *adagio* are common in everyday communication and did not always have the same permanent intent as when a composer set down "allegro maestoso" or "allegro vivace." If one compares the trumpet fanfares in bars 97, 99, 109, and 111 of no. 9 with the horn triplet in no. 1, bars 75 and 76, it is evident that no. 1 should not be performed at the speed of no. 9. Hence, the allegro vivace indication on the latter piece must be wrong. It is difficult to read an allegro vivace slower than an unqualified allegro. If the vivace alone were correct, it would mean that vivace also has a slower gait than allegro. The word *vivace* here can only mean "lively," rather than specifying a tempo. But there are hardly any examples in Mozart's music of a one-word expressive marking. It is most unlikely, therefore, that Mozart intended to specify any tempo, for the piece was self-evidently a march.

An equally puzzling marking is the moderato over Figaro's fourth-act aria "Aprite un po' gli occhi," no. 26. The authenticity of this direction has been questioned by all editors. The idea of moderation is absurd to begin with when one considers the content of the piece and the rage out of which it is delivered. We have three keys to proper speed through comparison with other pieces. First, the triplet parlando phrase in bars 61 and 62, as well as the same phrase when it is repeated later on, should be taken at about the same speed as Bartolo's triplet chatter in no. 24. (The rhythmic notation of the violins [♪♯♪] should be read according to traditional ways of "spelling," a generation after Bach's death.) The second reference, also to Bartolo's aria no. 4, is the violin figure in the rhythm ♪♪ ♩♪ (bar 44 in no. 26, bar 5 in no. 4). This is not a common formula. Since in both cases the second violins play continuing sixteenth notes—though here legato, there détaché—one must grant the relationship between the two pieces.

The third and clearest connection with other pieces that are not moderato is the rhythm ♩♪♩ ♩♩ in bar 37. This is one of Mozart's favorite formulas, appearing, for instance, a little earlier in the same act in Basilio's aria, throughout the allegro section that starts in bar 102. It is clearly derived from the opening of the marcia, no. 22, which has considerable psychological importance, particularly here when Figaro feels betrayed. The tempo of the wedding procession being that of a normal march, the jealous husband will certainly go faster here when thinking bitterly of that lilting rhythm. That very same rhythm appears prominently in the first movements of several piano concertos: K. 451, K. 456, and K. 459. In all the tempo is allegro; in the last, even allegro vivace. So it is puzzling that the main section of Figaro's aria is marked "moderato" (though Köchel, in his monumental volume and catalog, has "andante" in brackets). No editor seems to have seen the manuscript of the aria, and there are very few instances where a moderato alone can be found over a movement by Mozart. We can confidently conclude that this word does not represent the correct tempo.

Relationships to other pieces and its character of jealousy and frustration make an allegro far more appropriate. This is one more piece of evidence that a printed score must be read with the utmost caution, but with vivid imagination.

The only allegro section not yet mentioned is the maestoso portion in no. 17, the Count's aria. It is a fine character portrait of the Count and his terrible temper. The runs bespeak his choleric disposition; the many forte-piano effects indicate how he would fly off the handle more often if he did not suddenly remember "noblesse oblige." All these nuances require time to be heard and incorporated into the musical idea. The tempo will be under that of the unqualified allegro movements, with ample allowance for the ups and downs in the dynamic level. There are always variables within two tempos that are ostensibly alike, one being pushed ahead, another held back. (I do not even consider the third, a stiff adherence to a metronomelike beat, since it is rarely, if ever, appropriate in music.) There is no doubt that a piece such as the Count's aria will project its fullest impact if the maestoso portion is ever so slightly held back while the assai portion is ever so slightly rushed. This does not mean that the tempo gets faster, but that a certain rubato within each phrase invests it with the feeling of either stately grandeur or nervous tension and haste. All this under the blanket of "tempo giusto."

Among the pieces in a 4/4 (and 2/2) metrical pattern there remain five andante sections. The freest, and perhaps the calmest, is the very short section between the two allegros assai in no. 28. The Count asks his wife's forgiveness, and a warm and tender ensemble sung by all participants concludes the comedy. One could call this the archetype of a classic andante. More complex are the other four pieces. In order of their appearance in the opera, they are no. 16, a duet between Susanna and the Count; no. 18, a sextet; no. 25, Basilio's aria; and the first section of the finale, no. 28. The duet and Basilio's piece are marked with an alla breve sign. Comparing the opening section of no. 28 to no. 16, it becomes clear that the alla breve sign here means that the duet is double the tempo of the finale's beginning. We have then four pieces marked "andante," of which two are at half the speed of the other two. Since it is perfectly imaginable that with a not-too-skillful ensemble the conductor might take no. 28 "in eight," it is a matter of course that no. 16 would be in four. It is equally possible to take no. 28 in four and take at least portions of nos. 16 and 25 also in four—only the "four" will be twice the speed of the one chosen for no. 28. But I consider these matters of "taking" tempos in this beat or that irrelevant to the essential questions posed here.

My impression upon reexamining these pieces by the criterion of what the composer wanted is that Mozart had in mind a far greater intensity of expression than we are used to hearing in opera performances. If we relate the finale and the duet with the quarter note of the first equal to the half note of the second, both pieces gain in drive over the soapy flirtatiousness that they exhibit in more commodious speeds. Basilio's piece is to be weighed against the other two sections of his aria, of which the middle portion is clearly in tempo di minuetto. I mentioned the final allegro in connection with the formula in bars 106–09, which relates it to the piano concertos and to Figaro's outburst.

No. 16 is by far the most sophisticated of the andante pieces, for this one tempo covers a variety of dramatic and psychological nuances. The final sentence of Susanna in the recitative immediately preceding the duettino makes the Count believe that she is willing to revive the droit du seigneur that he has so nobly annulled quite recently. The Count, full of quickly lighted fire, rushes to her and, with the crescendo in the strings and flutes in bar 10, he is ready to embrace her. She escapes with the subito piano. For the following phrases (bars 14–22), she musically gives him the "runaround." This will be far less expressive if the violin sixteenth-note scales sound like solid, methodical exercises instead of flirtatious and deceptive expressions of the clever maid. The following portion in A major (bar 29) is built on the distracted answers of Susanna, who gets tired of constantly replying to the same questions from the Count. If all these exchanges happen in a stately type of andante, the piece loses some of its quality of the hasty rendezvous. After all, the Count and his wife's maid must not be seen in a lengthy conversation in his own reception room, which is ready for the later festivity.

In no. 28, bars 7–9 should reveal the best expressive tempo. The puckish humor alternates with a warmly singing phrase, followed by the incensed and embarrassed protests of the Countess. Just as the scales of sixteenth notes in no. 16 have to make a dramatic point and should not sound academic, so here the runs of thirty-second notes (from bar 13) will be fully effective if they whirr and buzz, a nuance that demands a fairly lively tempo. When we contemplate these two pieces, it should be clear once again that the Wagnerian tenet about the tempo extremes in classical music is just about the opposite of what one finds in a close examination and imaginative study. If so far there has been any general idea (though generalizations can lead one sadly astray), it is that the allegros are not as fast as they are customarily taken, while the andantes are not as slow. If this opening of no. 28 is right, then the next section, marked "Con un poco più di moto," will fall into place. Un poco più needs to be indeed very little—just enough to get from the scherzando type of staccato phrasing to a more cantabile and fluid phrasing.

The tempo marking in the sextet, no. 18, is once again not authentic. No indication has been found in the autograph. In modern scores I have found not only the usual andante but also one allegro moderato. This appears in the complete Breitkopf and Härtel score, considered up to recent times one of the most authoritative. For us it is sufficient to know that Mozart may have had no part in either marking. This is no surprise: the piece has probably more variety of dramatic emphasis and nuance than any other movement of comparable length. If I were asked to advise the publisher of a new edition on a tempo to be printed over this piece I should choose "allegretto." I base this decision on a comparison of Marcellina's opening phrase with the finale of the String Quartet K. 575, which Mozart did mark "allegretto." The sextet consists of several musical sections with contrasting meanings and dramatic connotations. On stage are two groups, one of four people who are happy (at first they are three), the other of the Count and the Judge, who are unhappy. The nobleman is furious, and his grotesque Don Curzio stammers wildly, though both use well-mannered whispering voices, while Susanna sings a most wondrously peaceful melody, "Al dolce contento di questo momento" (bar 103). The character of this phrase is most assuredly a broad andante alla breve, equal in tempo to no. 16. Not so the sections between bars 40 and 71, the character and phrasing of which, with its dotted rhythm, expresses Susanna's vexation, jealousy, and mortification at seeing Marcellina embrace Figaro. Nobody here could mark "andante" as the right signal. This has an allegro quality and is in four beats.

At the opening, then, Marcellina's phrase has an allegretto character definitely alla breve; otherwise the bass line would not have been composed as we find it. The violin phrase in bars 2 and 3 has the playful gaiety and lightness so right for this moment in which a fine solution has been found to a nasty conflict. This is suddenly interrupted by Susanna's dashing in (bar 24), mentioned earlier. The 4/4 character of her arrival has once before been manifest in bars 13–16, when the Count and Don Curzio exchanged in subdued voices their own feelings of frustration. One should note that 29–39 are identical to 13–23 (transposed, of course), a splendid example of how symphonic construction may be interlocked with dramatic composition. Perhaps the musical terms are better illustrated with the hint that Marcellina, Figaro, and Bartolo are still in a peaceful 2/2, while the discontented group (Susanna does not yet know what has happened; she only sees the nasty "hag" embracing her man) sing in a nervous 4/4. The art of the conductor is to bring all these diverse strands together in the same tempo.

Bar 40 is 2/2, but 44 is again 4/4; 48 once more gives Figaro happy, composed phrases, which float easily in 2/2. From 54 on the two groups mix, with Susanna and the Count having a rhythmical figure that is aided by the Judge (whose stammering is too often exaggerated, distorting the rhythm in favor of obvious humor). From 72 on we return to the opening theme and the general feeling of 2/2. At 80, when the incredulous Susanna needs confirmation that she has heard right, a humorous, bouncing 4/4 phrase appears. This is symmetrical to 24, where a very jaunty phrase in a buoyant 4/4 occurs. The phrase at 80 is almost a part of the recapitulation, only here the mood is happy, while at 24 it was not. After Susanna hears repeatedly that Bartolo and the elderly Marcellina are indeed Figaro's parents, the lovely interlude (bar 103) follows. (Dynamic balance between voices is here a major problem.) After this glowing mood has been established, the coda concludes the situation, happily for four, and frustratingly for two, of the six participants. From 124 on Mozart makes even the Count and Don Curzio blend in with the others so that the purely musical effect will not be disturbed by anyone's discontent.

This sextet brings to mind what Wagner wrote about the tempo in the prelude to *Die Meistersinger* in his essay *On Conducting*. When we recall that this overture (or prelude) is marked by Wagner "Sehr mässig bewegt," we can see that though a composer may indicate an overall idea of a piece, it is difficult if not impossible to translate this indication into exact terms of speed. It is the same in the sextet, no. 18.

2/4 and 4/8 Meter If we now proceed to the other duple time, the pieces in 2/4 or 4/8, we will find similar situations, only fewer of them, as the whole opera contains only eight sections in this metric pattern. The section from the great finale, no. 15, commencing at bar 398, has been discussed in its relation to the rest of the preceding and following movements and to Zerlina's aria from *Don Giovanni*. Of the seven pieces left, the first cavatina of the Countess (no. 10) is surely the slowest, and the middle section of Figaro's cavatina, no. 3, from bar 64, the fastest. The latter must have particularly satisfied Mozart, since he turned one entire piece for *Don Giovanni*—the aria "Fin ch'han dal vino"— around this same movement and same tempo. In both cases the spirit is one of excessive energy and vitality. The Don is anticipating more easy conquests, and Figaro is planning how to reverse the social order and injustice.[8]

The tempo marking "larghetto" for the cavatina no. 10 is once again not from Mozart's hand. Whatever its origin, it does make sense, for the same word appears over Tamino's first aria, "Dies Bildnis ist bezaubernd schön." There is so much of the same cloth in these arias that the tempos can be considered identical, though the young man is admiring a portrait of a beautiful lady and the Countess prays for the return of her husband's affection. Her prayer can be soporific or passionate, according to tempo and inflection. The smallest degree of dragging can turn her from an affectionate and full-blooded human being into a betrayed wife who tiresomely complains. The same is true of the andantino section of her aria in act 3 (no. 19, bar 26). We are constantly confronted with

8. I feel that both these arias have been made in our age into contests of speed, with a resulting loss of clarity. One of the more dangerous trends is to equate music with sports, where ever-faster timings amaze the world, be it in swimming or sprinting. Music (as a Rockefeller Foundation panel reported in 1965) is unchanged in its inefficiency: a Mozart quintet at the time of its first performance took five people thirty-five minutes to perform, and two hundred years later it still takes five people thirty-five minutes to perform it. And so it must be. Indirectly, the language question has a good deal to do with the tempo of the two arias and of other overdriven movements. Up to the early 1930s, the so-called Mozart style was determined by the German-Austrian establishment, which still claims to hold a lien on Mozart, Haydn, Beethoven, and Schubert. With the flowering of international music festivals, the idea of the original language emerged, and even in arch-conservative Austria, beginning at the Salzburg Festival, Mozart's Italian operas were now given in Italian, and the casts became international as well. The roles of Don Giovanni and of Figaro were given incomparable personifications by Ezio Pinza, a unique artist who possessed, in addition to an unforgettable personality and voice, diction that enabled him to speed up these presto arias to a point where he captured the public with wildly exciting renditions. The tone and speed were set, however, somewhat beyond the limits envisioned by the composer and outside the frame of the whole musical structure.

tempos that have tended to get slower (as the fast tempos have tended to speed up). It is tempting for a fine singer to show off her breath control, and the reprise of the andantino theme "Dove sono i bei momenti" presents an ideal opportunity (bar 62). It should also be noted that both pieces of the Countess—or at least the slow portions—are marked "larghetto" and "andantino," which carry us away from the grandly heroic largo or the comfortable andante. The suffixes are diminutives indicating, as it were, a more moderate largo or a quicker walking pace. It also indicates a lighter quality as compared to a slow movement in a symphony. Note that only Breitkopf and Härtel and Eulenburg have "andantino" over the "Dove sono;" Bärenreiter and Peters have "andante," and Köchel's catalog has "andantino."[9]

There will be several more instances where we find diverse markings in different editions. There are many reasons for this. For example, Köchel indicates that Mozart marked the *Figaro* overture "allegro assai" in his own personal listing of his works. Scores have presto. A similar discrepancy exists over the finale of the *Haffner* Symphony, K. 385. In *Figaro* so far we have encountered several cases of more than one tempo marking, and we will find a few more before this chapter is concluded. The actual differences between andante and andantino are not very great. (We are also reckoning with documents from an era where spelling of words and names was not uniform. We find the composer referred to as Mozard, Mozzart, and a few other versions of the name.) It is obviously important to know all the reputable editions, but one must keep in mind that the words for tempo are poor substitutes for insight and imagination. To follow the path of a genius who could write music in the same key, in the same meter, in the same tempo, and yet produce dramatic contrasts at will is a fascinating expedition. I need not emphasize its importance in gaining greater insight and achieving more authority as musical director of such a great score.

Cherubino's aria, no. 11, veers between the 2/4 and 4/8 phrasing. It is without surprise that we learn that here too the tempo marking in the autograph is not from Mozart's own hand. Considering the idea of the lute accompaniment to the page's poem and song, the natural tempo of the pizzicato together with the necessity of singing four-bar phrases in one breath make this a simple and uncomplicated tempo choice.

Susanna's arietta no. 12 and the song of the bridesmaids in no. 22, both the solo verse and the concluding tutti, are slightly faster than Cherubino's song. Here again a number of telling details make the right tempo fairly inevitable as long as all factors are kept in mind. There is a good deal of parlando chatter in no. 12, which needs the right timing to carry the flirtatious inflection, and in bars 95–96 and 99–100 there is so expansive a phrase that only allowing sufficient time to develop it will bring it to its fullest bloom. Whenever Mozart uses

9. Recently it was pointed out to me that only since Beethoven's time has andantino been considered faster than andante; until about 1790 it was slower.

such large interval jumps, whether in instrumental or vocal music, something unusual takes place. We find excellent examples, widely separated in time of composition, in the first movement of the Serenade with the Posthorn, K. 320, and in the part of Fiordiligi. The recitative preceding the aria "Come scoglio" (*Così fan tutte*, no. 14) and that aria proper are so full of wide interval jumps that this piece alone can serve to make the point that such magnificent and daring phrases must be timed carefully if all their potential is to be realized in performance. (Richard Strauss admired this particular feature in Mozart so much that he emulated it many times, especially in *Die Frau ohne Schatten*, where the three women are given some of the fiercest jumps ever demanded by a composer.) In Susanna's arietta the interval of the ninth (bars 95–96 and 99–100) has such a wicked significance that it would be more than a detail missed if it were lost through haste. The difference between the two phrases wonderfully illustrates both action and thought, as the maid glances up and down the feminine attire, while the page is the real object of her delight. Anyone who has seen a lady look at him in a certain way will be aware how graphic the interval of the ninth is in the context of this arietta's coda. (That the first Susanna was undoubtedly a superb and sophisticated actress is somewhat indirectly documented by Mozart's comment about the replacement piece he wrote for another singer—on condition that she sing it with real naïveté. The implication is clear that she could not emulate the ways of Madame Storace, so it would be safer to settle for the less demanding opposite.)

The duet no. 2 in act 1 stands in a relation to the preceding duet, no. 1, similar to that of a symphony's finale (in 2/4) to its sonata first movement (in 4/4). I suggest a good look at Quartet K. 465, Quartet K. 499, Piano Concerto K. 503, the *Prague* Symphony (K. 504), and Quintet K. 515. All these works show the same metric relation of a first movement in 4/4 and a last movement in 2/4. Mozart did not write many such examples, so it is interesting that after the composition of *Figaro* (and the closely related *Prague* Symphony) we find three more works with this pattern. Haydn used this combination much more, since most of his own final movements are in 2/4.

Of the works mentioned, the *Dissonance* Quartet, K. 465, is the most relevant. Peters and Bärenreiter mark the finale "allegro molto," while Breitkopf and Härtel has simply "allegro." I prefer the unqualified allegro for the usual reason that one must allow the listener time to hear what is happening in the music. In bars 147–49 of the finale, the harmony changes with each eighth note in such a manner that even in a moderately paced movement this dazzling progression must have the effect of a kaleidoscope. To hear eleven different chords in three 2/4 bars in tempo allegro is a quite sufficient feat.

The tempos of these instrumental works have a definite bearing on those of the duets no. 1 and no. 2. Earlier I mentioned how the first duet has been treated as an attacca to the overture, hence quite a bit overdriven in tempo. In consequence it would be too fast in relation to the second duet, which must sound faster and more jaunty than the first. While the first duet is all sweetness and lyrical well-being, the second duet establishes with one radical phrase (from bars 44 to 68) the entire conflict and dramatic intrigue of the comedy. This is not in form of a narrative exposition; it is conveyed by Susanna with the implication, "You, my dear Figaro, are a fool, because you never understood why the Count was so infinitely generous in offering us this marvelously located chamber as our bedroom." The repartee needs to be sharp, ironic, with a telling edge not found in the placid contentment of the first duet. There is hardly a better example to demonstrate how a seemingly harmless idea—playing duet no. 1 attacca to the overture—misfires, affecting a whole sequence of tempos far into the first act.

3/4 and 3/8 Meter In triple meter (3/4 and 3/8) we have nine sections, which, in order of their appearance, are: no. 3, Figaro's aria; no. 13, a terzetto; the sudden entrance of Susanna and that of Figaro in no. 15; the fandango in the third-act finale, no. 22; the arias 24 and 25; and the slow and fast sections in no. 28. We have discussed the two 3/8 pieces of the finale no. 15. The middle sections of no. 24 and no. 25, arias of Marcellina and Basilio, are, like Figaro's no. 3, minuet movements. The one of Marcellina is already a pre-echo of the famous *Don Giovanni* minuet, in many ways one of the musical highlights of that opera. Figaro's minuet is dictated by the text of his furious, though at first subdued, outbreak. He will teach a lesson to the Count, so what can be more convincing than to couch this plan in the Count's own aristocratic dance, the minuet? The prominent use of the French horns is an allusion to the scheme of cuckolding the new bridegroom. Horns were, then as now, the symbol of such betrayal, and Mozart, who was perhaps not unfamiliar with these suspicions, indulged here and in Figaro's aria no. 26 in a display of horns at symbolically appropriate moments.

Bar 132 in the finale to act 3 is, as the text says, a fandango. In opera performances the ballet takes the center stage here, which makes for a charming scene as long as the choreographer prepares the dance at a sensible fandango tempo. (This, as I have indicated earlier, depends on whether the responsible dance director is basically musical. The surprises that can await the fledgling conductor in dealing with choreographers are too numerous and too varied to be dealt with here.) Thus, we have four of the nine tempos well established, as long as the traditional movements of minuet and fandango are known.

The terzetto no. 13, like most pieces connected with the Count, carries a special adjective, *spiritoso*. This is perhaps in reference to the peremptory opening, which in an allegro assai might catapult this piece into excessive speed. The setting is unusual even for Mozart, with whom the unusual is the rule. There are hardly any related movements, the closest being a fragment of a piano concerto in C major that begins (though in 4/4) with the identical choleric trills as the terzetto (K. 502a). The tempo, as in most ensemble pieces that cover such a wide range of expressions, must take into account that the furious opening is immediately followed by the artificial restraint of the phrase from bar 8 onward, in which the women attempt to gain time by all means, fair or foul. The Count's prying questions are always accompanied by *fp* and, in bars 62, 64, 66, etc., by furious runs. The guide that can clarify the exact speed is once again that syncopated formula ♪♩♩♪ in bars 35, 50, 99, 114, and 129, which I pointed out in a different context in no. 15. If one holds the terzetto up to the first allegro of no. 15 it will be quite easy to see that the quarter notes of these two sections are in the same tempo.[10]

There remains the duet of Susanna and Figaro in act 4, no. 28 (from bar 121), and its immediate predecessor (perhaps we can call it an introduction), the short larghetto phrase of Figaro alone (bar 109). Figaro, ironically comparing Venus, Mars, and Vulcan to Susanna, the Count, and himself—a moment in which the servant indulges in allusions a bit beyond his probable educational background— is called to in hushed tones by a lady he assumes to be the Countess. The piece that follows is sung in a wild whisper and is the most rapid—by a considerable margin—of the triple meters. In Mozart's violin-piano chamber music there are several 3/4 movements in allegro molto which in spirit and forward-rushing drive are related to this section. I refer particularly to K. 481, which is also in the key of E-flat. Perhaps it will be helpful to look also at the opening duet of act 2 in *Don Giovanni*. Though its spirit is quite different, the cadential phrase in bars 41–44 and 50–53 can be related usefully to those of the Susanna-Figaro duet (135–38 and all similar places).

After the duet has been understood and properly related in timing and tempo, it will be a good double check to consider the preceding larghetto (bar 109) in a tempo slow enough that the triplet equals the whole bar of the allegro molto. Yet the larghetto should never drag. In the short larghetto, with its allusions to the Greek gods, the horns once again play a prominent role. It is also important to note that in over 150 bars of the fast section of the duet there is only one short spurt of "real" sixteenth notes, in bars 125–26. (The constant excited murmuring motive in the second violins is more a trill than solid sixteenths.) I find this singular use of the repeated, detached sixteenth notes most indicative of the sense of economy I mentioned as part of genius. At this moment Mozart has Figaro make one of the quickest decisions of his career. As soon as the (presumed) Countess appears, he gets the idea, represented by sixteenth notes, that he will take her along to surprise her husband with his own wife. If these two bars of repeated and heated sixteenths are correlated with the triplet movement

10. I should like to avoid a conceivable misunderstanding about such matters as these equations of tempo. Those checks and balances I suggest are of the greatest service in the preparation of the conductor. They should never be used in actual rehearsal. They help in acquiring a keener awareness of relative tempos and can provide, after a prolonged period of study, the authoritative assurance that a conductor must possess if he or she wishes to prevail. But these relative metric and rhythmic values must never deteriorate into charts or mathematical formulas.

of the preceding larghetto, the tempos ought to be ideal for the entire piece from 109 to 275.

6/8 Meter I have mentioned, in passing, the 6/8 scene (from bar 605) of the great finale, no. 15. It would be well now to have a closer look at this and other sections in 6/8 meter. Among these movements we find no. 8, the chorus of villagers; the above-mentioned section in no. 15; another choral piece, no. 21, in which the village girls present flowers, and just before it the letter duet, no. 20; the short cavatina of Barbarina at the beginning of act 4, no. 23; the conclusion of Susanna's and Figaro's duet "Pace, pace" in no. 28; and that masterpiece, Susanna's aria "Deh vieni," no. 27.

Mozart composed a tremendous number of important pieces in 6/8, and within that meter there are at least three different types. There is first the purely lyrical for slow movements, most admirably represented in the *Linz* and *Prague* symphonies (K. 425 and K. 504) and the G-Minor, K. 550. In quartets we have such movements in K. 421 and K. 428. (This latter will be important in relation to the duettino "Pace, pace mio dolce tesoro" in *Figaro* no. 28, bar 275, where the characteristic rhythmic formula [♪♩♪♩] in bars 289 and 291 is directly descended from the slow movement of K. 428.) In operas we have the finest flower in Susanna's aria "Deh vieni non tardar," in *Figaro*, act 4, no. 27, and in *Don Giovanni*, the terzetto in act 2, no. 2. (Eulenburg starts a new count of the numbers with the second act.) Among concertos there is the F-sharp minor movement in K. 488. These are only a few of the outstanding examples of Mozart's lyrical use of the 6/8 meter. The second type, with equally numerous examples, is the fast, "hunting" rhythm. This is mostly found in final movements, except that the *Hunt* Quartet, K. 458, uses this bracing 6/8 as an opening movement. Examples include all four concertos for horn, the clarinet concerto, and several piano concertos (K. 450, K. 456, K. 482, and K. 595), Quartet K. 589, and Quintets K. 516 and K. 593. The third pattern lies between these two and encompasses such marvels as the variation movement of the Quartet K. 421 and the famous Piano Sonata K. 331 (with the rondo alla turca), the serenades of Pedrillo in *Die Entführung aus dem Serail* and the Don in *Don Giovanni*, and the three B-flat major pieces in *Figaro*—first the section in the finale of act 2, then the letter duet, no. 20, and the above mentioned "Pace, pace" in no. 28. The vocal works have at least one nuance in common: they all feature a certain degree of puckish humor. The serenades need no explanation, and all the pieces in *Figaro* are full of wit, though some false sentiment has come creeping into a few spots of these ensembles and has gradually distorted the letter duet.

The chorus no. 8 is a simple rustic allegro, which should be contrasted most judiciously with the women's chorus, no. 21, lest the two pieces sound exactly the same. Both are in G major and 6/8, yet there is a considerable difference in emphasis and thrust. The appearance of the girls with their flowers for the Countess in act 3 is a gesture of genuine affection for the lady. This floral tribute before the great party provides a gentle little interlude. The first-act presentation has been staged by Figaro. We have learned in the recitative after the second duet (bars 32–33) that the Count is sorry at having abolished the droit du seigneur and wishes to revive it with Susanna. Like all good politicians, Figaro aims to nail the Count's promise to abolish the hated "right" by having as many witnesses as he can collect. Thus, there should be a certain aggressive quality to the harmless little G-major tune. This spirit can easily escape unless the tempo is just a shade fast and a bit on the relentless side. Here, as in the bridesmaids' duet in no. 22 (bar 61 in the orchestra and 74 in the voices), the idea must come across that the villagers have been coached and carefully prepared. Their delivery should suggest a school production at the end of the year, with more zest than talent on the part of the participants.

Although the tempo indication that appears over a movement needs to be weighed against the total musical message of the piece, the puzzle of what the composer intended in the duet no. 20 has not been solved. Over the decades it has increased in popularity but has sadly run down in tempo, from a spirited little trick by the two women into an exhibition of floating piano singing. This treatment can produce a pretty piece, but it tends to divorce itself from the comedy context, as if the actors stepped forward to deliver a comment to the audience. I have rarely experienced a performance of *Figaro* in which this delightful allegretto was not dragged down into a maudlin vocal parade piece, with the two sopranos competing as to who can sing more slowly, more softly, and with greater affectation. Only a determined, persuasive, and patient conductor of tremendous authority can ever correct this misinterpretation. (It is only fair to add that in this piece, as in several others, the large modern opera houses have contributed to the problem. Slowing down is necessary to project a piano tone in a large house, but not in theaters such as the Drottningholm Teaterswald or the court theater in Schönbrunn, which have acoustics like those of 1786.) We have correlated the other two B-flat 6/8 sections, in no. 15 and no. 28, both of which are andante. The letter duet should be, by any standards of musical or dramatic judgment, somewhat livelier in tempo, but in performance it is invariably slower and gets slower as it progresses toward the close.

The two solo pieces in act 4, Barbarina's little cavatina and Susanna's aria no. 27, have tempo markings that various sources agree are not Mozart's. In Köchel's catalog both andante designations are in brackets, which is the scholarly way of expressing doubt of authenticity. I am very much inclined to question this, too. First, it is patently unmusical to even attempt to fit these two pieces to a similar last. The Gardener's daughter is highly agitated at not finding the pin, and I am fairly sure that Mozart did not make great concessions in tempo to the vanity of the original singer of this role, who was all of twelve years old. Unless today's children have different biological properties, I cannot imagine that a twelve-year-old could sing as slowly as our present-day Barbarinas are wont to do. But the singer has only thirty-six bars in an evening that spans nearly four hours, and she wants to make the most of it. Consequently, she sings as slowly as the traffic will permit. But the piece is agitato and should be performed accordingly.

Susanna's declaration of longing has been subject to protracted speculation. The recitative leaves no doubt that hers is a deliberate attempt to arouse Figaro's jealousy: "The rascal is hiding and watching. I'll amuse myself by letting him have the just desert of his doubts." Those are her words before the accompagnato recitative begins. The end of the next portion is further proof that hers is a show for the hidden bridegroom: "Come la notte i furti miei seconda" ("How the night helps my intrigues"). Then begins a song that may be still part of the intended comedy, especially at first. If the second half of the piece and its ending were still part of the attempt to deceive Figaro, this girl would rank with the most astute actresses of all time. The consensus has been either that she is overcome during the progress of her song by her true emotion of longing for her husband, helped by the enchantment of the garden at night, or, far more likely, that Mozart himself was overcome by musical inspiration. He found himself in the same quandary later—and for much longer stretches—in *Così fan tutte*, where there are considerable discrepancies between the coolly calculated text and the deeply moving music. Fiordiligi and even Dorabella are treated thus on several occasions, and there is no reason why Susanna could not have shared their fate. The first interpretation—that Susanna starts in a spirit of playacting that gradually gives way to sincere feeling—is the only one that can be represented on stage. Therefore, singers take the 6/8 section at a reasonably gauged tempo but allow it to slow down until it is almost impossible to recapture the spirit of the orchestral postlude after the vocal part. It takes a great singing actress—preferably one with a superlative low register, such as the original Susanna must have possessed—to reconcile the varied expression in this great aria with the right tempo.

Perhaps the solution can be found in a parallel problem of tempo marking in the Piano Concerto in A, K. 488. Breitkopf and Härtel mark the second movement (a slow siciliano) "andante"; Bärenreiter and Köchel's catalog have it as an "adagio." While no edition ever suggested adagio as the right tempo for Susanna's F-major aria, the existing andante is certainly questionable. If we consider the aria to be the same adagio as the F-sharp minor slow movement of K. 488, we need not look further for psychological shifts of Susanna, but can confidently let her sing the incomparable piece with all the warmth of which she is capable. This idea is predicated on the principle that the adagio in K. 488 is not the same as the adagio of the prelude to *Tristan and Isolde*, to name one great example of the romantic adagio. Between these 6/8 movements of Mozart and Wagner there is no resemblance save the meter; the term *adagio* has entirely different meaning. To stay within the classical frame of reference, I cite the 6/8 slow movement of the Piano Sonata Opus 106 by Beethoven, which has a metronome marking. (It is in F-sharp, as is K. 488, and has a 92 meter for the eighth note.) As long as these indications are used not rigidly but as guides, there is a distinct relation here between K. 488 and Opus 106. If one wishes Susanna to move from comic trickery to real affection during the orchestral introduction rather than later, there is no reason not to conceive the whole of her 6/8 aria as an adagio. This necessitates a proper adjustment of the staccato figures in the wind instruments.

Conclusion

In this study of *The Marriage of Figaro*, with many excursions into other scores by Mozart, I have attempted to show that only the comparative method will bring home the original meaning of the composer's tempos. This method is the only one that can balance the inadequacy of the few words that were at the disposal of the composer to indicate how movements should be taken. There are so many discrepancies in different editions, between andante and adagio, andante and allegro, allegro assai and presto, and many other tempo terms, that one cannot rely on those words without more searching. It is of little use to the conductor to know whether a marking has been found in manuscript *A*, or copyist's score *B*, or parts of the first performance *C*. He is faced with two editions of the *Linz* Symphony, K. 425, one of which has a marking "andante" over the second movement, the other showing clearly "adagio non troppo." No footnote in either version explains the discrepancy. Thus, the performer has to do his own work until the text is so familiar that no word will be more than a corroboration of what the music has already told him with clarity.

Before continuing with the subject of tempo, we may summarize some of the conclusions the discussion has so far suggested:

1. The words indicating tempo have often been subject to changes, to counteract misreadings or to correct an initially misstated term. Actual speed differences between neighboring expressions, such as andantino and allegretto or allegro assai and presto, are not great. These terms are often only expressive suggestions: the feeling of an allegretto is quite different from that of an andantino, though their speeds may be the same. If a composer felt that a slow movement sounded too flippant as an andante, he wrote "adagio" over it; if, on the other hand, the musicians dawdled, he abandoned the adagio sign for an andante. But neither term necessarily refers to speed per se.

2. Only a wide acquaintance with a composer's work will answer questions raised in any single composition. The demonstration of this in a long opera with many different tempos may have shown an unusual number of relations with other compositions, but the principle is the same for all major works.

3. There is, to my knowledge, no book on any composer treating his work with this degree of cross-reference. The purpose of a biography is quite different

from that of a guide to reading music. Although there are some searching works available, they usually stay within one field of a composer's creative output. Either the operas are treated, or the string quartets, or some other category. The unending study of cross-relations between all types of composition will eventually bear fruit in performances of authenticity, without any dry rot or pedantic historicism.

Six
Knowing the Right Tempo: II

The Metronome

In many conversations with professional musicians I have found that most do not recognize the existence of the metronome. If they notice the curious figures at the heads of sections, they seem to consider them some kind of ornament. There are a few fanatics of the metronome who believe these directives to be sacred writ.[1] Far more common, however, is the willful, almost capricious, way of ignoring the metronome marks of any composer who used them.

, How can one explain this phenomenon? There is complete documentation that Beethoven saluted Maelzel's invention after initial skepticism. Thayer, in his biography of Beethoven, quotes a letter from Beethoven to Mosel:

> I am heartily rejoiced that you agree with me in the opinion touching the time designations which date back to the barbarous period in music, for what, for instance, can be more nonsensical than Allegro, which always means merry and how often are we so far from this conception of time that the piece says the very opposite of the designation. As regards these four chief speeds [*Hauptbewegungen*], which by no means have the correctness or truthfulness of the chief winds, we gladly allow that they be put aside, it is a different matter with the words used to designate the character of the composition, these we cannot give up, since time is really more the body while these have reference to the spirit. So far as I am concerned I have long

1. Rudolf Kolisch, "Tempo and Character in Beethoven's Music," *Musical Quarterly* 2 (1943):169–87; 3 (1943):291–312. In 1943 a well-reasoned and important essay by Kolisch broke a lance for the accuracy of Beethoven's metronome markings. It remained without effect in the world of musical education, since in general the obiter dicta of the group around Schönberg have been considered more irritant than enlightenment. This attitude, caused by the sententious manner and clannish ways of the Schönberg circle, is unfortunate. Ideas that are significant and need clarification have been disregarded because of personal foibles that have nearly erased the vast knowledge and useful contributions of eminent musicians such as Kolisch.

thought of giving up the nonsensical designations Allegro, Andante, Adagio, Presto; Maelzel's metronome gives us the best opportunity to do this. I give you my word that I shall never use them again in my new compositions—it is another question if we shall thereby accomplish the necessary universal use of the instrument— I do not think so. But I do not doubt that we shall be described as task-masters, if the cause might thus be served it would still be better than to be accused of feudalism.[2]

Beethoven's use of the metronome has been denounced unrelentingly. Critics have either discounted the composer's ideas of tempo because he was deaf or denigrated the validity of Maelzel's instrument because of its inaccuracy and unreliability. What these critics and skeptics fail to explain is the flagrant disregard of metronome marks of Debussy, Bartók, and others. Bartók was more than specific about his timings: not content with metronome figures, he added up the minutes and seconds needed to perform each section in a given tempo. Yet rare are the performances that heed Bartók's markings. (I cannot forgo one personal recollection here. After my first rehearsal for the Concerto for Orchestra with a group that performs under many maestros, a number of the players commented that this was the first time they had been able to play the notes of the opening section of the fifth movement. That section, from bar 8 to bar 160, is marked "Presto, the quarter note 134–46." This rather comfortably playable concept is commonly replaced by one so much faster that it becomes blurred and not so bracingly gay.)

I have had little success in explaining to musicians that Beethoven was deaf only to the outside world; as a composer he was never deaf. The argument that he heard for enough years in his youth to write through memory is simplistic and does not allow for the complexities of the human mind. The fact is that composition is a mental process, not a physical one. As I mentioned earlier, most composers do not use a piano: they work inside their heads and hear with an inner ear. Thus, there is no excuse to disregard what Beethoven wrote.

Among the innumerable canards on Beethoven's metronome markings (and hence his tempos), one of my favorites is the entry under "Tempo" in *The Oxford Companion to Music*, edited by Percy Scholes. It begins with an excellent first paragraph containing discerning and valuable ideas on the general subject. The second paragraph, dealing specifically with the tempo of the funeral march in the *Eroica*, ends memorably with the statement, "But everybody would agree that the composer's marking is too fast."[3]

There seems to be a reluctance to accept what may be uncomfortable, and there are many metronome marks that do not suit the ingrained habits or the immediate instincts of the performer. One of these curious habits that work

2. Alexander Thayer, *The Life of Ludwig van Beethoven*, ed. Henry E. Krehbiel, 3 vols. (New York: G. Schirmer, Inc., 1921), 2:386.

3. Percy A. Scholes, *The Oxford Companion to Music*, 9th ed. rev. (London: Oxford University Press, 1955), p. 1021.

against the metronome is the rush to make decisions from the opening strains of a section with a new tempo. The beginning is rarely the best place to make any judgment of tempo. I can single out Brahms as one composer whose initial phrases are rarely a clue to the right tempo. I contend that three-fourths of his movements in orchestral works are, at the outset, deceptive as to speed.

Perhaps this is one reason why Brahms wrote as he did to George Henschel, the first music director of the Boston Symphony Orchestra. In 1880 Henschel had written to Brahms, asking if the metronome markings in the *German Requiem* were meant to be taken strictly at face value. Brahms replied:

> The question received in your letter today is somewhat obscure, indistinct; I hardly know what to answer: "If the indications by figures [metronome] of the tempi in my Requiem should be strictly adhered to?" Well—just as with all other music. I think . . . that the metronome is of no value. As far as at least my experience goes, everybody has, sooner or later, withdrawn his metronome marks. . . . The so-called "elastic" tempo is moreover not a new invention. "*Con discrezione*" should be added to that as to many other things. Is this an answer? I know no better one; but what I do know is that I indicate (without figures) my tempi, modestly to be sure, but with the greatest care and clearness.[4]

It is true that the second edition of the score did not carry the metronome markings that were in the 1868 first printing.[5] One has to consider the lapse of fourteen years between the composition of the *Requiem* and the writing of this letter. We know that in the orchestral works following the *Requiem* (Opus 45), the variations, and the symphonies Brahms did not use metronome figures. But once again, the unmentioned issue is the relativity of tempos, not necessarily their absolute speed.

As to the original metronome readings of the Brahms *Requiem*, the facts are that the first and seventh movements are in the same tempo, the fourth and sixth movements have the same tempo, and the episode ("Siehe ein Ackermann wartet") from the second movement is in the same tempo as the first movement. The fugal sections in the second, third, and sixth movements are all related to the preceding portions. In the second we find the same relationship between the 3/4 and the 4/4 as in Beethoven's Ninth Symphony (see example 48); in the third movement, the only proverbial problem has been conductors' reluctance to agree with Brahms that the entire movement proceeds in one tempo; and the sixth movement shows a clear connection from the 3/4 into the 4/2—if the vivace portion is taken at the right tempo, which equates the eighth note of the 3/4 with the quarter note of the 4/2.[6] That Brahms was very conscious of such relation-

4. George Henschel, *Personal Recollections of Johannes Brahms* (Boston: Gorham Press, 1907), pp. 78–79.

5. They are found also in *A Thematic Catalogue of Brahms' Works* (Simrock, 1904).

6. Comparing the openings of the first and last movements from the Brahms *Requiem*, one cannot tell conclusively that these two tempos are identical. This is one more indication that opening themes need not be taken as the guide to tempos. Later on, however, we find the identical music, at the close

ships will be demonstrated several times over when the discussion turns to these matters. I believe that every composer wants first and foremost to have his tempos properly understood; that such understanding is not always, perhaps only rarely, achieved; and that disappointments, for which we have documentation, lead to spontaneous pronunciamentos on metronome marks that need not be taken as canon.

If one knows how many misinterpretations of even the most explicit directions are possible, any seemingly contradictory remark by a composer can be evaluated for what it may have meant under the specific circumstances in which it was made. The only certain factor is the composition itself. In my quest for right tempos I have found the metronome indications extremely helpful, though most of the time I do not consult the little clock. There were many years when I did not own a metronome, and still I found it to be of aid and comfort. If this statement seems contradictory the following examples may explain it.

Verdi wrote a most eloquent endorsement of the metronome and its proper use over the scores of his *Te Deum*. I translate:

> This entire piece ought to be performed in one tempo as indicated by the metronome. This notwithstanding, it will be appropriate to broaden or accelerate in certain spots for reasons of expression and nuance, coming back, however, always to the first tempo.

There are more than a handful of pieces where this rule applies. Altogether I cannot conceive of a more admirable statement to encompass in two sentences the essentials of classical tempos, or perhaps even of all music making.

The figure 80 that stands at the head of the *Te Deum* also appears over the *Requiem*'s beginning (with the direction andante) and at several other places. (As an aside it is worth mentioning that 80 is not far from a normal human pulse.) The *Messa da Requiem* (as its full title reads) has, not unlike Brahms's

---

of both movements—allowing for the rescoring of the last movement, where violins and trombones are added. The meter change at bar 206 in the second movement shows one of the favorite explicit relationships of tempo that can be found in all of Brahms's compositions, be they for solo piano or orchestra. How much awareness of these tempo relationships is required from the conductor is even more pointedly demonstrated in the sixth movement. At bar 82, the forceful sixteenth notes from the 4/4 continue into the 3/4, thereby making the relationship explicit. (The term *vivace* here is an expressive confirmation, since for purposes of tempo no word is necessary.) Where the mastery of these tempos will show is in the handling of the accelerando that starts at bar 68. Up to that point the tempo of the andante opening of this movement prevails. From the metronome table it is clear that the opening of the fourth movement is in the same tempo as the opening of movement six, no matter how different the character of the two sections. Thus, after arriving at bar 68, the task is to increase the speed gradually to the point where, with bar 76, the new tempo has been reached. If, finally, we consider that the eighth notes from bar 204 are equal to the quarter notes of the fugato (bar 209), the conductor should have the final fugue of this movement set in his mind as he reaches bar 76. To me it is quite understandable that Brahms would have been discouraged by Henschel's queries, for he believed that nobody could have been more clear and specific in marking tempo than he was in the score of the *Requiem*.

A German Requiem, a duplication of the opening strains toward the very end of the work. The first time it is played by the orchestra, with murmured interpolations from the chorus; the second time it is sung by the whole chorus, with the soprano solo a capella and half a tone higher. Again the composer writes andante and 80 for the quarter note (crochet). Not since the retirement of Toscanini have I heard a performance that heeds this explicit and logical direction.

Considering its utter simplicity, it may be hard to understand why anyone would willfully disregard this important instruction. My explanation has always been that the desire to make a special effect out of some detail often becomes more important to the conductor than the overall architecture of the work. When a conductor takes the opening string passage a lot slower than 80, there will be a startling effect of an eerie pianissimo, a hardly audible whispering of the chorus. It is indeed startling—and it is totally out of style, for two reasons. I have hinted at the potential damage to the grand line of any work when such parallel tempos are violated. To this argument one could reply that the conductor might conceivably take the a capella portion just as slowly as the opening, but this becomes impossible, for voices have a way of leading even the most autocratic of conductors back to nature's normal way of doing things. The breathing apparatus of a large group of people will gradually make a shambles of any but the right tempo, and that tempo will be 80. Or the solo soprano will gently protest that in "that tempo" she cannot properly sustain the floating pianissimo. In a word, no matter what the fancy ideas on the podium may be, the mass of singing humanity will drive everything back to Verdi, who composed primarily for the human voice, with the instruments imitating it rather than the other way around.

Like the opening of the *Requiem*, the "Dies Irae" is marked 80—but of course for the half bar (minim). Some conductors make up for the unduly slow tempo of the opening by taking the second movement much faster than asked for. This may appear terrifyingly effective to the casual listener, but it has the disadvantage that the greatest transitional passage in the work, the passing of the "Dies Irae" reprise into the a capella *Requiem* reprise, is ruined. The second disadvantage of overstressing the quietness of the beginning is the historic one: Verdi never conceived of such artificially hushed dynamics. According to Toscanini, who knew and worked under Verdi, the composer always wanted his piano phrases sung by the instruments in a natural cantabile sound. Knowing, however, that the playing of Italian orchestras was only moderately accomplished, the master felt that they needed special warning. He sometimes used the marking "pppp" in the hope of obtaining from them a single piano instead of the ubiquitous mezzo-forte which was, and still is, the clearest signal of mediocrity and indifference in performing music. Similarly, Verdi did not mean the triple or quadruple forte in strong passages; that too was a psychological ploy to obtain normal contrast.

The instrumental dynamic range is duplicated by that of the human voice.

Example 46. Wagner, *Siegfried*, act 1, scene 3 opening

There, too, considerable differences exist between the German and Italian methods of voice training. What in German music is a soft piano will usually be produced with a controlled falsetto, called *Kopfstimme*, or head voice. The Italians, at least up to recent times, detested and rejected this, much as we would not consider the barbershop tenor fit to sing Tamino in *Die Zauberflöte*. If we speak of style, there is no doubt that the proper sound of the *Requiem* orchestra will not be found with a nearly inaudible pianissimo for the opening.

As related tempos will be a major consideration of this chapter, it should be clear from the outset that they are more than a mathematical whim of the composer. Structural unity is here the issue. All great compositions have an element of symmetry, which may be less apparent when observed than it is disturbing when missing. Often we leave a performance that seemed unobjectionable in all obvious elements with some puzzling sense of dissatisfaction. The kindly disposed person will blame his own mood, a bad meal, or sudden fatigue, when the true cause may have been a lack of balance, an assymetry. Compositions, especially instrumental pieces, are described in their titles in formal terms. Sonata, rondo, and variation are principles of structure, and those come before all other considerations for the performer who studies a work. It is strange that recognizing the basic connection of tempo relations to structure has yet to be emphasized as the first step toward producing a balanced performance of any large-scale composition.

It seems ironic that Wagner wrote so eloquently about the freedom of tempo (and according to Hanslick put this theory into practice with his *Eroica* performance) and yet set down a series of related tempos in many of his music-dramas more strictly than did any operatic composer before his time. In order to show some of Wagner's tempo relations in full I would have to reprint here the entire third scene from the first act of *Siegfried*. It should suffice to direct the attention to some key spots. Of the two examples, the first (example 46) is invariably played correctly in performances. It contains a quite obvious relation with the last two sixteenth notes, indicating that the quarter of the 3/4 equals the eighth of the previous 2/4. The other example (example 47) has been misinterpreted for as long as I can remember. The easiest way to read it is to have the singer of Siegfried consider his first bar ("He, Mime") with the following moderato bar as one 3/2 measure. Then it combines perfectly the increasing nervousness of the dwarf with the contrasting address, peremptory but calm, by Siegfried. But the biggest advantage of performing this as Wagner wanted it lies in the succeeding tempos, all of which derive from this moderato in explicitly established relationships.[7]

7. Here is another example of why even highly successful recordings should not be followed instead of the composer's directions. In operatic recording sessions, as well as the opera house, the vicissitudes of indispositions, last-minute replacements, and other uncontrollable factors can frustrate the finest ideas and concepts of conductor and record producer. It is stated in John Culshaw's book about the great *Ring* recording project under Georg Solti that the directing forces wanted a new tenor as Siegfried. Unfortunately, this man proved unable to learn the role. While they were already in

Example 47. Wagner, *Siegfried*, "Forging Scene"

The disregard shown Beethoven's relative tempo indications plays havoc with many of his symphonies. In the Sixth there is a 66 for the entire bar over the first movement. There is also a 132 for the quarter over the trio. But conductors are frequently inclined to consider Beethoven wrong on the first tempo and decide to take that whole movement considerably slower, disregarding the fact that the phrasing is obviously a "one in a bar" and not a 2/4. Why should the composer have indicated his figure for the half note? Why did he indicate for the trio a quarter-note speed of 132? Are these not the same figures jotted down differently? Yes and no. What goes wrong for every conductor who disregards this relation is the contrast between the first and second movements.

I recall a highly regarded conductor who got out of this dilemma by playing the first two movements without pause, making it the longest opening andante in history. Notwithstanding a beautiful sound from the orchestra, the movement was dull, as it should never be, because his insistence on a steady 2/4 throughout the development section of the allegro made an exercise of it, rather than producing the kind of all-embracing elation that one feels in the midst of a lovely landscape. Taking the first movement too slowly and cutting it into two beats, the conductor decided on a tempo for the second movement that was faster than

sessions a veteran whom they had not wanted was begged to fill in. This established his indispensability and thus his right to do things his own way.

Beethoven's decreed speed, as are most renditions of this piece. Here then was a slightly livelier brook, but what one missed in that motion was the stillness inherent in the very slow tempo asked for by the composer—a stillness recognized by anyone who has ever sat at or wandered along a small stream in a setting so peaceful one can hear oneself think. There are moments when man's potential oneness with nature becomes almost tangible—but not when an etude is replacing the great mixture of nature's sounds.

In more technical terms, it is always dangerous to perform passages where a triple and a quadruple or duple rhythm go together. Throughout the development of the first movement there are long sequences of triplets against the motive of the principal theme. When this section is played in a tempo even slightly too slow, these two figures do not mix as they should but clash.

Here is only one of many cases in symphonies and string quartets where Beethoven sets metronome figures that relate one movement to another. Yet over the 150 years since the composer died, every argument against the metronome has been used, every sophistry has been applied, in preference to examining with open mind and with imagination what the composer wanted. The following examples show how some great moments are spoiled by flagrant violations of such relative tempo markings.

My most notable encounter with the next example goes back to the early 1970s. The section leader of the second violins in the London Symphony Orchestra, who is now the conductor of an Australian symphony orchestra, accused me at one of our rehearsals of nearly causing him to drive into a tree. While driving home the night before, he explained, he had been listening to the radio. When a recording of Beethoven's Choral Symphony was played he got such a shock that he nearly lost control of his steering wheel. He had performed the work numerous times under a variety of conductors, but never as he was hearing it now. When my name was announced as the conductor he couldn't wait to get home and look at the score. When he did so he had to admit that this was the way the passage appeared. The difference between the concept he had stored in his fingers and ears and the one on my recording was so startling that he wished to know why the obvious was ignored.

At the point in question (example 48), the score shows quite clearly that one quarter of the 3/4 bar must be equal to one entire bar of the 2/2 prestissimo. In other words, the thirty-second notes of the strings continue uninterrupted as eighth notes after the double bar. Or, to explain it a third way, the notes on the word "Funken" must be exactly alike on the second quarter of bar 919 and the first of 920. This is the way it is written—but not usually the way it is done. I have been told that Erich Kleiber did perform the transition this way. Wherever I check my own recollection by asking other musicians, the reply is always the same: the maestoso (bar 916) is generally taken much slower, so that the prestissimo begins in a completely new, and hence unrelated, tempo. In my first ventures in conducting this awesome score, I fell in with the customary manner

Example 48. Beethoven, Sym. No. 9, 4th mvt., mm. 916–22

Prestissimo

of doing it, but I recall the awkward feeling it always gave me to drag out the maestoso measures. It takes time and perhaps also maturity to acquire enough courage to counter accumulated habits and follow one's own conviction. This was my answer to the young violinist-conductor. It is not easy for anyone to disregard nearly every important "model" and take at a crossroads a seldom trodden and seemingly questionable path.

Why then have generations of formidable musicians taken this transition in a manner contrary to what is written? I never interviewed Furtwängler or Walter on this subject. When I could have asked them I did not know the question, and now that I know the question, they are not here to give the answer. I did show my example to the concertmaster of a great orchestra. In the first flush of his surprise he wanted me to allow that "one can do it our way, too." This was no doubt a declaration of loyalty to his conductor, and perhaps of liberality. But in such matters liberality is not germane. One *can* do anything and probably get away with it. It is the clear difference between right and wrong that is at stake here.

The first reason why so many generations have missed this transition lies in the purposeful disregard of the metronome marks. What can be clearer than the figure of 132 for the half note at the prestissimo (bar 851), which turns into 60 for the quarter at bar 916, allowing just a shade of relaxation between the mathematically accurate 66 and the calmer 60. With the strings in fast-moving thirty-seconds, the tempo is speeding up imperceptibly until it has again reached the 66, which is the same as the prestissimo's whole bar. This elementary argument is further buttressed by the way the 3/4 maestoso has been prepared by Beethoven. The section beginning with bar 851 is built on even-measured periods up to and including bar 909. With bar 910 the phrasing goes into two three-bar periods, thus preparing for the 3/4 measures. I can only surmise that this is too simple; it is more "metaphysical" or "profound" (terms much beloved by seekers of mystification) to make a special feature of the four maestoso bars. This habitual but wrong way of performing this section can also be traced to the Wagnerian thesis that slow must be too slow and fast too fast.

Perhaps a skeptic will ask why Beethoven did not continue in the 2/2 meter, after establishing the three-bar rhythm from 910 onward: to write twelve 2/2 measures instead of four 3/4 bars would give the same results. Not quite, and for reasons that lie deep in the spirit of music. Throughout the Middle Ages, the figure 3 was considered the perfect entity, representing the unity of Father, Son, and Holy Ghost. This idea found musical expression in a tradition that the most significant portions of the mass should be in triple time. When I first learned this, it struck me as quite extraordinary that in *Lohengrin*—famous as the squarest of scores, with more than three hours of music in duple time—the single exception is the prayer in act 1, which is in 3/4. In the finale of Beethoven's Ninth one need only glance at the variation, starting with the words "ihr stürzt nieder, Millionen," to realize that Beethoven at that moment moves toward an ever higher realm of spirituality, the brotherhood of man. Later on the ode speaks of God: "Über'm Sternenzelt muss ein lieber Vater wohnen" ("Above the starry canopy must dwell a loving father"). All of this is in triple meter.[8] Thus, it should not seem surprising or out of context if the one moment of repose before final tumult is a maestoso in 3/4. I started this argument about the maestoso by stressing that accumulated habit had made it into an adagio. It is invariably conducted "in six." But once the deeper significance of the Trinity, or triple meter, has been recognized, anything "in six" would be ruled out.

Let no one imagine that the way in which a conductor groups the beats in a bar is a mere mechanical device to bolster good ensemble. A triple time must be in three or it loses the triadic sense. Six is double-edged, since it can also be a composite duple meter, which of course most 6/8 or 6/4 movements are. Consider some important slow movements in triple time in Beethoven's late works: the Piano Trio Opus 97, the Variations of the Sonata Opus 109, and the adagio in the Quartet Opus 130. None of these must ever be thought of or phrased in six.

We come back to the basic question raised by Richard Wagner's notion of tempos. Unless one is convinced that the great classic pattern of musical proportion demands exactly the opposite of Wagner's ideas, namely, an allegro not too speedy and an adagio not too slow, none of these comments will make any sense.[9]

There is one symbol of musical notation that may be an additional cause of misunderstandings: the double bar line. There are several meanings to this symbol, but it seems to me that it is nearly always interpreted as a watershed between two sections. This is not so. First we have to look at the meaning of bar lines in general. They are a musical version of the grid on a map. When we walk in nature, there are no lines of longitude and latitude crisscrossing the ground. Such markings are for plotting and survey but not for the enjoyment of nature. It is the same with bar lines; they are our grid, convenient for the mechanical progress of rehearsal and performance, but they must never intrude on the hearer's consciousness, unless of course there is a special reason in rhythmic design. In our great reservoir of classic and romantic music, the bar line is one of the indispensable devices for holding things together. How it has been misunderstood will become amply evident in the section on bowing and phrasing (chapter 7).

When considering relative tempos, one should read a double bar line as the exact point at which a transition takes place. In the Ninth Symphony the passage

---

8. In *Fidelio* the prayer of thanksgiving in the finale of act 2 is also in triple meter.

9. An odd contradiction appears in the oft-quoted Wagner essay. He stresses that his own performances of the overture to *Tannhäuser* went much faster than those of other conductors.

from bar 919 to bar 920 must never be interrupted; it should not even be noticed that a different meter commences in 920. The voices finish the second "Götterfunken" exactly like the first. In other words, the double bar is inaudible in any case where a definite relationship between two bars is expressed explicitly.

In the same movement of the Ninth Symphony there is a good example of the type of error that has led to the denigration of Beethoven's metronome marks. It involves the principal theme of the finale, the "Ode to Joy." It appears several times, being the theme of a set of variations. Its first appearance as a motto, in bar 77, carries the directive "allegro assai" and the metronome marking 80 for the half note; its reappearance on the next page (bar 92) has the identical markings. In bar 237 the vocal portion starts in the same allegro assai. We can take it, therefore, that the metronome reading should also be identical with the previous appearances of this theme. In bar 655 the theme appears in a 6/4 configuration, as one of two subjects of a fugue, and again the metronome is 84 for the dotted half. Because of the changed rhythm, this is the near equivalent (four beats faster) of the half note in the previous appearances of the theme. In bar 331, at the alla marcia, the theme also appears, this time in a 6/8 garb where, to carry musical common sense a step further, the metronome would have to be 80, or perhaps 84 for the dotted half—in this case the whole bar.

At the start of this particular section we find "allegro assai vivace"—but the metronome here is 84 for the dotted quarter note. In numerous editions over a span of a century and a half, no publisher has examined this anomaly and come to the simple conclusion that in some early copy the half note got some ink into its center and became thereby a quarter note. Once this commonplace little deduction has been made, everything falls into place. But it has seemed simpler to denounce the composer and his deafness for incompetent metronome markings than to correct an obvious misprint.

This, alas, is not the only trivial misprint to have bedeviled generation after generation. In the same Beethoven symphony a singularly unfortunate error of metronome marking has been bequeathed to us. The correct marking over the trio of the scherzo should be the half note 116, yet until recently several editions had the whole note 116.[10] Here was another 100 percent error, only this time in the opposite direction. The whole note carries a tempo connotation that is totally absurd. All that is needed to discover the composer's intention is to ask with a critical and open mind what might have gone astray in the processes of copying and printing.

10. Since I thundered in my little German essay against this misprint over the trio, the Peters edition has made a new printing of the Ninth and corrected the sign. A little later the Philharmonia in Vienna revised the same spot when they reprinted the work. But somehow the publishers have left the task incomplete. No mention is made in either a preface or a footnote that this constitutes a change from an otherwise identical earlier printing.

Many sages still argue that Beethoven meant the whole note to be equal to 116. If not, they ask, why the accelerando leading into the presto? And why presto? To these two queries there is only one good reply, a purely musical one. Anybody can take up the opening of the scherzo in any suitable tempo of his choice and then transfer the same beat to the trio. It is amply documented that the composer had the same figure in mind. In the facsimile of the Ninth one can still see that the trio had been written at first in 1/2, or double the number of barlines; then, of course, the metronome 116 applying to the entire bar was correct, but the bar was only half as long. As the result of several errors, the entire sequence of the transition to the trio has been misjudged.

This brings us to the center of the topic of relative or "related" tempos. I suggest that the reader jot down (without peeking into scores of the Beethoven symphonies) the relative speeds of the eight scherzo movements (the third movement of the Eighth Symphony is not a scherzo) in order, according to Beethoven, of fastest to slowest. This quite elementary mental exercise may produce some surprises.

The first surprise will be that the scherzos of the Third and Ninth symphonies are to be taken in the same tempo (116). Most musicians to whom I gave this quiz without warning replied automatically that the fastest scherzo was that of the Ninth Symphony. Perhaps in the United States there is an explanation for such an assumption; the theme was used as a "signature" on the popular Huntley-Brinkley news broadcast in a super-rapid version.

If we examine the openings of the eight scherzos in question—setting aside for the moment all the nonsense about faulty Maelzel and deaf Beethoven—we find a 132 in the Seventh, a 116 in the Third and Ninth, a 108 in the First and Sixth, a 100 in the Second and Fourth, and a 96 in the Fifth. Only two trios of the six in 3/4 meter—we leave out the 2/4 barn dance of the *Pastoral* and the 2/2 of the Ninth—are in a tempo slower than that of the respective scherzos. In practice we are used to hearing the trios of the First, Third, and sometimes the Fifth also taken slower than the scherzo portions. This has two reasons: Beethoven's tempos are generally disregarded; and the trios of the First, Third, and Fifth are as compelling in the right tempos as the a capella section of the Verdi *Requiem* mentioned earlier in this chapter. It hardly ever occurs to convention-bound performers that the right tempo of the horn-dominated *Eroica* trio or the double-bass–dominated trio of the Fifth could be made the tempo of the entire movement. Add to this the simple argument that Beethoven was perfectly capable of writing the word *meno* when he wished to do so. The fine point of asking in the trio of the Fourth for un poco meno allegro (from 100 to 88) and in the Seventh for assai meno presto (from 132 to 84) has also been totally ignored, this time with the result that the trio of the Seventh is done so slowly that it deteriorates to a pompous affair, so dragged out that most conductors omit one or both of these trios' repeat signals. These are sure signs that a tempo has been badly chosen. Compared to 132, 84 is already assai meno, but discontent with the metronome figure and obsessed with the assai, many conductors have brought it down to 60 or even less. Yet this trio is a dance movement with a lovely lilt. When the tempo is reasonable and musically appropriate, both repeats will be right, necessary, and in proportion.

That these repeats, particularly in the third movement of the Seventh, cannot be treated as optional is more than proved by the three examples of the composer writing out other sections twice (albeit with variants). Anyone doubtful of his firm purpose need only take the score to find that in both trios (they are identical) bars 165–80 and 425–40 represent spelled-out repeats of the preceding sixteen measures. How can anyone then omit the repeat of the section that follows (bars 180 and 440, respectively)? To buttress this argument further, we find that in the first run of the scherzo a repeat sign in bar 24 demands that we go back to the beginning. In the second run the composer wanted this repeat as an echo, so instead of placing the signal in bar 260, he wrote out the twenty-four bars with several admonitions "sempre p" to stress his idea. The third time around he did not want the twenty-four bars repeated at all. This sequence appears clearly in all scores.

Who then dares to leave out, as is usually done, the repeats of the bars 25–148, 181–220, and 441–82? All those who are bored by repeats. The possibility that this boredom might be owing to wrong tempos was never allowed to interfere with habit until the trio of the Seventh was performed in the German-speaking citadels of the Beethoven cult by a foreigner, Arturo Toscanini. At the other extreme was Leopold Stokowski, who skipped (after making no repeats) from bar 236 to bar 497, omitting one scherzo and one trio, and thus saving his Philadelphia Orchestra perhaps two-and-a-half to three minutes' work and his subscribers the annoyance of having to put up with the compulsive strain in Beethoven's character.

Returning to the trio in the Ninth, it seems again elementary on the evidence of musical articulation that the half bar of the trio must equal the bar of the scherzo. The basic motive of the octave jump downward in a dactylic rhythm becomes contracted in bars 412 and 413 into a two-syllable octave jump, no longer dac-ty-lus, but simply dac-tlus. If the whole note were intended to indicate the tempo, even the greatest group of horn players could scarcely perform the four octave jumps in bars 412 and 413 if the speed were the same for the four quarters as for the scherzo's three. And finally, most significantly, the fabric of the trio's phrases, especially in the second part, is so clearly a "two-in-a-bar" pattern, with all the repeated chords, that it stands to reason that the basis of the trio must be the half note and not the whole note. This is one more indication carefully thought out by Beethoven, giving the basic beat and not mere speed when indicating a metronome figure. On this basis the first movement of the *Pastoral* is "in one" (as mentioned in some detail earlier); so is the last movement of the Seventh, which in most performances gets wildly driven, yet "in two," which makes a Germanic march out of a highly syncopated movement that is not terribly fast.

If I emphasize certain movements that are habitually taken faster than Beethoven's indication, it is to show how baseless is the general assumption that Beethoven's metronomes are "too fast." One can easily investigate how many of Beethoven's movements are taken faster than his metronome markings. We wade here in one of the most treacherous musical quagmires, where a large number of comfortable habits are at stake. I still propose approaching this whole topic of tempo on the basis of relativity. Taking anybody's choice of tempo for the scherzo of the *Eroica*—however it may differ from the actual 116 of the metronome—one should compare another movement in the same work, the final presto, which bears the identical 116 for the quarter note. It is only simple reason to accept the same figure as valid for the composer's idea of the same beat for both sections. Then, after this relationship has been established satisfactorily, one can ever so slightly slow down to arrive at the eighth note for the poco andante section, which the composer marked "eighth note equals 108." One can then take the 108 and compare and apply it to the scherzos of the First and Sixth symphonies.[11] (These checks can and should be made without a metronome, since it is my contention that more often than not one will arrive at the composer's figures, after all is said and done.)

In the First Symphony of Brahms, relations of tempo are often sought between the first poco sostenuto and the main section, where none exist, while the compelling proportions of the finale are generally ignored. In the first section of the last movement (adagio), many conductors arrive at the bar before the più andante in a state of ecstasy, aided by the timpanist, who has his day in the sun, pounding away with his roll; the conductor stands transfixed, in awe of his own and the kettledrummer's creative strengths. The roll goes on and on, until the moment when the protagonists have calmed down sufficiently to allow the horn

11. There are some most intriguing equations and similarities in the quartets. Opus 18, No. 5 is in A major and has a 6/8 meter in the first movement. Opus 92 is in A major with a 6/8 meter for the main section of the first movement. In both, the dotted quarter is set at 104. Opus 18, No. 6 is in B-flat and C; so is Opus 60 (of which more will be said). Both are marked at 80 for the bar. In both cases the words of tempo and character are different, while the figures are identical. The Quartet Opus 18, No. 5 has "allegro"; the symphony, "vivace."

A few examples can demonstrate that Beethoven wrote quite different words over identical metronome marks. The scherzo of the Quartet Opus 74 has a dotted half note of 100. So have the third movements of the Second and Fourth symphonies. But the words are quite different: Opus 36 has "allegro"; Opus 60, "allegro vivace"; and Opus 74, "presto." This recalls the examples from the *Pastoral* Symphony, where the identity of two metronome marks does not preclude the existence of a world of diversity between the two movements. Here is my main disagreement with Kolisch, who correlates certain verbal tempo markings with specific metronome figures. I maintain that words and numerals belong to separate categories, the former to expression and the latter to speed.

Example 49. Brahms, Sym. No. 1, 4th mvt., mm. 28–31

player to launch into his glorious solo passage. What the maestro has overlooked is the way Brahms wrote the timpani part, without any hold whatsoever (example 49). He wanted explicitly this equation: six notes in the last half bar of the adagio are six notes in the andante, or eighth = quarter.

The timpanist of a leading London orchestra told me, when I asked him to do the passage as written, that in a career of twenty years, spent with major orchestras, nobody had ever bothered with this detail, and everybody had performed in a freewheeling manner. Yet this is a most carefully planned transition, with metered notes in the drum preparing the new tempo for the più andante section. It establishes the proportions and relative tempos for the entire finale. In the più andante we come to a choralelike passage of trombones and other winds (bar 47), which is duplicated in double values in the più allegro coda of the movement (bar 407). In other words, the più allegro section is twice as fast as the più andante, which is twice as fast as the opening adagio. The tempo of the main section of the movement falls between the più andante and the più allegro. Anyone who prepares this work in such a manner will have no doubt (after studying these relationships) what the right tempo is. If one gets sidetracked by some indulgence in this or that mannerism, the structure falls apart, or at least shows cracks not of the composer's making.

In the quest for the great design that is in every composer's mind from the first, the single most important directive for performers to look for is the relationship of tempos within a work. Since Wagner himself has consistently done that in his scores, particularly from the time of *Tristan* on, it has been doubly unfortunate that his thesis on tempos in classical symphonies has miscarried badly. I repeat that he may have meant something different from what appears to be his message. One never knows with Wagner how much of his prose was prompted by polemic urge and how much represented his genuine artistic ideas. But if we take the composer's scores rather than his words as our guide, we find them filled with the type of tempo relationships (though most of them are customarily disregarded) that the above examples from Beethoven's Ninth and Brahms's First have illustrated.

It may come as a surprise to learn that Dvořàk can be as sophisticated as Stravinsky in his use of tempo relations and in the way he set them down. In his Violin Concerto, his use of horn triplets as the lever of a transition conveys the clear message that the main tempo of the movement should not be excessively fast. This is corroborated by the admonition "ma non troppo" next to the allegro giocoso, but the technical prowess of a virtuoso fiddler could easily set a speed quite a bit faster than the theme in 2/4. The composer is even more explicit, if that is possible, in his Variations Opus 78, a work that is, alas, insufficiently known. It will be useful to glance at the first variation, where the tempo marking is supported by a metronome marking of 84 for the quarter note. The third variation features triplets as countervoice to the theme in the woodwinds. The fourth variation bears the metronome marking 126, in simple arithmetic another way of saying that the motion of the triplet eighths simply continues as eighth notes, which in turn automatically establishes the "new" tempo, più allegro (84 times 3 equals 252 divided by 2 equals 126). Yet, a conductor preparing the work once asked me to explain some of the tempo transitions—in particular, this one—that he could not grasp. I believe that the general disdain in which the metronome has been held accounts for such failures to comprehend composers. Stravinsky's *Symphonies of Wind Instruments* offers little except this type of metronomic relationship as a guide for the tempos.

Richard Strauss has so many comparable transitions that one could quote from virtually any of his works, symphonic or operatic. *Till Eulenspiegel* is built on a most straightforward tempo relation, with the dotted quarter being equal to the eighth in the 2/4 portion. This is clearly printed on the first page of the score and prevails also at rehearsal figure 14, page 27, where each transition is carefully explained with "twice as fast" and "again half as slowly." At figure 26, page 58, where the dotted quarter equals the quarter, the preparation has been an accelerando for the four bars preceding. In short, there is a most meticulous organization of tempo relationships. As if all this were not enough, after figure 39 the ratio is once more explicitly stated. Here again it seems that the composer repeats what was quite clear from the outset, as if to convey to posterity that his meaning had been misunderstood too many times for him to trust his luck any more. (See Strauss's letter to his parents about *Don Juan* cited in chapter 3.)

The next example, also from Strauss's work, I show for a different reason (example 50A). In the overture to his *Bourgeois gentilhomme*, it is once again

Example 50A. Strauss, *Bourgeois Gentilhomme* Overture, following rehearsal no. 8

fairly obvious what the composer desired: the motion of sixteenth notes (at 138 for the quarter) continues unchanged as thirty-second notes, when the meter changes into the 3/4, largamente; the sign that the quarter equals the half note is easily visible. In returning to the 4/4, Strauss made things unnecessarily difficult by his manner of spelling out the transition. The effect he desired can be realized, as set forth here in example 50B. (Here again it is evident that bar lines are only for the performer and not for the listener.) The remedy is to go back to the 4/4 and the sign that the sixteenth once again equals the thirty-seconds from one bar earlier and invest the first quarter note and the second quarter note with a dot. Of course, the molto accelerando is eliminated as a signal and replaced by a sign indicating "the quarter equals the eighth."

The real purpose of this entire demonstration is to focus attention on the uncanny ways in which great composers indicate the right tempos by establishing relationships. In *Till Eulenspiegel* one cannot go wrong if the transitions are made according to Strauss, because each section is balanced against the other by means of the relative tempos. Specifically, one will find, I trust, that the principal 6/8 sections of the tone poem will be far more humorous and less overdriven if the tune in B-flat major (the 2/4 between 12 and 13) is weighed against all the other relative tempos. Similarly, in the *Bourgeois gentilhomme* overture (I am now referring to the complete music for the play, not only to the suite commonly

Example 50B. Strauss, *Bourgeois Gentilhomme* Overture, following rehearsal no. 8 (as rebarred by author)

performed) the motive in 3/4 depicting M. Jourdain and his woul '-be-aristocratic pomposity will be right only when balanced with the 4/4, which has also been metronome-marked.

Although we have read Brahms's disclaimer of the metronome, at several points in his life he used these little numbers, and a study of the thematic catalog that prints them is of greatest value. It is revealing that in the Trio Opus 8 the whole bar of the finale (dotted half equals 66) is closely related to the adagio, which the composer marked with 63 for the quarter. There are works from all the composer's periods in which he insisted on marking equations of time values (Sonata Opus 2, Quintet Opus 34, *Academic Festival* Overture, and so on). The short choral piece *Nänie*, Opus 82, is in ternary form, the outer sections in one of Brahms's loveliest 6/4 motions, the middle part in 4/4. Perusing first the return from the middle part to the recapitulation of the opening, where no metronome figures influence the mind, it seems quite natural that the half note of the 4/4 equals the half note of the 6/4. I tried this once after having no contact with *Nänie* for several years, curious whether anything earlier in the score would support my feeling about this transition. I found that the beginning was marked 100 for the quarter, and the middle part 76 for the quarter. Half of 76 is 38 and the half note of the first section (one third of the 6/4 meter metronome) is 33. An ever so slight relaxation of the tempo for the four a capella bars (137–40) would bring the tempo to 66 for the quarter, not a great ritard from the 76 of the start. Without much bending, the equation or relationship of the tempos of that work is set.

In the finale of Brahms's Fourth Symphony a crucial tempo relation—the quarter equals the quarter at the start of the flute solo at the section in 3/2—is most notable for being disregarded. This damages the entire grandiose structure of this movement. As I indicated earlier, neither in this movement nor in Beethoven's comparable work, 32 Variations in C Minor, are any changes of the main tempo intended during the regular 31 variations of eight bars. Yet the common approach is to retard gradually as one approaches the 3/2 and then let the first flute player have his arioso. There are at least two reasons why this is wrong (not counting the dull and Beckmesserish one that no ritard or other change in tempo is printed). The variations starting with that of the flute solo are in 3/2 and not in 6/4. Earlier I set forth why a 6/4 is not necessarily a triple meter. Here the languid treatment by most flute players creates a 6/4 in which the sighs of strings and horn fall on actual beats instead of being felt as syncopations, or afterbeats. Thus they lose the quality of anxiousness that Brahms intended. The solo—to come to the principal argument—is a dramatic flight of some hunted soul that tries laboriously to ascend, only to collapse at the end. The following variations are in several ways like expressions of comfort and healing, all of which ought to proceed without dragging. The final reason that one needs to remain in 3/2 comes in bar 113 with the trombones, whose phrase must never bog down through a quarter rest (on the third beat). This is one of those frequently encountered moments where the vocal style, interrupting a word, can be misread for a real pause, which it is not. All this is involved in that modest little equation ♩=♩. What a succession of consequences results when it is disregarded.

Several great opera composers also used carefully balanced tempos. A few examples might tempt any opera lover, whether singer, stage director, coach, conductor, or impresario, to search further. I can promise that it will be a rewarding expedition. In Verdi's *Otello* the final duet of the first act, after the demotion of Cassio, is introduced at a point (p. 141 in the Ricordi score) where Verdi asks for a 132 metronome speed. This transitional section prepares the opening strains of the divided cellos (p. 144) in exactly half the speed—or, if we have gradually felt the phrasing to veer to the half bar, the tempo remains the same. With the start of the voices, a slight speeding up to 72 (from the cellos' 66) is asked for; on page 146 it goes back again to 66, and on page 147 to poco più agitato. Page 150 once again has tempo I, which is 66. After another poco più largo (the most lyrical expression of the love between Desdemona and Otello), there is a poco più mosso with an 80 metronome marking on page 156, leading through a stringendo to 88 on page 162, and back again to 80 for the final pages. Between pages 141 and 166 (over a relatively short span, in terms of musical duration) Verdi uses the word *poco* seven times. This is, I submit, a most vivid illustration of the idea in Verdi's own heading over the *Te Deum* score, where he explains that one tempo with its accelerations and ritards is what he wants. One cannot get more specific without cramping the performer.

Perhaps more surprising still is the discovery that Puccini balanced his scores in a similar manner. If I suggest surprise, it is for two reasons. Like Dvořàk, this great composer has been somewhat cavalierly denigrated by the sophisticated because of his enormous popular appeal. Yet popularity is fully compatible with a fine hand for the most subtle nuances, though many of them have often been sacrificed on the altar of underrehearsed, overdriven, or overdragged performances. The second scene of *La Bohème* sets a tempo with 112 for the quarter, in this case the entire bar. This basic movement is the same (allowing the normal nuances) for a full thirty pages, through several changes of meter, phrasing, and expression. Yet I defy anyone to recognize this unity in any performance of the second scene. Typically it will start out too fast and gain momentum as if it were a jet racing down the runway. If these first thirty pages are built on 112, the next section, including not only the "Parpignol" shouts but also the entire entrance of Musetta, is built around 132. The third large section starts with Musetta's waltz, which at the grand climax slows down in six stages, marked by the composer to the point where the tempo, which was set at 104, is down to 66. This is the moment when the military music starts at rehearsal figure 27. That march is, not surprisingly, set at 132, which means that the several earlier themes—the entrance of Musetta, the brats shouting "Parpignol"—are all in their original tempo (132) under the blanket of the military march. This whole scene is organized like a Swiss clockwork. If prepared and played in such manner, it has a sweep and form not usually associated with Giacomo Puccini.

When Wagner's scores are considered critically, the word *symphonic* will nearly always come up, and with good reason—not only because of the fabric and technical complexity, the sheer weight, but also for the type of architectual organization with related tempos. That Wagner, like any other great master, was completely aware of what he created is manifest in his treatise *On Conducting*. In this short essay the composer, whose theories on classical tempos have been critically viewed earlier, expresses essentially the same view as does Verdi in his comment at the head of his *Te Deum*. It is particularly important to this whole chapter on related tempos that Wagner considers the same 4/4 of the *Meistersinger* prelude as representing three distinctly different types of phrases— a marchlike opening, a scherzando development, and a combination of motives in a "churchlike andante" to conclude, he admonishes, exactly as it started.

Wherever one looks into the music dramas, whether *Tristan and Isolde*, *Die Meistersinger*, or the *Ring* tetralogy, this type of interrelation is the base of the entire structure. To appreciate such attention to detail, look at the start of the "Fire Music." For some critical musicians those few pages have seemed examples of Wagner's disregard of technical execution: the violin passages have been considered unplayable. This is true only if the tempos are wrong. The composer did not take pains to write at least 128 notes for the violins in some hundred bars, including much other detail, only to obtain an al fresco effect. The meticulous care with which the winds and harp change harmony on the eighth sixteenth note while the violins with their thirty-seconds go precisely at the same point into matching harmonies is not just for show, nor are the players expected to fake their way through. In Bachmann's *Encyclopaedia of the Violin*, the author mentions the fact (illustrating it with an example from "Siegfried's Rhine Journey") that in modern orchestral parts there are difficulties far greater than those contained in the solo concertos of earlier decades. These passages of the "Fire Music" are indeed difficult—but they are playable and meant to be played. Of course, the violinists must practice them and the tempo must be right.

The beginning of the "Fire Music" seems to me ideal for setting the right tempo. After Wotan has sung for the last time, and the brass have repeated his warning, we hear in the violas, cellos, and second quartet of horns the sleep motive (example 51). Its appearance here is in note values exactly twice as long as the passage where Wotan sings "Zum letzten Mal letz' es mich heut'" (example 52). This second statement of the motive, to which the "flames" have been added in the violins, harps, and piccolo, is a broad andante passionato, compared to the earlier molto adagio.

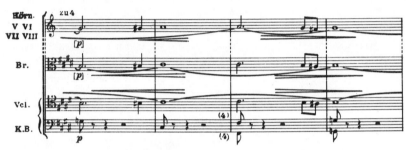

Example 51. Wagner, *Die Walküre*, act 3

Example 52. Wagner, *Die Walküre*, act 3

The adagio tempo was likewise anticipated a few measures before, as the violas continue the cellos' motive in halved note values (example 53). Here the eighth is equal to the preceding quarter. Wagner uses the 4/4 meter while the motive features the seventh in the major key (the euphoric feeling), going to the slow 8/8 as soon as the diminished seventh proclaims the melancholy expression that introduces Wotan's great peroration—the heart of the "Farewell." The 4/4 section (the same basic tempo as the "Fire Music") is linked to the "Farewell," for the figure in the violins and violas after Wotan's "der freier als ich, der Gott!" (example 54) is derived from the violins' motive at the outset (example 55). Once again the second appearance is in half the note values of the first—but quite evidently in the same tempo as earlier. The 2/2 of the "Farewell's" opening is followed by the "Etwas langsamer," where Wotan announces that only a hero freer than a god will have Brünnhilde, a heroic utterance repeated in the brass after Wotan draws the magic circle around the rock.

As shown, all the counterpoints are interrelated in such a way that the half

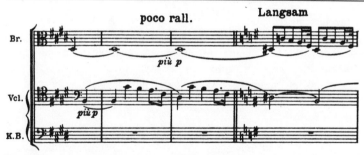

Example 53. Wagner, *Die Walküre*, act 3

Example 54. Wagner, *Die Walküre*, act 3

Example 55. Wagner, *Die Walküre*, act 3

note of the "Farewell's" beginning equals the quarter note in the section after "der freier als ich, der Gott!" (led into by a poco ritenuto from the "Etwas langsamer"). This in turn equals the eighth note at "Der Augen leuchtendes Paar" (shown in example 53). This adagio section, the heart and soul of the finale, is thus flanked by two faster sections and introduced by the great opening passages when Wotan promises the ring of fire around the rock. Tonalities too show the organization of the piece, which lands in the key of E major (first E minor) only when Wotan's decision has been heard.

There is one very real practical problem here: most heroic baritones in our day do not fancy this slow adagio of the "Farewell." If I have discussed the interrelations in this piece at length, it is partly because I know the difficulty of realizing them in practice. A conductor has many functions, and one of them is to bring out the best in the participants while covering weaknesses wherever possible. Thus, it is not his function to show up singers who can't deliver, but to disguise this fact, while still maintaining as much as possible of the marvelous balance that was in the composer's mind. In the seventh bar of the adagio portion, it is possible to let the tempo become more fluid and allow the singer a tempo that will not overstrain his vocal apparatus. The paramount concern is that the transitions be right.

There is another strong reason why it is of particular importance to entrust Wagner to the care of the best musicians: his works have become in the second half of our century playthings for willful and eccentric stage managers. They have been distorted and made ridiculous, and few musicians have had the courage to defend the composer. The unflagging enthusiasm for his work is basically a musical enthusiasm; and thus it will be mostly musicians who decide how Wagner's scores will survive.

I stated above that there is no end to the passages and spots that could serve here as illustrations. Perhaps a couple of beautiful interrelations, not instantly recognizable, from *Die Meistersinger* will round out this discussion of Wagner. In act 3 the music of the quintet in scene 4 begins in a moderate 4/4. The passage itself is a variant on the violin phrase in the prelude to the act and is descriptive of a dramatic-poetic content that subtly shows the development in Hans Sachs between these two points of the work. That prelude to the third act is all about Hans Sachs. Its first theme becomes later the opening of the "Wahn" monologue; then comes the chorale that will be sung by the populace in the final scene as a tribute to the poet Hans Sachs; and next a recollection of his cobbler's song from act 2 that brings back the whole curious and beguiling comedy of the midsummer night. There is no doubt in the text that Sachs has felt more than fatherly or avuncular affection for Eva, and the change of the high violin phrase from its appearance in the prelude to its appearance here preceding the quintet is the final change in Sachs, who "found the right man for Eva" and now stands as godfather over the baptism of the prize song.

From the end of Sachs's lines there are five bars leading the tempo to Eva's phrase in such manner that the eighth notes of the 4/4 become equal to the sixteenths of the 6/8 phrase. The postlude of the quintet (the lyrical climax of the whole work), which elaborates the motives of the prize song and the quintet once more, leads to a robust motive (heard before) in one of the classical transitions, "Die Viertel wie zuvor die Achtel." This music brings the enchanted group and the equally transformed listener back to the more bourgeois pleasures of a holiday in Nuremberg. Sachs himself commented on his "beloved Nuremberg" to this same music in the first scene. This passage coming so early in the third act seems to me like the first of two towers that support a bridge: the entire scenes between Sachs and Walther (in scene 2), Sachs and Beckmesser (scene 3), and Sachs and Eva, and finally the quintet (both in scene 4) are as if suspended between these points. There is within this brief reference to that bourgeois world of four-square order another brief reference when Sachs suggests to Walther that the final stanza of his poem might be invented at another place soon (near the close of scene 2).

Another wondrous metamorphosis happens to the chorale, when the curtain opens after the first prelude to act 1. I am sure that it has been noticed before that this chorale melody is formed out of the main subject of the prelude itself, leaving out three notes and, of course, changing the rhythm and emphasis. The opening line of this chorale returns in miniature form when the apprentice David sings his little verse in act 3, scene 1. And when Sachs announces in his own brand of poetry and humor, "A child was born here" (act 3, scene 4), the baptismal ceremony is accompanied by a quotation from that opening chorale. It is worthy of note that the "original form," in act 1, is in values twice as great as those for the baptism of the "child," the prize song; and that phrase is again twice as great in values as David's miniquotation. Needless to say, these variants have their proper meaning in relation to tempo.

Another composer of whom this type of tempo relation is not expected but who offers us some of the most intricately organized relationships is Claude Debussy. In every work, from *L'Après-midi d'un faune* to *Jeux*, one can find explicitly marked transitions, establishing equations between tempos in different sections.

Ritards and accelerandos are legitimate means of transition; we have seen that Wagner often asks for them, and so, indeed, do most composers. But if there is one single habit of conductors that has most blatantly distorted composers' intentions in transitions, it is the tendency to make uncalled-for ritards. When unwanted and unplanned, they produce exactly the opposite effect of what they are supposed to do. What may need emphasis is the preparatory nature of ritards and accelerandos. An equation of tempos tries to avoid such preparation. To insert a ritard before a surprise change would be like warning the audience at a mystery play that a shot will soon be fired. Ritards may often originate in a conductor's doubt as to whether his tempo of the moment is the right one to pass into the next section, or they may simply represent the course of least resistance. Whatever the cause, an unwanted ritard or accelerando in a transition passage can be inept and unsettling.

The conclusion to be drawn is that when composers equate two sections, either by marking the same metronome figure or by other means, they mean exactly what their various symbols say: *A* equals *B*, or *C* is half as fast as *D*, or the quarters of the preceding part are the eighths of the next. In those indications are embedded the balances between sections, the structural unity, the guiding designs of scores, the symmetry and proportion. When this is understood one need not quarrel about absolute speed and tempo.

Among the phenomena of great music, the last quartets of Beethoven are supreme. Here, as in the Ninth Symphony and in other landmarks of our cultural heritage, respect and awe sometimes get in the way of clear musical sense and

simple musical instinct. One of my favorite test cases has been the slow movement of Opus 127, the Quartet in E-flat. Every time I have asked a quartet player
about the transition from the 12/8 to the 4/4 (example 56), I have received either
a convoluted speech or an uncertain guess as a reply. And whenever I tell cham-
ber-music players the solution to the puzzle, they recognize that they have
missed a rather elementary point. If one takes a look at bars 58–76 (example
57), the other two transitions, it becomes quite clear that this entire movement
is conceived to be played in one speed. In other words, each complete bar equals
the next complete bar. Therefore, bar 38, in which the andante con moto starts,
is in its total extent equal to bar 37 and, ipso fact⁷, 39 is equal to either. If it
were not so, bar 38 would be shorter and so would bar 76, where the return
from the adagio molto expressivo to the opening 12/8 occurs. The movement is
a variation (not unlike the slow movement of the Ninth) with the 12/8 section
the first and last portion and the very calm E major in the center.

Example 56. Beethoven, Opus 127, 2nd mvt., mm. 37–39

To get to the core of these great musical statements one should study the entire
set of compositions that have gestated in the mind of the composer. This Opus
127 slow movement is part of the awesome group of pieces that started with the
Trio Opus 97 (slow movement in variation form), continued with Opus 106, a
slow movement of unusual extension, and culminated in the "Benedictus" of
Opus 123 and the adagio of the Ninth. In the slow movement of Opus 127
Beethoven gives us a curious signal. No matter how far he has developed away
from the orthodoxy of classical periodic composition, he still insists on finishing
this movement on the eighth eighth note because it has started on the ninth
eighth note, thus adhering to the old principle that all the bars and fractions of
bars must add up to a whole. Hence, it is reasonable to assume that he wanted
bars 38 and 76 also to be complete bars. In terms of expressive meaning it is
quite natural to obtain the andante con moto character, with its almost dancelike
inflections, by considering each fourth of the bar as a unit and not equating the
eighth note of the 12/8 with the eighth note of the 4/4. When this habitual
mistake is made, bar 38 becomes a 10/8 measure, a most unlikely event.

   This entire problem originates (not unlike the example of the maestoso-pres-
tissimo in the Ninth) with a wrongly conceived basic tempo for this movement.

Example 57. Beethoven, Opus 127, 2nd mvt., mm. 57–77

The admonition ma non troppo after adagio once again carries the decisive mes-sage.[12] The custom in this movement has been to start very slowly; then, by equating the eighth notes (in bar 38), to set a faster tempo for the andante con moto variation. A big ritard becomes necessary in 58 to return to the adagio tempo and, with another uneven bar, 76, we have tempo primo—which, how-

12. Such moderating words as *poco*, *pochissimo*, *quasi*, and so forth have, over years of trying for more gallery-pleasing effects, been blown into molto and assai and other blatancies, when mere hints had been intended. But I should not use the "gallery" in a pejorative sense, since the jaded people are more often downstairs in the expensive seats.

ever, is usually faster than the opening. Another test for a perfect tempo is in bar 118. If that pause of half a bar becomes absurdly long and cannot carry the tension, then the tempo has been too slow. Moments such as these are decisive indications of whether a performance is alive or dead. Of course the players themselves often realize this, and various accelerandos and adjustments are made. These become superfluous if the whole concept starts with the overarching idea of the piece, into which the details are fitted.

It is indeed unusual to find in one movement several tempo indications. As I tried to show with three scherzo movements (Opus 36, Opus 60, and Opus 74), tempo indications are words for the expressive spirit of the respective sections and not for a change of speed. I suggested that this movement has suffered a lot from original dragging. And yet, if quartet players would tune their imaginative antennae they would recognize that the adagio ma non troppo e molto cantabile is a close relative of the Benedictus Opus 123, Missa Solemnis, andante molto cantabile e non troppo mosso. Here a cautionary non troppo mosso, there a ma non troppo adagio and (is it magic, mystery, or just one of those "coincidences"?) the one consists of 126 bars, while the other is 124 bars long—both in 12/8 and both invoking and bestowing *blessings*.

I have taken extra pains to elaborate on this quartet movement, partly as a precaution. Young conductors often find the existence of so many relative tempos, of such intimate inner relationships, to be persuasive, even seductive, to the point where many begin to find equations everywhere. This is theorizing, not reading the composer's intentions. The quartet movement has been a prime example of what happens if the wrong equation (eighth equals eighth) is followed as an a priori principle. It will be most helpful not to adopt theories, not to make up one's mind beforehand, but to let the composer be one's guide.

It is particularly tempting, yet rarely valid, to look for definite relationships between the introductions and allegros of classical first movements. A beguiling case is the Symphony No. 104 by Haydn. A study of three different editions shows that there is an unanswered problem. Breitkopf and Härtel has at the end of the slow introduction a rest of one quarter with a fermata; Eulenburg has no rest, but only a fermata over the bar line; Robbins-Landon has a quarter rest without a fermata. So here we have three variations of the same passage. Which is right and what does it mean? The two editions that feature the fermata, whether over the quarter rest or the bar line, are more or less identical: what is the difference between a bar line and a quarter rest if we assume that the fermata extends a silence (or a note) at liberty? (In fact, such an assumption is not always valid.) The third edition, without the fermata, seems to me the only one that makes sense. Since the quarter rest is not needed to complete a bar or a period, it must have another significance. What can it be? A tempo relation between the opening adagio and the following allegro? There is one explanation for the existence of the quarter rest: the eighth note of the adagio equals the half note of the allegro. The fermatas were evidently window dressing by editors and publishers who could not make head or tail out of the rest.

There is a similarly tempting relativity of tempos between the introduction and the allegro in Mozart's Symphony in E-flat, K. 543. In both instances, if these relationships are observed, the introduction becomes less pompous, while the allegro gets a more moderate pacing than is customary. This is, as explained earlier, the essence of the classical line: the avoidance of violent extremes of speed and slowness. In most other symphonies that have slow introductions it is not advisable to search frantically for definite relationships. In the First and Fourth symphonies of Beethoven the upbeats leading into the allegro sections should be taken in relation to the allegro, which means either slightly increasing the basic tempo of the introductions (both of which are metronomed in unrelated speeds) or, in the case of Opus 21, by holding the long note G (sol) as if it were double-dotted until the four notes running into the allegro will fit that tempo.

The spurious fermata in the introduction of the Haydn Symphony No. 104 brings us to another, this time authentic, set of fermatas that have greatly puzzled musicians. I refer to the opening measures of Beethoven's Fifth Symphony. As shown in example 58A, the first and second holds are different; there is an "extra" bar before the latter. I have asked every musician I could find what Beethoven meant by that "extra" bar. (It is repeated as a pattern each time these two sequences occur.) Invariably the logical answer to my question was: "He wants the second one longer." Good. We must assume that "he" wanted it longer by the length of one bar. But how can that be heard unless the fermata has a definite duration? And here the answers dry up. One day, on a flight from the East to the West Coast, I devoted the entire journey to this enigma and came up with an explanation that still appears to me the only one that answers the question posed by the extra bar (example 58B).

The phrase as sketched here spans an eight-bar period. Beethoven's decision to spell the phrase as we know it may have had something to do with the highly unusual rhythmic character of the theme. Later in his life the composer did not hesitate to write "offbeat" ideas in an offbeat manner. The explanation I offer

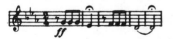

Example 58A. Beethoven, Sym. No. 5, 1st mvt., mm. 1–5

Example 58B. Beethoven, Sym. No. 5, 1st mvt., mm. 1–5 (as rebarred by author)

168
169 Più mosso. 𝅗𝅥 = 𝅗𝅥.
Fl. I. II.
III.
Ob. I. II.
Ob. III.
C. ingl.
Cl. picc.
Cl. A.
Cl. bas.
Fag. I. II.
III.
C. fag.
Cor.
I. B.
Tr-be II. III. A.
Trb-ni e Tuba
muta in Fl. piccolo II.
a 2
sff sempre
sf
f sempre

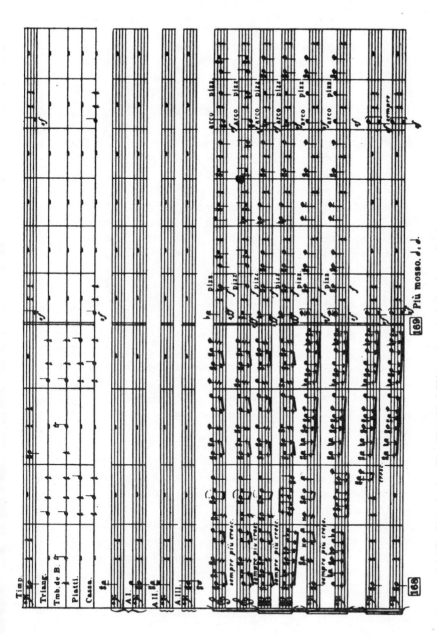

Example 59. Stravinsky, *The Fire Bird*, Più mosso (original version)

here would also do away with the whole body of legends connected with this opening. There is no reason whatever why these three notes should be pounded out as if some monster were announcing its arrival. There is no reason why these three notes should be played in a slower tempo. Somebody might as easily do the same with the four opening notes of the Violin Concerto. Why did the composer write "rit." before the holds in the third movement of this symphony and not in the first?

Earlier, when I offered the quiz on the relative tempos of Beethoven's eight scherzo movements, I suggested that tempos will become ever clearer if a musician studies the entire output of a composer and cross-relates the findings. This idea is fundamental: certain patterns of phrase and thematic invention are conceived as being in the same tempo. In the outline of the tempos in Mozart's *The Marriage of Figaro* it was helpful in several cases to turn to other works of the composer that were marked with more clarity than to heed contradictory opinions of the piece under discussion. In the Haydn example we can only get to know all existing editions and, when we see important discrepancies, use our own judgment as to which is right.

Let us make similar comparisons with *The Fire Bird* by Stravinsky. The transition to the faster portion of the dance (number 169 in the original, 29 in the Chester, and 132 in the Leeds edition) is different in all three editions. In the earliest setting (example 59) there is no accelerando and a definitely metered più mosso, with two quarters equal to three at the turning point. For some reason we can only surmise, the composer changed this in the suite (1919) to an accelerando poco a poco to the point 29, which is identical with the point 169 in the early version. In the latest version (example 60), the accelerando has been canceled while the più mosso advanced four bars earlier. A presto with a metronome marking replaces the più mosso of the earlier version.

Going back to the beginning of the dance, one can see that for the 1945 edition the tempo has been lowered from the 168 (in 1910 and 1919) to 152; hence the added più mosso and the presto with the 82 for the whole bar. In the original configuration, where the main part of the dance is 168 for the quarter, the più mosso comes out as 84, the same as in the 1945 edition. My personal guess is that the original transition proved too difficult for ballet conductors (not all of whom were Ansermet and Monteux), and the composer looked for a simpler way. What the relation "two quarters equals three quarters" demands is a conductor and a principal trumpet player who will count in their heads the four bars preceding the new "one – –". It is a tremendously effective and exciting sudden shift into a higher gear, not replaceable by the smoother acceleration, which is more gradual.

While Stravinsky is the subject, I should tell a story that may be of assistance to readers torn between the master's scores and his own recordings. Ernest Ansermet informed me one evening that he and Pierre Monteux had been quite hurt when Stravinsky disavowed "their" tempos of the early ballet scores. According

Example 60. Stravinsky, *The Fire Bird*, Più mosso (Leeds edition)

to Ansermet, the criticism coincided with the composer's energetic assumption of a conductor's career. When he found that some of the things he had written were not so simple in practical execution with orchestras of varying caliber, he changed them (which a composer indeed has the right to do), but was nasty enough to accuse his old maestros of Ballet Russe days of falsifying his ideas. Ansermet ended the tale with firm assurance that after all their rehearsals with the dancers there was nobody who knew the right tempos better than Monteux and he. (Believe, when in doubt, a composer's first version.)

Earlier I complained of Scholes's cavalier dismissal in *The Oxford Companion to Music* of Beethoven's metronome marking. He is not alone. In Joseph Kerman's admirably searching and well-written *The Beethoven Quartets*, he acknowledges the composer's gigantic stature throughout. Yet even a man of Kerman's deep sensitivity to the genius of Beethoven comes up with these sentences concerning Opus 18, no. 6:

> If so, he was going much too fast, for he clocked his Allegro con brio at 80 for the whole note, a pace allowing for little leisure. Many of the metronome marks for the B flat Quartet tend to extremes. This one is fast; the Adagio very slow, in spite of the qualification ma non troppo; and the Finale so fast (dotted quarter equals 88) that Allegretto quasi Allegro should have been piùtosto allegro or plain Allegro to achieve the desired effect. When Beethoven came to issue metronome marks for the early and middle quartets, around 1819, it may be that his ear had grown impatient with some of his old music.[13]

What strikes me here is the notion that one can lift a tempo out of an entire context and question the composer's judgment—especially a composer known to have been extremely painstaking in his sketches, drafts, and corrections.

In a most beautiful essay on my own favorite slow movement, from Quartet Opus 127, Kerman makes a curious comment: "Variation 3 is a hymn-variation of the melody, slowed to Adagio molto expressivo and simplified into alla breve time."[14] What does "simplified" mean in this context? What would a young quartet player looking for guidance to the late Beethoven works gain from this? The sign for cut time (alla breve) has been misunderstood, as I mentioned earlier. It means in the slow movement of Opus 127 the same as in the overture to *Die Zauberflöte* or the overtures to *Don Giovanni* or *Così fan tutte*. Wherever it appears together with a slow tempo indication, andante or adagio, it means *in the larger rhythmic value and not in the smaller one*. In the case of an even meter it simply tells the player that there are four beats to the bar and not eight.

Kerman, by the way, considers the Beethoven B-flat Quartet, Opus 18, a close relative of the Piano Sonata Opus 22. While it is easy to spot certain duplications of motives in these two movements, I find the relationship at best very distant. The character and tempo of the two pieces are built along entirely different

13. Joseph Kerman, *The Beethoven Quartets* (New York: Alfred A. Knopf, 1967), p. 72.
14. Ibid., p. 216.

rhythmic lines. The quartet's first and second movements have indeed a close relative in Beethoven's works, but it appears a few years later—in the Fourth Symphony, Opus 60. Their opening movements are built on a phrasing of the whole bar as a unit, while that of Opus 22 has a far more lyric and less boisterous phrase of "two," and sometimes "four," in a bar. By a further "coincidence," these movements of Opus 18 and Opus 60 carry identical metronome marks.

If I keep returning to the blithe criticism of Beethoven's metronome markings it is because it involves a double fallacy. It fails to consider the entire structure of the movement, and by insisting on a quota of leisurely moments in Opus 18, it ignores the possibility that Beethoven may have felt more boisterous and less leisurely than is supposed. Neither in Opus 18 nor in any other work did anybody compose a tempo to be a straitjacket. Moreover, this kind of criticism is inconsistent, for it fails to challenge every similar phrase and piece on the grounds that the tempo is wrong.

Most musicians today and for some time past have gone further than this. They have simply disregarded the existence of metronome marks, not only in Beethoven's works but in those of modern composers as well. I recall a conversation with a very precise conductor, who is quite at home with Stravinsky and with Elliott Carter. Speaking of one of the four movements in Ravel's *Rapsodie espagnole*, I remarked that I felt a metronome mark had been victim of a misprint similar to the one I pinpointed in the 6/8 portion of Beethoven's Ninth. There the discussion ended, for my colleague said that he never bothered with metronome marks. Still, the example is worth considering. The first three tempos given in the *Rapsodie* are perfectly natural when played as marked. On the other hand, the fourth, at 40 for the quarter note, may well be impossible to perform. This habanera probably suffered exactly the same type of misprint as that dotted quarter 84 in the Ninth: a half note accidentally was filled in and became a quarter. If we take the habanera at 40 for the *bar* (80 for the quarter) the tempo is right, close enough to the other well-known habanera from Bizet's *Carmen*, which is marked 72.

We have been conditioned to read figures indicating tempos with far less attention than words. About the words we have a variety of documents to show that they often varied. In many of Mozart's works (in addition to the examples from *Figaro* discussed earlier), the wording of the tempo indications depends on which edition one looks at. One edition of K. 488, the Piano Concerto in A Major, has adagio and allegro assai for the second and third movements, while another edition has andante and presto. The slow movement of K. 425 is variously headed andante and poco adagio. I am not suggesting, however, that it is of any practical value for the interpreter to become a research expert and make tempo changes only if a different term has been discovered in a copy heretofore unknown. As I have said earlier, I believe that the comparative method of studying the composer, of looking at related phrases and movements and themes, should be a part of preparation for any work. I have never felt that we missed information because Bach was more than sparing with tempo indications in his headings.

That words have many meanings is evident in Debussy's *La Mer*. Over the opening bars (6/4) the composer wrote "très lent" and the figure 116 for the quarter. In bar 31, after an acceleration of the tempo, we arrive at a 6/8 section marked with 116, this time for the eighth note. Since both passages are "in six," we are clearly asked for the identical speed; yet this second passage is entitled "modéré, sans lenteur." Most performers see only the "très lent" and indulge for the first five measures in a much slower tempo than the 116 would indicate. Here then is a case of the metronome clarifying the words.

There is no error involved. In the opening bars nothing happens but a brooding haziness, and the words *très lent* express the meaning, rather than the beat. (One will hardly need to "beat" those bars to make them come out right.) The other section has gentle movement, light and quite lively, with slightly accented second and fifth beats, hence the note of moderation without slowness. Returning to Kerman's equating of Beethoven's Opus 18 and Opus 22, the words over the first movements are the same, allegro con brio, but the meaning and thrust of the two pieces is not alike. The piano sonata gets closer to the lyricism of the *Spring* Sonata, Opus 24, than to the hammering quartet movement.

Kerman's comment that the words over the finale of Opus 18, no. 6, "allegretto quasi allegro," do not represent the proper tempo is also questionable. What about Opus 31, II, which has a finale marked "allegretto" in which a veritable storm is developed?[15] Wherever we have metronome marks, they are most eloquent in revealing to us the interrelationship between movements of a work and, in a wider sense, the connections between different works by the same composer. When Brahms withdrew his metronome figures, he did not mean that they were ill-considered when he wrote them down. Modern composers' markings have been ignored, disregarded, and, in general, misunderstood, but that is no reason to conclude that the author was making a mistake when he set them down.

In a publication called *Wiener Vaterländische Blätter* ("Viennese Patriotic Pages"), there appeared on October 13, 1813, an article from which I quote:

> Herr van Beethoven looks upon this invention [Maelzel's chronometer, the forerunner of his metronome] as a welcome means to secure the performance of his brilliant compositions in all places in the tempos conceived by himself, which to his regret have so often been misunderstood.[16]

It seems quite clear that Beethoven was not always happy with the way in which his music was played. And now Wagner from *On Conducting*:

---

15. If I argue excessively with Kerman, it is because of my tremendous admiration for his book, which is one of the few, if not the only one, that attempts an encyclopedic consideration of Beethoven.

16. *Wiener Vaterländische Blätter*, 13 October 1813.

I have often been astonished at the singularly slight sense for tempo and execution evinced by leading musicians.[17]

In my earlier operas I gave detailed instructions as to the tempi and indicated them (as I thought) accurately, by means of the metronome. Subsequently, whenever I had occasion to protest against a particularly absurd tempo, in *Tannhäuser* for instance, I was assured that the metronome had been consulted and carefully followed. In my later works I omitted the metronome and merely described the main tempi in general terms, paying, however, particular attention to the various modifications of tempo. It would appear that general directions also tend to vex and confuse capellmeisters, especially when they are expressed in plain German words.[18]

Beethoven wrote on the autograph of his song "Nord oder Süd": "100 according to Maelzel; but this must be held applicable to only the first measures, for feeling also has its tempo and this cannot entirely be expressed in this figure."

Conclusion

It is awesome to imagine such star witnesses as Beethoven and Verdi arguing for the metronome against Wagner and Brahms, who oppose it. In one single respect there appears to have been no disagreement: all complained, as did Strauss, Stravinsky, and Bartók among the more recent composers, about being misunderstood by too many interpreters, including people of fame and distinction. Thus, the contemporary student (an artist and interpreter remains a student all his life or else ceases to be a true artist) finds an open field unconstricted by a body of approved rules.

Anyone can argue for and against the metronome, but no one questions the crucial importance of right tempos. Wagner, expressing his views radically, as usual, writes: "The whole duty of a conductor is comprised in his ability always to indicate the right tempo."[19] It is of course not the whole duty; there are a few others, of which more anon. For our colleagues who prefer to believe that a score is a vehicle for the ingenuity of an interesting interpreter, we have quite enough documents to show that composers considered *the* right tempos for each work to be singular and not variable. Those factors that vary—acoustics, environment, instruments, size of choirs, and so on—have been well summed up in *The Oxford Companion to Music*. But because of a universal instinct of humanity, whenever a new idea threatens comfortable assumptions, it may be either quietly ignored or resolutely resisted.

The old and oft-discussed issue of Beethoven's metronome markings has been

17. Richard Wagner, *On Conducting*, trans. Edward Dannreuther (London: William Reeves, 1897), p. 25.
18. Ibid., p. 20.
19. Ibid.

dealt with mostly in an objectionable manner. Publishers of the quartets have simply omitted the existing markings. The one edition that includes them, the Philharmonia, is not easily available and, to my knowledge, does not issue the quartets in parts but only in pocket study scores. If an eminent musician (Rudolf Kolisch) and a fine scholar (Joseph Kerman) can debate these metronome markings, how can a publisher omit them as if he had the right to censor the composer and to deprive the student of authentic information? The act of omission in itself symbolizes the dodging of this whole topic.

A further proof of an even odder sort is to be found in Thayer's biography of Beethoven. The letter to Moscheles from Beethoven was the composer's final written document; he died a few days after writing it. That letter contained the metronome readings for the Ninth that were intended to be given to the London performers of the work. According to temperament, a reader will find it either funny or shocking that in neither of the two prominent editions of Thayer's work can one find these markings correctly reprinted. Somebody, if not the authors themselves or the editing experts, would have discovered the inaccuracies—which in this case amount to absurdities—if they had been proofread. But, so the thought probably went, these metronomes are no good anyway, so why bother? Perhaps it is significant that Verdi believed in the metronome. Unlike Wagner and Brahms, he was scarcely, if at all, influenced by German musical philosophy and was perhaps unaware of the disrepute into which the metronome figures of Beethoven had fallen. In any case, the method that will lead each performer to the right tempos is the comparative one, with an awareness of all available authentic directives, including the metronome figures.

Seven
Knowing the Conductor's Role

The Conductor's Image

One of the differences between evaluating performers who sing or play instruments and those who conduct is the inability of most lay people to understand what conductors are doing. Many music lovers can easily distinguish a first-rate tenor from an indifferent one, an outstanding pianist from a routine performer, or a truly fine string player from a scratchy practitioner. Uncertainty of pitch, shortage of breath, or sloppy banging on a piano can be detected by most listeners. Yet these same listeners are at a loss to judge the capabilities of a conductor. The qualifications for this elusive art and craft are a mystery to all but a very few experts.

How vague the general concept of conducting is was brought home to me in a letter from a record buff who fancied himself a born *chef d'orchestre*, though he admitted never having studied music. From his resumé I visualized my correspondent spending many hours cutting a graceful figure in front of his speakers as the glorious strains poured from the magic machine. Many students have practiced baton technique in such a manner, but this gentleman had come to believe that his choreography was actually the cause of the wondrous beauty that sounded forth. He was convinced, moreover, that he could produce the same results with a group of musicians on a public platform. Not for a moment did I consider the man deranged. He had merely confused cause and effect, as many do when they try to imagine the task of the musical conductor. Anyone with some musical instinct can follow the outlines of a symphony with appropriately synchronized gestures and create the illusion that the follower is the leader.

The mystery of conducting is perhaps increased by its one item of paraphernalia, the baton. Reminiscent of the sorcerer's wand, Aaron's rod, the prospector's Geiger counter—in short, the symbols of extraordinary powers—it recalls abracadabra and Open Sesame. A number of genuinely talented persons prominent on the international music circuit who have a dash of the prestidigitator in them have deepened the confusion over the conductor's function. Although illusion alone could never ensure success, there is no doubt that even the best conductor owes much to its unfathomable magic.

It is a very individual magic. If two accomplished conductors facing an orchestra not previously known to them were to perform the same piece of music without prior rehearsal and without giving verbal directives, the very sound of the orchestra and the music would change from one conductor to the other. Similarly, two violinists will coax different sounds from the same fiddle, as will two pianists from the same keyboard. Some wonderful singing artists make do all their lives with an indifferent timbre of their larynxes, while an uncultured extrovert produces a timbre that drives audiences wild with joy. Sound is an extension of human personality, and this truism is just as evident when the instrument consists of one hundred instrumentalists as when it is a pair of vocal cords.

The simple fact that sound is a part of personality has, from my earliest acquaintance with conducting, made me dubious about so-called baton technique. I have always refused to teach conducting, supporting my refusal with the argument that the motions are of no consequence. Yet no one, at least in my experience, believes the simple statement that there is no such thing as a technique of conducting. Richard Strauss is said to have told a would-be conductor who wanted instruction, "What there is to learn I can show you now." With his right hand he drew a diagram of the four-beat, then the three-beat, then the two-beat, and finally the six-beat. That, he commented, was all that was teachable. The rest one either acquired by oneself or not at all.

The well-known violin teacher Ivan Galamian considers his only real accomplishment as a teacher to be his insistence that his pupils practice. If they do not do so, he expels them. Thus, though their musical and artistic merits vary widely, all his disciples are marvels of technical proficiency. This should prove that only the technique of instrumentalists should be credited to their teachers. Conductors, alas, have no chance to practice. Orchestras, whether their members are students or fully paid professionals, do not tolerate being treated as guinea pigs for experimenting conductors.[1]

Gesture is of crucial importance in conducting as long as it carries a message. But that message cannot be determined in advance. It is born out of a need that arises only during music making. It is pointless to prepare an eloquent quieting

1. In Moscow in 1976 I witnessed a session of an orchestra engaged solely to serve as a practice instrument for student conductors. Whether this socialist method of training musical leadership will produce more and better conductors will have to await the test of time. More recently the Juilliard School in New York established an orchestra as a body for conductors to practice with—or should I say "on."

motion for the left hand if one fails to know when or whether it is required. I suspect that the belief of serious musicians in conducting technique grows out of the tradition of the operatic routinier. The best of this breed are able, with little or no rehearsal, to hold a show together, steering it with imperturbable assurance past cliffs and narrows and through stormy passages into the safe harbor of the final curtain. These are the prototypes who pass for "technicians of the baton," relying on the unequivocal clarity of their signals. At the opposite end of the scale is the conductor who at first sight seems awkward, whose every upbeat or start of a new tempo causes a minor nervous crisis—and who yet produces without fail performances of distinction.

Perhaps an illustration from the recent past will help to make this distinction clear. Gennaro Papi, a conductor at the Metropolitan Opera for many seasons, maintained a singularly calm manner as he piloted his usually unrehearsed performances through to the end. He never used a score; he cued every instrument and singer accurately; he knew music perhaps better than his antipode. Yet outside the tiny circle of insiders who marveled that he could get through a complex Puccini score without rehearsal, without disciplined singers, without the minimal artistic wherewithal, Papi passed for just another maestro who was useful in keeping opera managements afloat in time of financial calamity. On the other hand, Serge Koussevitzky, the long-time conductor of the Boston Symphony, was not gifted with an easy conducting arm; he needed help on the musical side to prepare himself; he performed by the standards of some observers superlatively, for others only intermittently so. Yet he has been welcomed into the halls of fame, having been a figure of musical importance.

My conclusion is that a conductor is effective if intent and result are identical, or as near to it as possible. I doubt that Koussevitzky would have made it through *La Bohème* without ten rehearsals, if then. Papi would have been able to learn all of Koussevitzky's repertoire and go through it without a score. Yet when Papi finished, no one would have learned anything new about the works he had played. The performance would have been unexceptionable but routine. Papi had been conditioned by circumstance and his own personality to confine his great knowledge of music to solving the dire practical problems of repertory opera. Koussevitzky, whatever his shortcomings, brought his own personal insights and emotional response to the music. If Papi possessed the "technique of conducting" that the other lacked, Koussevitzky was nonetheless the musician of consequence. In the bluntest terms, one handled traffic, the other made music. The worlds of opera and ballet possess and need many traffic directors. One should not be surprised, however, if other conductors, some of whom cannot match their dexterity, nevertheless achieve greater success and, more important, just renown.

This kind of conducting is a relatively recent development. The time-beater who does little more than provide the coordination to help a group of professionals synchronize their playing and avoid breakdowns belongs to an older tradition. In earlier times the conductor was also one of the performers. He might conduct from the keyboard of a harpsichord while playing the continuo or, like Haydn's Salomon, keep time with his bow when not using it on his violin. Most music written before 1800 requires no more attention from a conductor than this. Even the music of Bach, though as complex as any, can be conducted from the continuo instrument as it was two hundred years ago, when cast with the limited forces used by the composer.

The requirements for this kind of conducting are quite different from those with which this book is mainly concerned. In recent years a number of small chamber groups have won wide success under leaders who are playing participants. Often they became known first through recordings, and then had their reputations confirmed in the concert halls. The directors of these groups are first-class instrumentalists who can prepare a choir or chamber group to perfection and perform in masterly fashion the music of Bach and his contemporaries. They generally eschew that element of romantic inspiration which is indispensable in post-Baroque music. The eloquence of Bach can be well conveyed by such a stylish and cool delivery, whereas Mozart and Beethoven would perish under it.

The type of personality that properly refuses to impose itself upon the music of Bach's time is not often well adapted to the demands of a large group performing music of a later age. The greater freedom of the music and the greater size of the forces both require a stronger and more visible kind of direction. If players are insufficiently skilled or badly prepared, no amount of imploring or imperious gesturing during the performance will make it sound any better. But how the conductor "acts" does make a difference. The most experienced musicians can be alienated or exhilarated by the aura, the stance, the charisma of the person on the podium. The musical results will still depend on the caliber of the orchestra. Nevertheless, the conductor has both a musical task (which is what this book is mainly about) and an inspirational one that can raise the level of any group beyond the limits of painstaking preparation. Unfortunately, from fire and involvement it is but a small step to hysterical carryings-on, dervish dances, leaps and stabbings in the air, and other forms of uninhibited behavior. These may impress unsophisticated audiences, but the poker faces of the players will tell a different story. There is a classic middle course in which neither masklike indifference nor obsessive miming prevail. The only guide to this golden mean is good taste—not a strictly musical talent but the product of fine education.

The advent of television has brought with it changes in podium manner and stance. Although this book will provide no help toward winning an Emmy, it would be churlish and unrealistic to deny the impact of our most powerful communications medium upon the art of musical performance. The show-biz aspect of television conducting may not make a lasting contribution to the interpretation of music, but it does heighten the entertainment value for a large segment of the public. Recently a well-known conductor with a splendid orchestra played a great overture on television. It was a first-rate performance all the way through, the director was totally absorbed by the music, and everything went wonderfully and simply. At the final page, however, it seemed that the conductor became conscious for the first time of the camera's presence. With a start he began to play up to it. As the music drew rapidly toward its last powerful chords, the only effect he could still manage was one wild spasm of emotion in face and body, lest anyone forget that the music truly swept even the maestro off his balance. The hilarious element in the incident was the conductor's sudden realization that he had nearly wasted the opportunity of his career.

The Conductor's Authority

The position and philosophy of a conductor today may need a good deal of rethinking. Throughout the past century conductors held posts of wide responsibility, with a great deal of economic power and the responsibility for hiring and firing. This filled many a head with exaggerated ideas of self-importance. It may be a blessing in disguise that contemporary economic and social developments are rapidly diminishing this power of conductors. No longer are they employers. If present trends continue, the chief of an orchestra, no matter what his title, will have only his musical authority left, and even that is already reduced in regard to selecting personnel. All this will bring a new balance, quite different from the remnants of nineteenth-century structures, into musical organizations. To me it means that a conductor will take a new and better place as one of those who are only performers, only interpreters, concerned alone with the meaning of music and how to present it.

There remains, however, the vexing problem of how to cope with unsatisfactory players. The pendulum has swung all the way from one extreme, when conductors brutalized musicians and dismissed them without warning for real or imagined failures, to the other, in which ideas of social justice take precedence over concepts of excellence. The only hope is that the swinging pendulum will in the near future come to rest in the center.

When I first arrived in the United States in 1937, a musician at the Radio City Music Hall would recognize that he was being given notice if the conductor raised two fingers of his left hand while continuing to beat time with his right. It meant that the unfortunate person had two weeks of employment left. Caprice and whim ruled so unpredictably that corrective moves had to come. After the end of the war, in 1945, American musicians obtained ever greater job security. In England, on the other hand, conditions became more brutal. Unlike their colleagues on the European and American continents, the English had no government, private patrons, or foundations to pay their salaries. They functioned in cooperatives, with the same risk as a shareholder in an enterprise. London attained the status of being the recording capital of the world, and the London orchestras made their living from the recording dates their managers could secure. Gradually, the once-easygoing English musicians became so strict with their own colleagues that any slight lapse in a recording session might lead to instant replacement of the erring player. In most orchestras in all other countries, after a newcomer has passed a trial period of varying length, he is assured of virtual tenure. There are no provisions for dealing with sudden deterioration, and there are few exceptions to the rule of calendar-dictated retirement. This problem is even more significant and unresolved than that of the pension plans, which are still far behind the times.

For the modern conductor, the best counsel is to remain on the sidelines and not get involved in insoluble personnel problems. Like a bridge player, a conductor stepping in front of an orchestra has been dealt a random selection—not of cards but of talented people—with which to make the most of his "contract." The better player will produce better results with the same deal, but with a deck of treys and sevens nobody can make a slam. At the time when many German musicians had to emigrate, George Szell appeared as guest conductor in northern Britain. He was known to be an exacting master. The manager of the orchestra, anxious to please, appeared during the first intermission and asked Szell if he could bring him something. "Another orchestra" was the prompt reply.

A shrewd and knowledgeable talent agent once stated in an interview that after he had placed young conductors with young orchestras, he had to watch for the right moment to pull them out. As soon as they began to make music "around the difficulties of the orchestra," it was time to terminate the contract. In reference to the finale of *Die Walküre*, I stated earlier that it is not the conductor's task to expose shortcomings and weaknesses of the cast, and we have to try hard to bring out the best. This is quite different from playing *Petrouchka* slower because the trumpet can't manage the solo, or beating 12/8 in the adagio of the Ninth because the players can't stay together "in 4."

Arturo Toscanini, a man not known for timorousness or vacillation, once commented that at a first rehearsal a conductor should always listen with an open mind to the way solo players in the orchestra handle their important passages before making suggestions or criticisms. Within limits, there is more than one valid way of approaching a solo. As long as a player does not do anything contrary to the composer's idea of the whole, it is best to grant him his own manner, because he will play with more inner conviction. It is not necessary to force every detail into one's own predetermined pattern.

In the same spirit, it is also perfectly proper, not to say advisable, to give in occasionally when an orchestra feels a tendency toward some fine new nuance, either in dynamics or tempo. My only emphasis is on the word *fine*. An ensemble of good musicians possesses a collective instinct that must not be disregarded. Not included in this recommendation of liberalism are mindless ritards in wrong places, or any other excesses. A rehearsal should above all else establish a relationship between conductor and players. Our contemporary time restrictions and limitations often give an undue advantage to the sheer professional competence of a conductor, while others who need longer to get to the essence of musical and personal contact may not achieve their own potential. There is a world of social change involved in the various new problems that gives them more than specialized interest. Musical organizations are part of a structure that grew around the industrial revolutions—a paradoxical situation.

Before turning to the more fundamental aspects of how a conductor conveys his musical ideas to his forces, I would like to deal briefly with areas of potential conflict that do not necessarily include incompetence. In performing concertos, there are many instances when politeness and experience mask basic disagreement between soloist and conductor. That this solution does not always work was proved one night when the music director of the New York Philharmonic Orchestra appeared together with a well-known, somewhat eccentric pianist to perform the First Concerto by Brahms. The conductor explained to the audience his total disagreement with the interpretation of the soloist, but urbanely added some polite words about the highly serious purpose of the soloist—which did not clarify how the team settled their differences.

I have often been asked who controls a concerto performance. This depends on the procedures that govern the engagement. Soloists for orchestral subscription cycles are cleared with the music director and with prominent guest conductors. If a soloist whom nobody fancies has been engaged because of box-office considerations, the manager will assign him to a conductor who is in no position to demur. In any event, relations between conductor and soloist can vary widely. When Vladimir Horowitz agreed to play a concerto with the New York Philharmonic after a hiatus of decades, it was he who chose the piece, the hall, the conductor, and the time of the event. In rehearsal, moreover, he gave plenty of advice to the conductor so that his own ideas should prevail throughout. At the opposite extreme of the superstar soloist are conductors who accept only soloists willing to submit to their wishes. Between these poles every kind of relationship between soloist and conductor exists. My own experience has varied from the despair of finding myself totally at odds with a soloist to the bliss of a perfect meeting of minds that leads to a nearly wordless rehearsal followed by an ideal performance.

My usual procedure as a guest conductor is to submit a list of some fifteen pianists, violinists, and so on with whom I find it agreeable to work. I also have a small index of concertos that I will not conduct because the orchestral role is so subordinate that the resources of a fine orchestra are wasted on them. The same is true of some choral works. The best orchestras should be reserved for music that needs the best players. In a Chopin concerto, a great orchestra is wasted, for a secondary group can do full justice to the score.

When, instead of a single instrumental soloist, several strong-willed singers are competing for control of tempos and nuances, it becomes clear why unified opera is so rare. I consider interpretation of opera no more complex than that of a string quartet, but it is beset by more human conflict and hence by greater

obstacles. Confronted with a singer who was unwilling to change a vulgar misinterpretation of *Salome*, my only choices were to put up with it or walk out on
my contract. There was no meeting of minds. Toscanini solved this problem in
his performances of operas at NBC in New York by casting them with nonstar
singers. In this way he achieved the unified interpretation he could not get with
performers whose minds were set in concepts different from his own. I was
present in 1936 at a most embarrassing confrontation between Toscanini and a
world-famous heroic baritone who had been engaged by the Salzburg Festival
to perform the role of Hans Sachs. Rehearsals showed the total incompatibility
of conductor and protagonist, with the result that a parting of the ways was the
only remedy. As in the case of the Brahms Concerto at the Philharmonic, the
conductor had accepted an artist on the recommendation of others rather than by
his own choice. Under such circumstances, conflicts often are past conciliation.

A conductor who performs only symphonic works apparently has the easier
task. Why, then, do many mediocre people make their mark in the opera house
and fail on the concert podium? Because, having no concept of their own to
begin with, they do not generate the friction connected with operatic personalities. They consider a score to be a set of purely technical problems and believe
that their whole task is simply to hold a rather complex mechanism—singers,
chorus, stage band, and orchestra—together. That mechanical task is reduced to
a minimum when only a symphony orchestra is involved. Many observers will
easily recall cases of aging conductors of stature (I have at least three in mind)
who were well able to give distinguished performances of symphonic works,
while choral works added a hazard, and operas were a constant brush with dis-
aster. Perhaps one may devise a formula: opera is easier for a routinier who has
no strong opinions, whereas a musician with a concept encounters fewer personal conflicts in conducting symphony.

On the other hand, an easygoing opera conductor used to accommodating
diverse temperaments and unifying the disparate elements will come to grief if
he presents himself alone before a symphony orchestra. The reason is quite
elementary: while even a capricious opera singer brings some kind of interpretation to a performance, an orchestra is a blank as far as reading beyond the
notes is concerned. In the opera house the typical maestro must conduct only a
short prelude, without too many interpretive problems, before the curtain rises.
(Even the giant Verdi wrote very few orchestral sections requiring any particular
depth of musical insight. The "typical" operatic conductor rarely gets to Wagner,
Mozart, or Strauss, whose demands are more taxing.) When such a musician
steps in front of a symphony ensemble, he is like a fish on dry land. The stage,
with its varied populace, is missing. Nobody sets the pace for him by either
rushing or dragging, as singers are wont to do. On the symphony podium, the
conductor is quite alone, with no help to be expected from the orchestra. And
that holds true regardless of an orchestra's skill. When a hundred or more mu-

sicians play together, they lose their individual characteristics and become indeed a collective.

The Conductor's Task

Having considered situations that can lead to conflict between conductors and musicians, let us turn to the basic task of the conductor on the podium. Most of this book has been devoted to the conductor's preparation for this task, but that preparation will ultimately count for nothing if it is not translated into performance. The conductor must find ways to convey his own sense of the music to his players. Unfortunately, the division of brain and muscle work that is fairly routine in the relations between singer and coach, instrumentalist and master teacher, or dancer and choreographer is much more difficult for conductors to establish with orchestras.

Let us begin with some suggestions about the practical, daily routine of the profession. For convenience, I will compress them into ten admonitions. I make no claim that any or all are infallible guarantees of success.

1. *Be prepared.* Today, this Boy Scout motto is more appropriate than ever for a conductor. He or she must be securely in command from the first moment of the first rehearsal. There was a time when rehearsals could be prolonged at the conductor's whim. Some conductors learned new scores during rehearsals, relying on quick reading and routine to conceal their lack of preparation. But that was before musicians were represented by unions and each hour of rehearsal meant a charge to the management. Today no conductor can afford such indulgence. Being prepared means knowing exactly what should be heard and diagnosing the problem if it is not heard. Nearly all new works, especially at first performance, have mistakes in the parts that will result in wrong sounds or wrong silences. The conductor should be able, through prior knowledge of the right sounds, to point to the error as precisely as possible. If he is unsure what it is, he will do better to say nothing, but check the score later or consult with the composer.[2]

2. *Work with the librarian.* Working on orchestral parts with the librarian in advance of rehearsals may be the single most time-saving and productive activity a conductor can engage in. If possible, it is best for the conductor to own the parts for standard works by Haydn, Mozart, Beethoven, and others. Otherwise, he is faced with two alternatives, both equally unsatisfactory. If he is a guest

---

2. If the composer himself cannot hear the mistake, the chances are the first mistake was to accept the work for performance. Before 1800, both composers and artists involved their students in producing new works that were required in a hurry. Mozart had Süssmayr write the recitatives for *La clemenza di Tito,* and many great painters let their pupils paint the lesser figures in their huge canvasses or murals. I suspect that a few contemporary composers employ a similar device when they accept more commissions than they can handle. As a result, they do not always know their scores.

conductor, he must accept the bowings and other editing he finds in the orchestra's scores, for he has no right to change those of the regular conductor. If the orchestra is his own, he must waste preparation time while the players write in changes—unless he and the librarian do this before the rehearsal begins. Current restrictions on rehearsals have increased the importance of the librarian and his responsibility for improving the quality of parts, choosing the best editions, and other contributions not obvious to the outsider. A conductor who cooperates closely with the librarian will be able to rehearse more efficiently and also learn a good deal about his orchestra.

3. *Plan rehearsal time.* As might be expected, there is a definite relation between rehearsal time and quality of performance. And some works require more rehearsal time than others. All things being equal, the Sixth Symphony of Beethoven takes more time to prepare than his Seventh; Brahms's Third needs more preparation than his Second. Most orchestras have collective contracts with fairly rigid schedules. It is essential to plan rehearsals in advance so that every piece on a program will be equally well-known to the orchestra by the time it is played. One way to do this is to arrange programs so that an unfamiliar or complex work is balanced by one easier to prepare. How well this works depends somewhat on prior knowledge of an orchestra. Some have better-trained violin sections that can learn certain classical patterns quickly; others require tiresome sectional practice. If worse comes to worst, a piece that seems to require more time than is available can be dropped in favor of a less demanding one.[3] When a good orchestra is rehearsing standard works, it should not be necessary to take time to go through the entire piece. It will be more useful to concentrate on the difficult passages. In Beethoven's Fifth Symphony, one might begin with the trio of the third movement, at least in orchestras where not all the basses are virtuosos. In Strauss's *Also Sprach Zarathustra*, it is wise to start with the passage preceding figure 18. This method will show the musicians that the conductor knows the music and that the rehearsal is intended for their benefit, not his. Even the most jaded orchestra members will be grateful for the chance to do well, especially if the conductor establishes a positive mood.[4]

3. Even the best-laid plans may go wrong. In the 1970s I began rehearsals with one of the best London orchestras and found to my astonishment that they had never played Prokofiev's Fifth Symphony, which was on the program. No music was available for substitution, and we had only one day to rehearse. The score, written by a pianist, is most unidiomatic for the strings, and not even this quick-reading group could master its enormous difficulties in time. The performance was, to say the least, undistinguished. On another occasion an orchestra in Prague, less brilliant in most music than the London group, knew the intricacies of the Prokofiev score. Consequently the symphony sounded better at first rehearsal in Prague than it did in concert in London.

4. A relatively new problem mainly concerns the string sections of many orchestras. When a contemporary work is to be prepared, it requires good judgment to place it not only in the best part of the program for proper effect and success, but also to schedule it wisely within the rehearsal timetable of the orchestra. Some contemporary compositions turn the musicians off. Not all such hostility can be laid to the usual human conservatism that objects to the new out of sheer inertia and lack of curiosity. There is often some very good cause for these feelings. Many composers today do

4. *Speak little*. Speeches are heard but seldom listened to, so they contribute nothing to better performances. Players resent lengthy talk as a waste of their time. Comments should be kept brief and always to the point. How much an orchestra needs to be told can be judged quickly by the knowledge they show of a work when playing it. The conductor should let the orchestra play for at least five or ten minutes without interrupting. If the work is unknown to the players, they should be allowed to play it through in order to become familiar with it before work is begun on details. With a group of first-rank professionals, relatively little correction may be needed. After directing such a group, however, a conductor can seriously underestimate the amount of work needed when he faces a less expert orchestra.

5. *Stop seldom*. It is a normal function in a rehearsal to stop the music when necessary for correction or other comment. This should be done, however, only with great discretion. Stopping interrupts the flow of a work and prevents the players from feeling its long line. The best way to minimize the resulting frustration is to make mental notes of points needing correction and stop the orchestra only when you have collected several of them. When bowings are to be marked for a particular passage, this should be done at the same time for repetitions of the passage, which are commonly found in classical works. In some great orchestras players manage to signal a conductor that they know they have made a slip. When this happens it should be unnecessary to stop at all for a correction.

6. *Do not keep musicians idle*. Plan rehearsals so that musicians who have nothing to do in all or parts of certain works may arrive late or leave early. (For example, in the Brahms Second Piano Concerto, the trumpet and kettledrum players should not be kept after the second movement unless the first two are to be repeated.) This will avoid debilitating waits for those players and distractions for the others, both of which lower concentration and morale.

7. *Stand to conduct*. Unless a conductor has a health problem that precludes standing, he should not sit during rehearsals. Rehearsals should match the conditions of performances as far as is practicable. They should be held in the hall where the concert will be given so that instrumental balances can be properly judged. This practice establishes the correct sound for the final performance, just as a conductor's stance helps to convey the correct attitude. The visual message conveyed by his seated body may be reflected among the ranks of the

---

not know how to write idiomatically for string instruments or do not wish to do so. They assign to the string sections tasks that render the whole training and schooling of a string player fairly senseless. The violinist who has been brought up to play phrases finds now that his only task is to count bars of rest, now and then interrupting them for a single pizzicato note, a glissando, or a scratch on the back of the fiddle. If a conscientious conductor rehearses such a piece for an hour and then ventures into a Mozart symphony, it will be a big struggle to get the demoralized string players back on track. From the standpoint of developing an orchestra's best playing, it is desirable to compartmentalize this type of contemporary music so that it does not get mixed up with the standard repertoire.

orchestra in crossed legs, surreptitious smoking, and other manifestations of boredom or indifference instead of an eagerness to perfect the ensemble and make spirited music.

8. *Understand players and their parts.* Understanding players demands an acquaintance not only with psychology but also with the materials with which the players have to work. The conductor, who has the full score in front of him, should keep in mind that the players can be expected to grasp only a limited sense of the whole work from their individual parts, which are just that—parts. To do more than produce a meaningless succession of notes a player must be helped to see their interconnections with those that other players are producing. It is up to the conductor to enlarge the players' awareness of the work as a whole. This can range from pointing out that a certain player must be in unison with another whom he can scarcely hear to demonstrating the complexities of "broken line" work. A good example of the latter that is too little understood by even the most experienced orchestral players is in the first movement of the Third Symphony of Brahms (bars 50–64).

9. *Do not fake.* By "faking" I mean calling for repetitions of a passage that has been well played simply because the conductor is himself uncertain about how to bring out some extra nuance of which he is fond. This way of passing the buck to the musicians is sensed with uncanny accuracy and is resented.

10. *Do not delude yourself.* When a young (or old) conductor steps before an orchestra, he is sometimes thinking, "Now they will play this work for the first time as it should be played." This may be an accurate self-assessment or it may be megalomania. In either case, it is a grave mistake to betray the thought by word or implication. For one thing, although individual players may prefer one interpretation to another, an orchestra has no collective opinion on how a piece should be played. It can and will, however, quickly form an opinion of a conductor's knowledge, his musicianship, and his behavior. Boasting should be eschewed, especially boasting by denigrating the work of other conductors.

The first of these admonitions deserves a further word, which also applies to the ninth. Regardless of a conductor's age or experience, the lack of total familiarity with a work shows clearly. The lay listener may not notice it, but to one acquainted with the work, nothing can conceal a merely routine approach. It is particularly evident in the recurrence of involuntary nuances, mainly ritards which allow the conductor time to prepare a new tempo or adjust a transition. Such ritards are not structural and intrude into the playing through a collective uncertainty in the orchestra caused by the conductor's own.

In symphonic literature written before 1900, there are long stretches that move ahead in such regular patterns that the lack of conductorial assurance is less keenly felt. A movement of a Mendelssohn work, for instance, runs practically on its own momentum. The tempo is firm; the orchestra plays on with only a minimal time-beating necessary for good ensemble. In performing such scores, a clever follower is almost indistinguishable from a real conductor. But as soon as he comes to a change in tempo, a new meter, or any other variant to a steady pulse of a straight 4/4, the fat will be in the fire. Suffering most will be slow movements that have no firm pulsation, or composite meters such as a broad 6/4, 6/8, or 9/8. The opening movements of the First Piano Concerto by Brahms or his Third Symphony are classic examples of pieces where real mastery is a sine qua non. These are the works that prompt musicians to speak wistfully of stick technique. I should prefer to call it *knowledge* technique, for it has little, if anything, to do with the stick.

A great test of conducting ability with soloists and without lies in successfully distributing subordinate roles. Music is made of a fabric that combines leading and accompanying voices. Even a work for piano consists of such elements, with the lead moving from the right hand to the left or appearing in a middle voice. An ideal illustration is found in the Eighth Novelette of Robert Schumann. In the first twelve bars, the upper voice leads; from bar 13 on the melody moves into the bass; and from bar 24 on it continues in the middle voice. This is basic to all music: at any given moment a more important voice is accompanied or matched by less important ones. In complex music this lead can change within a single bar. String quartets offer wonderful examples in which to study this. But voice leading involves not only series of notes but also the human beings who produce them. Here interplay of egos may severely tax a conductor's tact and authority.

A good look at the slow movement of Beethoven's Violin Concerto shows that the solo instrument actually provides an accompaniment, albeit a most important one, for the entire first theme of the movement, playing heavenly turns around a tender melody. But the melody is the leading voice, whether in the horns, the clarinet, the bassoon, or the strings. If a soloist's ego has swollen beyond control, the roles in the movement will never be properly distributed. As a result, the interpretation will be quite wrong. In opera this constant shifting appears mostly in ensemble numbers. Schönberg formulated the situation succinctly when in one of his scores he explained the H and N signs, for *Hauptstimme* and *Nebenstimme*, with the footnote "The human voice is always Hauptstimme." So it is in Verdi, in Mozart, and in Wagner. In the third-act sextet of Mozart's *The Marriage of Figaro*, a passage occurs where, from bar 103 through bar 111, Susanna should be at all times heard clearly in the lead; she sings a most endearing melody, with the other voices forming a soft background. The problem is to convince the five other singers, especially Marcellina and Bartolo, that they must subdue themselves. The difficulties are compounded by the fact that most Susannas nowadays have light soprano voices, while a heavy mezzo Marcellina and a burly buffo Bartolo happen in this ensemble to have notes in their best (loudest) range. It takes a convincing conductor to make singers with strong egos realize that at times they sing accompaniments.

A conductor needs stubborn determination to set his performances free from

Example 61. Beethoven, Sym. No. 3, 2nd mvt., mm. 180–81

the ingrained habits of the experienced orchestras who play so much music that they tend to play by rote. Typical of such tendencies is bar 180 in the funeral march of the *Eroica* (example 61). There is hardly an orchestra that does not make a ritard on the third and fourth eighth notes of this bar, coaxed by the low strings. This compels the first violins to play the upbeat to the next bar longer than they should. (The violins who have the lead there should play it as they do the upbeat before bar 17.) I do not think that this slowing down of the triplets in bar 180 (or similar gross effects) is the result of mere inertia. More likely it began as an elegant turn of phrase, fortuitously discovered, at first admired, then imitated—and gradually exaggerated until it became a meaningless mannerism. My efforts to erase such bad habits are usually successful for the first, perhaps even the second, performance. But when a work is repeated several times in a series or on tour, the old accustomed manner creeps back. Wide-awake alertness gives way in the backstands to an attitude of "Again the *Eroica*," and playing by rote takes the place of playing with thought. The French call such return to earlier habit "la nostalgie à l'écurie." Such habits make the more popular and better-known piece the more difficult to render freshly. Lesser-known works are never taken for granted, for they demand the players' attention just to produce the notes correctly. The mistake that musicians make with familiar works is to assume that reproducing the sequence of notes as they are accustomed to is all there is to knowing a work.

An unfailing test of how well an orchestra knows a work is to note how many rehearsal numbers have been written in its own set of parts. This will indicate whether the score has been rehearsed or merely played through. Concertos in particular suffer from the system of running through the music once, to give the soloist his minimum due, and letting it go at that. Yet some solo concertos rank among the great orchestral masterpieces, and they need proper work as much as does any symphony.

Certain problems that face every conductor deserve more detailed discussion.

The specific concerns of the string and wind sections are especially important, as is the achievement of balanced dynamics. The question of how much to edit is also a knotty one.

Bowing. Bowing is one of the most vexing subjects facing a conductor. The simplest view is that it should be left to the concertmaster and other string section leaders. This might be a perfect solution if the bowings were to be marked for a single group of players. But if the conductor were to take the most meticulously bowed material to another orchestra, within the first five minutes the leader would politely, though with a barely concealed note of disdain, ask, "Are these *your* bowings, Maestro?" The implication would be, "Of course, we *can* follow them—if this is your way." As my early cello studies were perhaps inadequate to teach me to arrange violin bowings, I would wonder at such moments if I might have made some glaring mistake. One day the concertmaster of a good, though not outstanding, group of strings asked the usual question with the usual trail of unspoken criticism. An hour later two young players from a back desk stopped me and wanted to know who had made these marvelous bowings—ever so much better than their own and easier to play! I told them that it was the redoubtable concertmaster of the Boston Symphony. This incident merely underlined the extraordinary difficulty of getting any two violinists to agree on the best bowing for any phrase.

A second problem is the custom of turning material for bowing over to the concertmaster without his knowing the music or what the conductor may demand. I recall a case when I prepared the parts for an act from a Wagnerian opera to be given in a concert by an orchestra who had never played it before. Before having the leading string parts with my bowings photocopied, I wanted the concertmaster to go over my handiwork so that he might object or change this or that technicality. He made a few perfectly appropriate corrections on points where only the player can be judge of what his section does best. When he proposed more bow strokes in a number of spots, I asked if he had any notion of the tempo involved. He did not. How then could he possibly judge how much bow was advisable? Bowing is a very important part of interpretation and ideally cannot be delegated. Perhaps the best situation is one in which the conductor meets with the string player who "does" the job, showing and explaining what his tempos are and, particularly important, how much crescendo he desires in any doubtful place.

A fine example of the relationship between crescendo and bowing is in the third movement of Beethoven's *Pastoral* Symphony. I once conducted an orchestra that had marked the parts for a passage (bars 215–18) to be played by the strings with three bows, one up-bow for two bars and then one each down and up for the following bars. When I suggested playing the four bars in one up-bow, the concertmaster immediately protested that this would mean "less crescendo." What I wanted was precisely as much crescendo as the thirty-four violins and twelve violas would produce with a single bow stroke. I explained that in this instance we did not need any large convulsion, that forty-six players going from a *pp* to a single *f* did not need more than one bow at the tempo of the scherzo, and that even in the best string sections three bow changes would make the legato less perfect. With crescendos, as with tempos and other dynamics, the idea of *poco* tends to be discarded in favor of *molto*.

Marking parts for bowing should not be undertaken by anyone unfamiliar with the specific ideas of the musical director. In many instances it should not be left to a string player, unless he is an exceptionally versatile musician who comprehends all the problems. Once a violin virtuoso arrived at the first of two rehearsals for the Brahms Concerto with his own string parts, marked by himself. As he was (and still is) a truly admirable violinist, I expected, if not revelations, at least enlightenment on the best way to do that work. During the first rehearsal I noticed a certain unrest among the players caused by their acute discomfort with the bowings. To my surprise, the concertmaster of this very fine and flexible orchestra came to me at intermission time to ask if the players might use their own material. It was a delicate situation. As I expected, the great violinist was quite offended when I tried with diplomacy and tactful words to convince him that perhaps his own bowings were too adventurous for a choir of orchestral players.

Not only may an eminent virtuoso's bowing fail to be accepted by orchestral players, but nearly every type of approach can encounter objections. Once, in rehearsal for the second movement of the Second Symphony by Beethoven (example 62), a player right behind the concertmaster commented loudly on the bowings: "That type of thing is unplayable." After such a remark, it is best to set matters straight and explain how and why such a bowing not only is playable but is the best for the way the phrases lie. Bars 18, 20, and 22 are the spots where the down-bow is most appropriate; and bar 22 is the third and strongest repeat of the same pattern; thus to achieve the best phrasing and dynamic range, it seems most natural to play bars 17, 19, and 21 with an up-bow. This presupposes that the upbeats in bars 16, 18, and 20 must be played with a down-bow. The short down-bow is one of the least popular with string players, since it demands a bit of thinking and estimating how much (or how little) bow will be used if one is to reach the point of the bow when the upstroke must begin. The same page of this score is another example of the laws of inertia and how they work. Left to their own resources, few string players will look far enough ahead to arrive at the end of bar 6 at the point of the bow. There are two ways of accomplishing this. The simplest solution is to begin right away with an up-bow—which is also near anathema for routine string players. Why is this so? One cannot generalize, yet it seems to me that Leopold Mozart's *Violinschule* has been uncritically accepted as gospel. There are some other fairly common habits affecting string playing. Conductors who venture to suggest bowing changes may encounter resistance in even the finest orchestras.

In this pattern ♩♫ ♫, found frequently in the *Pastoral* Symphony, the sec-

Example 62. Beethoven, Sym. No. 2, 2nd mvt., mm. 1–23

ond of the two slurred notes is commonly shortened. One can hear some violin-ists mumbling that Leopold Mozart had decreed it thus—though this does not mean that his dicta must apply to Beethoven or any other composer who came after the time of Leopold Mozart. I do not wish to set down any more general rules, because most bowing questions depend for their answers on the overall concept of the conductor. It is crucial to be firmly convinced that there is no rule that demands that the last note before a short one be abbreviated under all cir-cumstances. Altogether I have found that in most orchestras, with very few exceptions, short phrases interrupted by rests are rarely played through for all they are worth. One of the simplest ways to test this is for a conductor to locate in the score those moments when the entire orchestra has a rest. Up to the rest there should be a constant sound from the ensemble. Since much classical scor-ing is in the pattern of "broken work" (one instrument or group of instruments alternating with others), this particular problem arises frequently.

How meticulous composers can be in this respect is illustrated by Claude Debussy's second Nocturne, "Fêtes." Example 63A shows the passage in ques-tion in the first edition. In the revised version (*version définitive rédigée par l'auteur*) (example 63B) the fourth note of each figure has been omitted in the violins. This makes perfect ensemble more difficult but produces greater conti-nuity. In the first version it is inevitable that the fourth note gets an involuntary accent. That accent acts like a comma or a semicolon, where uninterrupted con-tinuity is intended.

This is a standard example of the most difficult type of broken work. The conductor reading the score hardly guesses why this is so. For him the page has no problems, because he sees the connection. For the player there are only visible in his part so many notes without a "piste" to land on. To have such passages played properly, much rehearsing is needed, with constant admonition

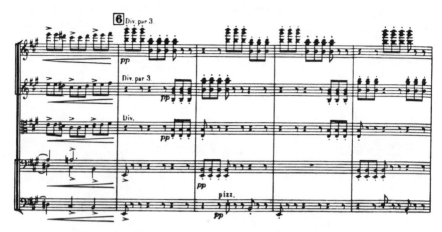

Example 63A. Debussy, "Fêtes," rehearsal no. 6 (first version)

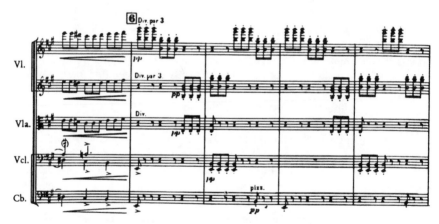

Example 63B. Debussy, "Fêtes," rehearsal no. 6 (revised version)

not to rush. The absence of a concluding note after each three- or four-note phrase somehow petrifies players. Fear of being still heard during a rest seems always keener than fear of leaving too much silence. Most of the time each phraselet will be played at first with a haste that leaves a noticeable gap between individual passages. Unless this widespread habit is not tolerated but promptly corrected, it will make a shambles of literally hundreds of passages that form one of the most characteristic elements of voice leading in classical chamber music and symphonic composition. As an example, one could reprint here almost any Beethoven symphony, particularly the slow movements of the Third and Fourth Symphonies.

This entire topic of short phrases, whether in leading voice or in accompaniment, is intimately related to the variety of staccato interpretation mentioned earlier. As in all matters of transforming the printed page into live music, the elements that affect this realization are many and not always controllable. Acoustics, size of string bodies, quality of players and of their instruments, and other such factors need to be considered, lest it all become an academic exercise. The first and crucial factor will always be the conductor's intimate relation with the work, without which the freedom to adjust and balance the diverse elements will be missing.

In this and other matters of string playing, it seems to me that in many orchestras the connection with chamber music has been lost. The sonority of any classical score is most definitely influenced by the middle voices of the string quintet, the second violins and violas. Accompaniments, no matter which instruments provide them, are the carpet on which the principal themes move. Decisions of playing on the string and/or off the string affect the end result radically. A wrong choice in this respect may change the character of a passage or even a whole section or movement.

There are two kinds of phrases, distinguishable only after careful study. In longer, more flowing themes, no accents should interrupt the flow. No matter how good a violin section's members, when eighteen or more players change their bows at the same point, some involuntary accent will be made. With an extended phrase beyond the possibilities of being played on one bow, it is better to stagger the bow changes so that they do not occur for more than a few players at the same time.

Leopold Stokowski preferred free bowing at all times, a method that begs the question, for there are innumerable instances where uniform bowing is preferable. Players of regular orchestras are not happy with free bowing, fearing that the public will consider the visual confusion a sign of insufficient preparation and poor musical discipline.

The whole issue becomes much simpler when the idea of breathing is introduced as a guide. Why should the chorale melody in the overture to *Tannhäuser* be punctuated by breathing? Why does one have three (and often four) trombones if they all stop together to catch breath? I am afraid that habit has accustomed the music listener to be served with melodies full of commas and dividing lines, which disrupt the melody by turning it into a sequence of a few notes. There are, of course, plenty of classical themes built on regular periods, where the punctuation justifies, even demands, the unanimous bow changes or breathing. The slow movement of the Second Symphony by Beethoven is built of symmetrical two-bar cells, which produce through the repeated rhythmic pattern the feeling of four times two bars. In contrast stands the theme of the slow movement from the composer's Fourth Symphony, where no two bars in the theme show any rhythmic resemblance. Here a staggered bowing should be preferred, for the uniform bow change on each first beat of the bar can tend to mar the freely floating melody. For the first three bars this will mercifully eliminate any involuntary accents, which, in a context with a highly rhythmic accompaniment, would be far too much "beat" in such a songful theme. The violas should also be considered for staggered bowing, since they are the lower voice of a rhythmic pattern nearly identical to that of the first violins.

One of the best examples of the advantage of staggered bowing I find in the third act of Wagner's *Tannhäuser*. There can be no doubt that the composer intended to produce, through seventeen bars, an expression of the weariness felt by the protagonist as he tells of his tiresome pilgrimage and its frustration. When on one occasion I asked that this passage be staggered to avoid punctuation, the musicians welcomed the suggestion, perhaps because we were in a covered orchestra pit invisible to the public, where no pedant could accuse the group of poor discipline.

It may be worthwhile to point out once again that printed orchestra parts are in most instances edited, and therefore the dull admonition "Play what's printed" rarely represents the composer's intentions. Most of the standard repertoire exists in the generally useful and widely available editions of Breitkopf and Härtel. At some point in its history, that venerable firm commissioned bowings for orchestra parts. If they are acceptable to a conductor (or a violinist), well and good; this is entirely a matter of taste and depends on many variables. But it is important that they not be considered composer's directives. Moreover, they may not be visible in all scores printed by the same publishing house.

Winds. Wind instruments need consideration and care as much as the strings, though their problems and requirements are of a different nature. It is not even enough distinction to speak of "winds" without going into subdivisions—double reeds, horns, trumpets, and so on—each of which has special characteristics. Their relative position in the orchestra has changed far more than that of the strings because so many startling improvements have been made in their mechanisms. If bowing is of the uppermost concern in relation to the sound of the strings and the whole interpretative concept, the wind and brass players need a conductor who is above all a breathing musician. It is not necessary that a conductor study the detailed intricacies of oboe or trombone, but he must have a close relation to singing. The human voice is a wind instrument, a fact recognized in our use of the term *short-winded* and other expressions connecting wind, breathing, and the human windpipe. Every orchestra conductor ought to sing enough, no matter how scratchy the voice, to know how to breathe between phrases and how to gauge tempos where the length of breath counts. From there it is a very small step to a proper appreciation of all instruments that are blown and how to treat them.

Wind players have often told me that few conductors understand their peculiar problems. Those maestros approved by the players turned out to have some exposure to singing, mostly through opera work. When this is part of a conductor's background and experience, the chances are excellent that all instruments blown, from piccolo to contrabass-tuba, will be more comfortable than if they are directed by a musician whose pulse beats for and with a keyboard or a violin. The crucial differences between strings and winds are response and phrasing. If bowing is an issue of prime importance for the strings, balances and articulation are the problems facing the wind choir.

Preparing scores for performance, the conductor will discover the differences between a wind choir of 1810 and 1910 to be so great that any resemblance is almost coincidental. It is perhaps a good start to deal briefly with the question of doubled woodwinds in classical symphonies. As with many musical questions, this one is partly legitimate, partly a matter of fashion and of following established patterns. To let four clarinets and oboes blow away in London's Royal Festival Hall is absurd, for its acoustics favor all winds to excess. What a judicious doubling can produce is improved clarity of themes in the weaker ranges of woodwinds. Some of these instruments have lost—others have gained—ease or prominence in certain parts of their range, and slight changes can often help to recreate the balances originally demanded. Perhaps the most important purpose of doubling players is to relieve the solo player of strain during loud tutti passages. These are tiring and may produce fatigue of lip and lung. These then may falter when an important solo passage must be played. Many times I have noticed in the lighter Beethoven symphonies (which are rarely doubled) that a woodwind principal simply stopped playing for a few bars of a tutti passage to rest for the next exposed portion of his part. At such times the extra wind player would be needed. A principal wind player with the stamina to go through an entire symphonic program alone is no longer common. Sometimes the demand for an alternate is an act of self-aggrandizement, but often it is genuine inability to sustain an eighty-minute program without help.

The dynamics of brass instruments must be adjusted, especially on long-held notes. A long note is stronger than any moving voice. It is a strange sensation to listen to music from a radio turned on lightly and placed twenty to thirty feet away. Ever so often one hears most clearly the unimportant accompaniment, the held notes of wind and brass, even the repeated notes of middle strings, while the melody is wiped out by distance and imperfect balance. Here the experience of the conductor is most crucial. The novice assumes that what is heard by the conductor on the podium is what the public hears. This is rarely the case. In many recently built halls the winds have an overwhelming advantage, and often the style and lack of force of string players puts the strings to further disadvantage. Thus, a conductor should begin weighing carefully where the long notes of the brass or woodwinds need to be toned down. Richard Strauss once observed, "Don't ever look encouragingly at the brasses."

A more complex symptom of changes in scoring over seventy or one hundred years stems from the development of brass instruments and from new techniques, such as those demanded in the works of Mahler, Schönberg, Stravinsky,

Bartók, and others. These have not yet been acquired by many orchestras, especially in Central Europe. A conductor who programs *Petrouchka* or Mahler's Fifth Symphony had better be a teacher of brass instruments or he will rue the day when he threw caution to the wind and selected such works. It should be known that the English-speaking countries have modern brass players in far greater supply than European orchestras. France has outstanding instrumentalists but rarely enough of them together to make a first-rate ensemble. Altogether there is a critical situation in most orchestras below top rank whenever instruments are required that were brought into use after approximately 1850. It has become a common experience to find the oldest and worst member of a flute section playing piccolo, with dreadful results in intonation and ensemble. The solo passages in *The Fire Bird* (the 1910 version) demand the highest skill and control, as do works by Shostakovich, who loved to give important parts to the piccolo. I was told in Vienna that musicians interested in playing bass clarinet must await engagement by an orchestra to get real experience with the instrument, for no young player owns one. What would King Marke say? Mozart's *Requiem* or *Die Zauberflöte* are often marred by terrible playing of basset horns. Here the London musical scene is the best. They have for each of the rarely used instruments a few specialists who turn up in every group as extras when works are programmed demanding Wagner tubas or basset horns or cimbaloms or other exotica.

The preparation of wind parts is far less time-consuming than preparing the bowing for strings, but an acquaintance with technique is desirable for those times when a conductor finds players who cannot manage the demands of the score. (This applies even more to the percussion department, which has been upgraded in importance by contemporary composers beyond anything dreamed of before 1900.) These few facts should explain why a goodly number of talented youngsters can score high with first-rate orchestras and not do so well when they appear with second-ranking ensembles. In such groups the task of bringing piccolo, bass clarinet, double bassoon, Wagner tubas, or bass trumpet up to a bearable level of competence demands resources of ingenuity not required when conducting the finest groups. For the generation of American and English conductors whose strength lies with the composers from the end of the nineteenth century on, it is not easy to make much musical impact on the European continent, where most orchestras have great troubles with that type of repertoire. Since this situation was the same fifty years ago, when I was a student in Austria, it would require the wildest optimism to expect an early improvement.

Editing. There is one place on the first page of the Brahms Second Symphony where only a churlish crank would refuse to add a note that Brahms did not write. As a convinced conservative and classicist, the composer left open a quarter where the note D-sharp in the basses would be in place. He evidently never considered a scordatura of the E string and avoided writing a note that did not exist on the regular double bass. In his work for orchestra we find numerous places where the double basses jump to the upper octave because they did not have the notes below the E.

No matter how persuasive one person may find the argument for substituting in those places the lower octave possible on the modern double bass, there will always be some who speak darkly of violation or introducing an alien, un-Brahmsian sound, and of other heinous crimes. I place myself cheerfully on the revisionist side, yet I find every day that there is no single case, no matter how logical or likely it looks to me, where some other person will not disagree. Therefore it must be stated in all fairness that the D-sharp in the Second Symphony of Brahms is the one and only example of editing, or updating, where I expect consensus.

Nevertheless I believe firmly that most composers would have added or altered in spots had not the limitations of their time made certain things impossible or at least inadvisable. Another example of a situation to be found hundreds of times is in bar 300 of the first movement of the Fourth Symphony by Brahms. The second trumpet, in its natural state before valves were added, could not play the (written) D below the staff, therefore the horn and trumpet parts of the classics are full of exactly the type of jump one finds here. I substitute the lower D wherever this switch appears. I had always assumed that the 8va sign here was as noncontroversial as the D-sharp in the Brahms Second until March 1978, when a learned horn player who played second in a good orchestra disagreed with my view. Clearly neither this question nor any comparable one is beyond debate, so I will confine myself to recommending changes that seem obvious or logical or compelling to me.

We may take as a random example the overture to *Coriolan*, Opus 62, by Beethoven and look for the places where the composer was frustrated by technical limitations of the instruments of his day.

1. In bar 19 the first flute could play the high A-flat, which evidently was a little high in Beethoven's day, especially in a piano attack.
2. In bar 26 the flute should do the same on G-flat.
3. In bar 42 (and 43) the idea of the harmonic progression would demand that the horns and trumpets play a (concert pitch) D. In bars 40 and 41 one can see how the composer distributed the notes of the diminished seventh chord, which should be exactly the same one half tone lower in 42–43. Lacking the notes on the brass instruments, the composer lets the second violins help out with the D.
4. In 62 one can see the problem of the second horn.
5. In 63 the basses should take the low C.
6. In 71 the basses should take the low D.
7. Second trumpet in 101, 103, 105, 113, etc. should play the lower D.
8. A grave question is whether in 188–89 the cello and basses should be led for the two notes D and C-sharp to the lower 8va. This would correspond to

the cello part in 196–97, where the basses also can be adjusted to go to the two lower notes.

9. The second trumpet in 276 should play the lower D.

There are numerous other places where Beethoven avoided assigning passages to instruments where a problem of fingering may then have existed. The technical problems have long since been solved.

This short list of a few fairly obvious points is given to show how much or how little can be done in editing important scores. There will never be agreement on this, either in principle or in detail. I can only declare my own ideas, which in general support updating. Perhaps ever deeper involvement in the music makes me sense what frustration these limitations must have caused composers. Especially in works where great dynamic and dramatic intensity is of the essence, it becomes quite compelling to me to add the notes now available to complete an incomplete phrase. In the adagio of Beethoven's Third Symphony, for example, I can think of no argument for *not* leading the third horn in bar 139 up to the (concert pitch) C in unison with the clarinets. I find it punishing to Beethoven if one sticks to the letter here. How can the violas replace the great horn sound just when the music modulates back to C minor?

Immediately after this point, in bar 142, one can see where the composer might have demanded the high A-flat of the bassoon. It would have been natural to have the two clarinets in unison with the two oboes and the two bassoons an octave below. Believing that the A-flat would not be manageable on the bassoon, Beethoven needed nonetheless to have the whole passage in octaves. Therefore he called the second clarinet to the rescue for the A-flat. Since the clarinets could no longer help the oboes all the way, Beethoven divided them as best he could under the circumstances.

Here then are some examples of editing and updating questions for the wind instruments. The danger of going too far is ever present. To do nothing is stodgily safe, a symptom of fear of criticism, an avoidance of the issue by hiding behind "We play only what's printed" or perhaps "We dare play only what Wagner before us retouched" (an attitude that in fact leads to questionable editing in Beethoven's Ninth). The proper criterion is that editing should remain within the boundaries of the original sound. To give an almost ludicrous example of what not to do, I again cite the difficulty that oboes of Beethoven's day had in handling the key of E major. If anyone were mad enough to add two oboes in the slow movement of Beethoven's Third Piano Concerto, the change of sound would be quite indefensible by any standard.

The very fact that the great masters concerned themselves with the technical limitations of their orchestras strengthens my own conviction that they would have welcomed complete phrases with no notes left out as unavailable or too risky. Toscanini did a great deal of editing. To my way of thinking this does not invalidate his claim of being concerned only with serving and interpreting the composer. Yet the belief that he followed punctiliously the letter of the score is quite mistaken. Indeed, his retouching went beyond notes not practical in 1810, for he made extensive corrections even in Debussy's *La Mer*.[5] He also changed the first note in the presto section of *Leonora No. 3* from C to D, arguing his view with heat and spirit.

Toscanini was also more liberal and pragmatic with transpositions in opera than anyone else in my experience. It has not been recorded that in *Fidelio* performances at the Salzburg Festival he invented a new modulation. The great Lotte Lehmann was incomparably moving and well cast as Leonora/Fidelio, but she had difficulties with the high notes of the aria. When the second run in 1936 came along, Toscanini wanted to relieve Lehmann's anxieties and transposed the entire piece one halftone lower. Everybody felt that although this was a most generous act to bring out the best in a great artist, the recitative preceding the adagio portion of the aria had suffered in the transposition. They particularly pointed to the phrase "So leuchtet mir ein Farbenbogen," which had its own color in C major, whereas in B major an exotic and alien element entered. In the third year Toscanini tried to combine the original key of the recitative with a transposed aria and "invented" this new transition: C major ("der blickt so hell, so freundlich"), C minor ("nieder, der spiegelt alte Zeiten"), 6/5 chord over A ("weider"), seventh over B-flat, 6/4 over B-flat ("und neu—"), arriving at the half-tone lower key of E-flat. Forty years later I can still see the raised eyebrows of the Vienna Orchestra and the cognoscenti who heard the new modulation.

There is no need to debate this specific change. My only purpose is to show the possible range of editing that may be done for a variety of reasons. Mahler's constant changing of orchestral detail, in order to bring out essentials more prominently, is one case of a composer-conductor who kept on editing his own work in order to improve it. He also updated the symphonies of Robert Schumann, which in the view of most conductors, including myself, need some such revisions. Other conductors of no small reputation insist on sticking to the original scoring. I can only surmise that the defenders of Schumann's original scoring are content with a muddy texture. Purists continue to regale us with pious admonitions, demanding the strictest adherence to the originals. Yet, in the interest of realizing the composer's intentions, every experienced conductor makes changes. My own preference is for adopting the extremely valuable rescorings of Mahler, but *without* the changes he made in the compositions per se. For example, Mahler omitted a bar in the coda of the last movement of Schumann's Second Symphony (which I restore), and he changed the notes in the opening fanfare of the First Symphony. Such changes are outside the limits of needed improvement and represent needless tampering.

5. They can be found in a score and in the orchestral parts owned by the New York Philharmonic Society. Since Debussy himself—no mean orchestrator—is known to have revised his scoring, Toscanini's improvements can be regarded as merely one more in a series of unnoticed revisions.

Perhaps the most widely publicized example of controversy over a brilliant but imperfect work of genius concerns the fate of Moussorgsky's *Boris Godunov*. When Shostakovich rescored this opera, the protests could be heard around the world of musicological purism, just as they could when Mahler set out to improve Schumann's orchestrations. *Boris* first became widely known in the version by Rimsky-Korsakov, who was famous as an orchestrator. But when Moussorgsky's original composition appeared in print years later, musicians everywhere condemned Rimsky's changes of harmony, rhythm, and essential ideas of the composition. They clamored for performances of the undiluted original. In their justified enthusiasm for the more starkly daring work of Moussorgsky himself, one fact was overlooked: the composer's setting for orchestra showed severe limitations in workmanship.

In recent years the Metropolitan Opera in New York has twice spent great effort and sums of money for editing and copying in the hope of salvaging an acceptable original *Boris*. Neither attempt has achieved that objective. In the 1950s the composer Karol Rathaus was commissioned to make Moussorgsky's orchestration work, but he was unsuccessful. The most recent new production was once again announced as the "original version," with the assurance that no strange hands had been allowed to interfere with the ideas of Moussorgsky himself. What happened is best described in the words of Schuyler Chapin, then the Met's general manager.

> We were committed to using the second Lamm edition of the score, which was really the 1872 version of the opera as revised by the composer himself. This decision had been made by Kubelik in our early pre-planning and I saw no reason to change it. The Rimsky-Korsakov and Shostakovich versions seemed to assume that the composer did not know what he wanted from an orchestral standpoint. Lamm, the musicologist, and other experts felt that Moussorgsky knew very well what he wanted and was, to a large extent, ahead of his time. The only problems presented by this version had to do with the actual sound as it would reflect in a theater as large as the Metropolitan. Too sparse and skimpy an orchestration would sound just that way and Schippers felt that we had to modify the score or beef it up in a way that would give the composer's sound to the audience sitting anywhere in the vast auditorium. The trouble was that he kept changing his mind on details and at every rehearsal he would make new changes and every night the librarians would be piling up overtime with modifications that had to be in all the orchestral parts by the next morning. This meant that every orchestra-stage rehearsal was a stop-and-start affair and progress was very slow.[6]

Any competent musician knows that no conductor worth his salt will refrain from correcting the orchestration of Moussorgsky's *Boris*; the only question is how far he should go. For this production Thomas Schippers did what any nor-

6. Schuyler G. Chapin, *Musical Chairs: A Life in the Arts* (New York: G. Putnam's Sons, 1977), p. 401.

mal, nondoctrinaire colleague would have done: he tried to make the score "sound." The irony in this story is that Mr. Chapin appears to imagine that an original version of *Boris* was performed.

This is, however, merely a part of a larger irony. The original *Boris*, like the symphonies of Schumann, requires—and invariably receives—editing in order to achieve a satisfactory performance that does justice to the composer's genius. Yet the Shostakovich "version," which outraged purists, presents the essential composition unaltered in a brilliant and idiomatic orchestral dress. (I found exactly one minute change in the voice leading of a choral piece.) The explanation of this absurdity is that the most puritanical musicians will accept any amount of doctoring or rescoring as long as it is not announced and credited as a revision. One can only assume that they cannot follow a score well enough to know the difference. The situation reminds me of recent scandals over the false labeling of French wines. To the average nonconnoisseur, the label *is* the wine. On the more highly trained palate it is the taste that evokes the response.

We are heirs to much editing by many generations of conductors. (Weingartner cites a note change made by Bülow in the trio of Beethoven's Ninth Symphony that alters the entire progress of a modulation.) The dividing line between improving a composition, to the advantage of the composer, and distorting it is both elastic and very thin. It is not a boundary that can be surveyed as if one were dealing in real estate. Flexibility, good taste, and above all reverence for a master are of the essence. The admonition "Play what's printed" will never suffice. Even without the emendations of conductors, there are considerable differences between printed scores. No firm rules can be laid down. Perhaps the most useful advice would be an example: every sensible conductor will add the low D-sharp to the double basses in the opening phrases of the Brahms Second Symphony; none will replace flutes with oboes in the second movement of Beethoven's Third Piano Concerto. Between these extremes lies a vast field for the exercise of thoughtful consideration.

Dynamics

A conductor may adjust balances between brass and strings admirably and yet fail to establish a gradation of dynamic levels as a whole. We have no sure criteria but our good taste, knowledge, and imagination to set levels. Perhaps it is because of the ubiquitous noise in our modern civilization that music too seems to get louder under all but the most stubborn musicians. Not only are the decibels higher than they should be, considering the total range of a work, but the real *pp* misterioso is very hard to obtain from most orchestras. In setting dynamics it is good to remember that in nearly every great score there is one climax that should remain the high point. The sign *ff* is, like the staccato dot, a many-faceted one. So is every other dynamic mark. Because overtones are differently activated, every instrument has a different intensity. Hence a *p* in front of a low C on an oboe is a different piano from that played on a muted violin.

What more urgently needs discussion is the relative loudness demanded by different scores. Here we face the basic question, raised in the earlier chapters, of the aim of a musical performance. If it is to recreate as far as possible the sound and spirit of the first performance, then the dynamic level of Beethoven's Seventh Symphony must not be confused with that of the large scores of Wagner or Strauss. I do not suggest any conscious attempt to shrink sound to fit a predetermined frame. I merely insist that overindulgence in the sonorities of trumpets, kettledrums, and horns or doubling the winds will only make more noise without increasing the impact of the music. The optimum effect is created by a well-considered scale of dynamics. Achieving it requires a firm resolve that nothing before bar 427 of the finale in Beethoven's Seventh Symphony shall reach the triple-forte level. There are many *ff* spots in the preceding forty minutes of play, and every one of them is a bit different. The scoring is different, the emphasis is different, and the impact should be different.

Perhaps the most decisive nuance in this whole reckoning will be the single *f*, which is, alas, often overdriven. The handiest example of this common sin is the opening of the First Symphony by Brahms. Rare are the conductors who have the restraint to wait for the second phrase (bar 25) to reach the *ff* level. It is easy and seductive to let the throttle out right away, with the C of the kettledrum rousing the audience to a fever pitch of excitement by the time bar 25 is reached. But what then? What is the meaning of forte and fortissimo? That the impact of the phrase in G, a fifth higher (not a fourth lower), should be greater.

A few problems result from the nature of the instruments as the composer used them. The principal difficulty is Brahms's strict adherence to natural horns. The E-flat horns have some of the notes for the first passage, but in the second, both pairs can only hold single notes. As a result, if natural balances are left unedited, the first passage comes through more powerfully than the second. The other grave disadvantage is that the roll of the kettledrum in the second passage, though it may be louder than the repeated notes of the first, cannot match them for grandeur and power. In the second strain the roll actually blots out the single notes of double basses and double bassoon, further jeopardizing the desired increase in tension and power. Yet it is obvious by merely glancing at violins and trumpets that such an increase was the composer's intention.

More difficult and more often ignored are consecutive dynamic markings that retreat in strength, especially a forte following a fortissimo. In both of the first two Beethoven symphonies there are such places, each time to take a new start at building toward a high point. In the finale of the First Symphony the one bar of slight dynamic relaxation will make the following thrusts and holds twice as powerful and effective, while in the coda of the Second Symphony the theme marked with a single *f* will proclaim it in dignity after the boisterous tumble of the preceding bars. Earlier in that same movement we find a simple *f* forming a dynamic bridge from a *ff* to a *p* phrase, or, to put it differently, four chords that are more casual in expression than the wild goings-on immediately before.

One of the most beautiful examples can be found in the Brahms *Requiem*. The sixth movement closes with a powerful fugato, yet the composer ends it—after many *ff* passages and climaxes—on the level of a single *f*. Once, after a performance, I was asked by a critic how I "defended" myself, since I was the first in his experience to observe that pull-back in dynamics. My pleasure is always acute when the finer points of a musical concept are noticed, the sense behind that simple *f* being quite special. The fugue in C is not the end of the work. To try to "bring down the house" with it would somewhat mar the profound and moving opening of the last movement. There should not be any wait between these movements, yet if the cadence of the sixth part shakes the rafters, one must have a hiatus that would be detrimental to the inner fervor of the phrase that starts the last section. Somewhat similar ideas should govern the ending of the first movement of Beethoven's Third Symphony, where the two final chords should match those that open the symphony.

All reductions or increases of orchestral forces, smaller strings or doubled woodwinds, aim to establish balanced dynamics. One very fine and thoughtful conductor used to perform the First Symphony of Beethoven with a full string complement—which I too have tried at times—plus doubled woodwinds—which I have never tried. This was done, one may presume, to make something "grander" of this work. I cannot tell from secondhand reports what this did to the work's spirit of buoyancy, but I do know that I tried the full complement of lower strings only in the first of four repeats, having noticed that the rapid passages in the first and last movements became muddy when eight basses and eleven cellos played them. There is also a question whether triple stops in the strings are best served by being played divisi. This, once again, depends on the total concept. If one likes chords to be short and hard, they should be played divisi; if one wishes them to sound somewhat broader, even broken, then each player should take all the notes.

How relative the scale and effect of dynamics can be is best illustrated by a comparison between the piano and harpsichord when the same piece is played on both instruments. If equally fine performers were to play Bach's *Italian* Concerto, the piano would be the stronger of the two instruments, particularly if heard in a sizable concert hall. If, on the other hand, our phonograph reproduces the same performances, the harpsichord will have the grander and more majestic sound. Such a comparison dramatically illustrates the relativity of loud and grand. Nothing can be louder than certain types of popular music, yet there is neither power nor grandeur in it. Decibels are a physical quantity that must be adapted to the sense, spirit, and meaning of the music at hand.

Our generation is intent on correcting the nineteenth-century concept that increased the physical strength of Bach's music by enlarging choirs and doubling or quadrupling instruments in an effort to do justice to the inner greatness of the music. There are still too many unregenerate believers in the blown-up Bach, particularly among amateur choral societies. Most professionals understand that Bach must be performed with limited numbers lest the clarity of his polyphonic writing be lost. The time is ripe to apply this lesson to other eras of composition. A concern for relative dynamics should aim for a means to intensify a performance to the utmost without breaking the frame. If we take thirty-four violins to play Mozart's Symphony in G Minor, K. 550, it will constantly be necessary to allow the seven woodwinds to come across a thick curtain of strings or else to double these seven winds—which leads to new complications. There will be a loss of clarity even in the best sections when the fast passages in the first and last movements occur. When we decide on a small string section, it is not to scale down the work into a quaint antique but, on the contrary, to allow every outburst to be delivered without restraint, without having to reconsider balances, and without loss of clarity in fast passages. The Symphony K. 425 calls for two trumpets and kettledrums. This might allow for a larger string complement, notwithstanding the fact that K. 425 is a work of light and humorous spirit, while K. 550 is intensely dramatic and violent. Yet there are passages where themes in woodwinds can be distinctly heard only if the strings are cut down drastically. Assuming a situation in which any wish for ideal musical excellence could be fulfilled, it would be splendid to use doubled winds for a few chosen bars, but few players would be content to perform the menial chore of sitting for a half hour to play a handful of notes.

An important aspect of orchestral balance lies in the seating arrangement. Here a basic compromise is necessary. It would be musically ideal for each type of scoring to have an appropriate seating arrangement. There is no doubt that the Seventh Symphony by Beethoven ought to have the old-fashioned antiphonal arrangement, with the second violins playing from the right of the conductor. This seating, by now largely obsolete, is quite wrong for scores such as Debussy's, with violins in six or eight parts. They must sit on the same side of the stage. Since the disadvantages of having that type of seating in Beethoven are fewer than if Debussy were played with the antiphonal arrangement, the prevailing custom is to have all violins together. Many younger music directors, more at home with the moderns than with the classics, have regrouped their brass sections with the trumpets on the opposite side of the stage from the kettledrums. This is quite impossible for any scoring up to and including Brahms. When I find this arrangement, I go beyond the privileges of a guest conductor and insist on reseating the trumpets and timpani side by side for all works with the classical orchestral fabric. In twentieth-century music, much can be said for the other seating, for around the timpanist are lined up large percussion sections and the trumpets are part of a vast brass choir. But in Mozart, Haydn, Beethoven, Schubert, Schumann, and Brahms, trumpets and timpani appear together and disappear together. In the slow movements of such works by Mozart as K.

504 and K. 543 and in Beethoven's Second Symphony, they are silent. In Brahms's Second Piano Concerto, Opus 83, they cease to play after the second movement. Thus, questions of seating cannot be solved permanently. There should be only a minimum of change. It is preferable to have musicians regularly hear the same people in their vicinity, and from a more mundane viewpoint, it does not look very good to move chairs and music stands between the works of a concert.

These variables of external and internal dynamics must be considered every time a classic work is restudied and prepared for performance. Within each work, one of the first objectives should be to locate the climax—or the several climaxes—in order to make appropriate gradations of subtlety and diversity. To close with a specific example from a supreme masterpiece, we find in the third *Leonora* Overture by Beethoven the archetype of a one-climax work. Every forte and fortissimo throughout the long piece is to be weighed against this summit (29 bars before the end).

Determining the numbers of strings in early music is the first decision of interpretation. If I play the *Third Brandenburg* with full strings (as Karajan does), I set up a concept quite different from a version with three players to a part. Sound is such an integral part of interpretation that it has become doubly important to scale down string complements for earlier works. This is not merely a matter of respect for historic precedent. (Even in Mozart's day there are variable string complements. It is known that Kapellmeister Bono played one of the symphonies, presumably No. 34 in C, with forty violins.) Balance within a program ought to be a sufficient criterion. It would be a bad choice to play the First Symphony of Beethoven with the same number of strings that are used later on the program for Brahms's Second Symphony or Bartók's Concerto for Orchestra, with their much heavier complements of wind, brass, and percussion. Within the pre-1800 repertoire it also matters whether a work calls for trumpets and timpani or only for two oboes and two horns in addition to the strings. Since the post-Wagnerian era has left us such mammoth pieces as Schönberg's *Gurrelieder*, Strauss's *Alpensinfonie*, and most Mahler symphonies, conductors have sufficient repertoire to allow constant indulgence in the "big sound," which can be so woefully wrong in earlier music.

Another kind of balancing problem arises from conventions of classical scoring and is sometimes apparent even in the early twentieth century. Composers often wrote one dynamic mark for the entire vertical scoring involved. Rare are the instances of graded dynamics in scores prior to 1850. They expected the performers to adjust their instruments' relative strength according to the primary or secondary importance of their roles.

To appreciate fully how composers' holographs looked, it is helpful to peruse some of the old oblong scores. A glance will tell more than a page can describe, how in some haste a composer hurriedly marked one *f* or *p* for the entire vertical sound, never stopping to consider individual gradation of strength. This is understandable: balances are so obvious most of the time that no composer writing in the classical manner dreamed of taking time for such minute and self-evident detail. Today we still have a few orchestras in which basic balance problems are adjusted fairly automatically on the simple assumption that held or repeated notes are subordinate accompaniments that should never intrude on the clear definition of the leading voices.

There are passages in nearly all classical symphonies where violins and high woodwinds lead, while the others hold or repeat the same notes. If the players play what is printed, not much of the theme will be audible. A sustained *ff* of brasses, a kettledrum roll, and the rest of the players observing the letter of the law relegates the lead passage to a pantomime.

While it is relatively simple to adjust such passages to satisfactory levels of balance, the immensely powerful entrance of the recapitulation in the first movement of the Ninth needs more sophisticated adjustments. I leave all decisions on how to make these adjustments to the performer faced by the problem. There is a need to edit this passage, however, as the general effect of the reprise will otherwise be a mere blur of sound without clearly profiled themes. To single out one vexing point: in bars 304 and 308 the trumpets, perennial companions of the kettledrums, play an A when the timpanist does, while in 310 they remain on the D. The flutes play the same note as the drums, so why not the trumpets? From 315 on the clarity of the thematic outline is severely jeopardized by the trumpets, who continue with their tonic and dominant while first the strings and then the winds try to set forth the main subject.

There is one fundamental physical law that bears repetition, since so many musicians are unaware of it: a sustained note is always stronger than a moving voice. How this simple physical law has played havoc at times is best illustrated in the scores of Gustav Mahler. I do not believe that anyone can ever establish quite what Mahler's original conception of balance was: a great performer and conductor, he made changes every time one of his scores was in rehearsal. Hearing the problems of each orchestra was enough for the conductor Mahler to make the practical adjustments in parts and score. Consequently, we cannot be certain which markings were ad hoc editings and which were due to some miscalculation in writing the orchestration. It is easy to imagine that an orchestra in Kassel, where one of Mahler's symphonies was first played, needed a lot more adjustments in instrumentation than did an orchestra in Berlin. In various privately owned Mahler scores, there are such contradictory retouchings, all from the composer's hand, that no other explanation seems satisfactory. A passage for bassoon may be for one solo player in one copy and be marked *à 4* in another. What could account for such diversity except a very weak principal bassoonist in one town and a very strong one in another?

There is so much to be decided by the conductor who cares for a balanced performance that no amount of detail can possibly cover the permutations presented by such considerations as: types of instruments (and players), size and acoustics of the hall, seating arrangements, types of scoring, and, finally, whether a performance is intended for a live audience or, via microphone, for transcription. Yet for all conditions the basic law remains that the long note is louder than the short. The sustained accompaniment is most frequently the cause of covering solo voices or solo instruments. While one hears more about these balance problems in opera, where the frail human voice can easily be swamped by seventy or more instruments, the technical reason is invariably the same: insufficient discretion from the players of sustained sounds.

There are two methods of scoring: the composer writes the end result, and we interpret in a way best suited to obtaining these intended effects; or the composer leaves not a *t* crossing nor an *i* dotting to the performer but dictates the performance of the smallest detail. The most extreme representative of the second school was Arnold Schönberg, who went so far as to prescribe the fingerings for harmonics. Many string players, including partisans of the master, assured me that not many of these prescriptions were obeyed, for easier and safer harmonics could be produced with different fingerings. The second group of composers has created special problems for the performer by being meticulous about details of execution without considering that different halls or musical organizations have different acoustics, different equipment, different characteristic sonorities. Therefore, the same specifications can achieve quite different results. It is as if a composer-pianist insisted that his own fingerings must be adopted by other pianists, no matter whether their hands respond well to them or not. It is fair, though seemingly paradoxical, to conclude that those composers who give only general markings indicating the desired effects will get better results than those who prefer to figure out the last and smallest detail of practical application. Dynamic balance is subject to wide variation caused by differing conditions.

Notwithstanding my refusal to give specific advice on how to adjust balances, I should mention the essays by Felix von Weingartner on these problems, especially in reference to classical symphonies. Reading through these suggestions will give the less-experienced conductor a general idea what a master conductor wrote in the score and parts to clear up textures. I do not recommend wholesale acceptance or rejection, but merely getting to know how modest editing may produce desired results. In the post-Wagnerian era it has become a custom to double the woodwinds in the symphonies of Brahms, Tchaikovsky, and, often, Beethoven. This has merit at times, depending on acoustical conditions. In halls built during the second half of the twentieth century, the strings are often at a disadvantage compared with the wind and brass. In such places, consistent doubling is counterproductive. There is no resemblance between the old halls, such as the Musikvereinssaal in Vienna, and newer ones, such as the Royal Festival Hall in London.

These varied necessities make it important to have thorough knowledge of performance practices in various countries and in past eras in order to read the composer as he intended to be read. The scores we have as authentic texts often contain not only a composer's directives but also his counterdirectives, added in the hope of compensating for bad habits in the ensembles of the composer's experience. In a rehearsal for *Otello* with the NBC Symphony Orchestra, Toscanini demanded a full-bodied piano from the strings in a passage marked *ppp* by Verdi. The principal cellist asked the maestro about this unexpected request, since Toscanini, who had worked under Verdi, was known to respect the composer with a reverence even more fervent than that he showed to other composers. He explained that the Italian orchestras for whom Verdi scored his works played everything in an unvarying mezzo forte, which forced the composer to write extremes for forte and piano in order to obtain nuances of any kind. It was a case of writing against ingrained habit.

Another example of regional practices is the frequent doubling of horns in twentieth-century Russian scores, particularly by Prokofiev and Shostakovich. The six horns in *Romeo and Juliet* in a Russian orchestra cannot yet equal four in an English or American orchestra. This will be understandable to anyone who has heard Russian orchestras and is aware of the weak sound coming from the French horn, which is overbalanced by the Russian bassoons. Another less easily pinpointed problem is the plethora of accented notes for the strings in scores by Tchaikovsky and Dvořák. These composers never knew exactly how many strings there would be. To ensure vigorous phrasing and emphatic articulation from the players, they sprinkled their pages liberally with little roofs, marcato signs, and sforzatos. If these directions were strictly observed by a large body of strings, the resulting quality of tone would only be ugly.

The famous orchestra of the Grand Duke of Meiningen, conducted by Bülow, consisted of forty-nine players. Since they performed Liszt and Wagner, music requiring a fair amount of woodwind and brass, it is easy arithmetic to figure out how many string instrument players the orchestra could have mustered. There is even an emphatic letter from Bülow to the young Richard Strauss, who was slated to be his successor, advising him to refuse the appointment "should the grand duke make good his threat to reduce the number of musicians from 49 to 35." Today, with as many as eighteen first violins and often a string body totaling sixty-eight, it is difficult for us to reconstruct what the sonic problems of balance and volume must have been.

Accents are not the only markings that strike one as "defensive" directives. I have already spoken of the overwhelmingly numerous staccato dots in Beethoven's orchestral scores. I am quite certain that the low caliber of instrumental performance in his time led the composer to many exhortations to "articulate, articulate, and articulate." This is something essentially different from our unimaginative interpretation of the term *staccato*. The conductor must be alert to the fact that a composer's directions for dynamics, phrasing, and other technicalities of execution may just as often be ad hoc warnings of what *not* to do as signals what to do. To distinguish between warnings and creative invention is synonymous with good reading.

On Recordings

Conductors who make recordings will discover that my caveat to professional musicians not to rely on the study of records and tapes has several bases. The reason that I mentioned at the outset remains the most important: if one studies a piece of music with someone else's performance, one meets the composer only through an intermediary. This stands in the way of a direct response to the music through the conductor's own knowledge and imagination. But there is another problem: reliance on recorded interpretation arrests the normal change and progression of the student's response. A professional musician and performer of talent and sensitivity represents his generation and the world of his era. I have shown how the ideas about Bach have varied through time. Eminent musicians born before the end of the last century could never catch up with certain changes of style and manner. My own recollection of performances by the heroes of my younger days is often totally wrong. Many times, to my surprise and vexation, I have switched on a radio program playing an unidentified recording and made egregious mistakes in guessing the conductor. These mistakes have resulted from gradual and unnoticed changes in my ideas of what a Toscanini Brahms or a Walter Mozart was like. The metamorphosis was, of course, in myself, not in the musical performance. The changing nature of this response demonstrates that a performer must mold his own direct, personal relation with the composers out of his own world view, his own temperament, and his own reading.

Listening to records is not the same as reading music, for music making, like reciting verse or prose, involves a variable translating of symbols. Thus, a constant recourse to models imposes severe limitations on a musician's individual development.

Other factors make even the best recording a questionable authority. Sound is the stock-in-trade of the record industry. Without constant development of new techniques and improvement of sound reproduction, the industry would have yielded entirely to jazz and rock 'n roll, for the nineteenth recorded version of the complete works of Beethoven or some other composer can be sold only by reference to ever-improved sonic factors. All this is perfectly legitimate in trade and in serving the public; it creates discussion and new interest. However, it has nothing to do with producing a more authentic reproduction of a composer's work. In the field of painting we are aware that fading colors can be skillfully restored, yet the finest restoration cannot ever equal the original. We can easily imagine that a spectator finds the restored colors of great painting A more likable than the original ones of the same painter's canvas B. It is more than likely that a splendidly engineered recording of a well-performed classical masterpiece may seem to many a listener perfection beyond Beethoven's wildest dreams. Yet it is not a way to know the ideas of the composer on the sound he originally conceived. It cannot be stressed often enough that every generation needs to find its way back to the past in order to perceive the great works of great minds in their pristine form. That form partakes of the nature of the work—and also of the seeker.

Recorded sound, like the picture on a postcard, has undergone several modifications. It is an accepted fact of musical life that recording artists are very much in the hands of the mixer and the splicer. It is well known among practicing professionals that the sound of a recorded performance need not be the sound the conductor has elicited from his orchestra. Thus, those who believe in learning from recorded performances may be doubly deluded. Aside from practical reservations, the idea of what constitutes "good" sound changes constantly, not unlike fashions. In 1962 the top executive of a leading American record company, with only an average amateur's musical perception, personally instructed a group of his company's engineers and producers on "what kind of sound their product should strive for." His ideas were dictated by purely commercial considerations. He assumed that as most playing equipment was mediocre, no extremes of dynamics were needed on the company's records. The main effort should be to tone down the loud and bring up the soft elements. That this is the opposite of what musicians seek did not trouble this official. This philosophy of sound, prevailing for several years, discredited his company. Unfortunately, it also injured the reputations of some artists involved, though they had no part in either the decision or the result.

Some years ago, a music critic of the *New York Times* indulged in a fantasy: a young record buff attends his first live concert. Knowing the music only from his discs and home playback equipment, he finds most of what he hears unsatisfactory. This satire was not far from reality.

As a final warning, I must report that on many occasions artists have approved records for release against their own best judgment. I have been surprised when conductors who I thought could forbid publication without injury to their own careers allowed quite unacceptable discs to be released. Whatever their reasons may have been, the student who eagerly takes a recording by Maestro X as the ultimate should be aware of the curious accidents that sometimes beset even the most highly touted electronically reproduced music. For example, at operatic recording sessions, some singer's indisposition may have required a later session at which the vocalist, with earphones, has sung to a previously recorded orchestral track. I heard once of a Puccini recording session for which the tenor was unavailable. His entire role was dubbed in later without either orchestra or conductor being present. I myself have recorded portions of an opera with the orchestra alone. Because of overwork, the tenor could not produce any acceptable lyrical sounds but did so (quite admirably under the circumstances) later. Whether this practice can result in a truly authentic or even fully persuasive performance I leave to more detached judgment. It is quite obvious, however, that such mechanical, piecemeal synthesis can be acceptable only as a technical feat of skill. The give-and-take essential to the best ensemble performance in music must be lacking.

A recording may mislead also because the conditions under which it was made cannot be reproduced in a live performance. Schönberg's Variations, Opus 31, was once recorded by an illustrious orchestra whose equally illustrious conductor thought that the nature of the scoring would be best served if for each variation a different and appropriate seating arrangement were established. Since in this work variations for a chamber group of diverse instruments alternate with variations for the full complement, this ingenious idea gave the musicians and the recording crew the most favorable chance to do justice to the utterly complex and wonderful score. But if a student believes that the piece will ever sound this way when he rehearses it—even with the same illustrious orchestra—he is in for a shock. The illustrious conductor, knowing that you cannot change chairs in live performance, has declared that he will never again perform the work in concerts, but will leave it to his perfectly set-up recorded version.

It is a common disposition of civilized man to give credence to the printed word above the spoken. In music today the record or cassette or tape holds the same place as the printed page. The implications of this for the preparation and development of the professional musician are immense. Earlier I have tried to show that the edited and printed score is not necessarily the most authentic copy of a composer's ideas. But the damage caused by mistakes and misunderstandings in a score is negligible when compared with the impact of a recording upon an impressionable youth.

The current obsession with sound for its own sake, divorced from context and meaning, shows curious parallels between music and stage. Since Wieland Wagner made it popular, *Lichtregie* ("staging through light effects") has become a concept to reckon with. It is a style of production that emphasizes a static behavior of the actors while great varieties of light effects throw the attention of the spectator where the producer wants it. Used occasionally, particularly for long stretches of exposition, it is a perfect device, but it has become a replacement for acting, which it is not.

In music too we have acquired a new word, *Klangregie* ("staging through sound"), which comes from the recording field but is also rapidly becoming a style of live performance. The basic idea is to treat the sound, or specific sonorities, as the first concern of the conductor and to subordinate to it other considerations, no matter how explicitly they were demanded by the composer. Concerned solely with *Klangregie*, a conductor may substitute muted brass for open brass (or vice versa); he may double violins with cellos to achieve a thicker sound; he may reshuffle balances, seating, orchestration, and rhythmic nuances if the sound ideal demands it. As a replacement for interpretation of a musical score it is unacceptable, yet a few very successful people have made it their battle horse and ride on it. Sound in music is a widely misunderstood element. For the maestros who have tended the Philadelphia sound there is one way of managing sonorities and no other. Whether the score is *Pines of Rome* or *Sacre du printemps* or Bruckner, the same sheen and gorgeous tropical moisture prevail—to the evident satisfaction of many faithful.

There are, of course, many works in which such sonorities are essential. For the conductor who struggles with program planning and learning, it is of vital importance to recognize all such problems, lest he subject himself and the public to inadequate performances with orchestras incapable of producing a fine sound. There are many ensembles of secondary rank where a work will otherwise be performed admirably, while the sound still leaves much to be desired. Here I must quote the American composer William Schuman, who once stated, "The sound of an orchestra improves in equal proportion to its budget."

When I assumed the post of music director for the Boston Symphony, I was asked by journalists if the orchestra would now have a "German sound," assuming that during the years of Charles Munch's incumbency, they had played with a "French sound." All this is nonsense. These terms are made up by slogan breeders who understand music simply in terms of clichés that, when scrutinized, prove to have no meaning at all. There is no German sound and there is no French sound. There is a right sound and a wrong sound for every work performed. If this is understood, sound takes an important role in interpreting music. A violinist, playing a very craggy work, was quite rightly offended when a leading critic found her tone lacking in sensuous beauty. The work would have taken on different significance altogether if its deeply introverted slow movement had been performed with a lush tone. If the violinist had been concerned with displaying a gorgeous tone she would have selected the Tchaikovsky concerto. A record producer expressed his disappointment to me, when he was assigned to tape a cycle of Beethoven's works, because "his orchestration is not good for recording." There is a story that Beethoven, when criticized for writing music that did not exploit the beauties of the violin, shouted, "Do you really believe that I think of his miserable violin when the spirit comes to me!" Today he might substitute "tape recorder" for "violin."

Sound is an integral part of the interpretive concept, for each instrumentalist as well as for ensembles. On two occasions a very fine string quartet of dedicated young men proved to me that they performed Alban Berg's music better than any other group. But in each instance they followed it with works by Schubert or Mozart using the same type of tone, producing something close to a caricature of a Schubert or Mozart sound. They had become addicted to the constant swelling and decreasing sonorities and to a hectically fast vibrato, which, when applied to a classical quartet, ruined the spirit and the concept.

Making Programs

It is impossible to give any rules for the selection of programs. Earlier, in discussing the differing appreciation of composers in different countries, I touched on one of the principal problems of program making. It is imperative that the young conductor remember that on the two sides of the Atlantic Ocean tastes in music and estimates of individual compositions vary widely. Some of the best young American conductors have chosen inappropriate selections for their European debuts and thus failed to duplicate the favorable impression they made in the United States.[7]

The reasons for this are twofold. The repertoire in the United States is much larger, broader, and less conservative in symphonic music, while in Europe there is far more adventure and contemporary repertoire in opera. Second, in most European cities the symphony concert is secondary to opera in importance. In the United States, however, there are few opera companies worthy of the name, and which enjoy a status comparable to that of the symphonic establishment. American conductors should be aware that to succeed in the European concert world they must have a considerable repertoire of classic and romantic standard works. In the United States this is far less crucial, except to conductors responsible for entire seasons, with dozens of programs to plan. Wherever symphonic music is performed, the classics are still the bread and butter of concert programs. Specialized programming and self-limiting selections may work for a festival or occasional appearance, but it will not carry the conductor through a season of even guest appearances. Programs in Europe need to be approached from a different viewpoint than those made for American audiences.

Unless a program is devoted to a single composer, it is essential to provide variety and contrast. Unlike some of my distinguished colleagues who favor programs in which one tonality dominates, I consider it important to avoid such uniformity. I should never put Mozart's E-flat Symphony on the same program with *Ein Heldenleben*. If a conductor finds that a soloist has chosen the Brahms Second Piano Concerto, he must decide whether to place it in the first or the second half of the program. If he chooses the first part, he had better make sure that part two does not produce an anticlimax. If the concerto is to go at the end, the first part of the program must avoid works in flat keys and works that will make the Brahms orchestra sound meager. A fine contrast with a big Brahms concerto will be one of Stravinsky's symphonies—perhaps the one in C—but never one of the early ballet scores. The lean texture of the symphonies will form a splendid contrast. Moreover, because the long concerto is well known to all orchestras, the orchestra will have the rehearsal time necessary to give the Stravinsky symphony adequate preparation.

The question of sufficient rehearsal time is affected by more than one factor. For example, the strengths and weaknesses of particular orchestras should be taken into account. If one conducts the SWF Orchestra in Baden-Baden, one can take for granted that Schönberg's Variations, Opus 31, will present no appreciable difficulty. The orchestra has been for many years under the eminent lead-

---

7. A very talented American conductor, who has successfully led some of the best American orchestras and appeared at the Metropolitan Opera House with fully deserved success, found himself at a loss when a major European engagement was offered with a request to include in each program one work by Robert Schumann. The young man was not prepared to conduct any Schumann at all, and the engagement was lost.

ership of Rosbaud and Boulez, both of whom have cultivated music that in other locales still presents nearly insurmountable problems.

Perhaps the best guide to program making is a clear awareness of one's philosophy as a performer. Everyone has it, but some do not realize that it is a philosophy. I subdivide it into three basic purposes: serving oneself, educating the public, and encompassing the great repertoire. The first goal is rarely acknowledged, but it is the most frequently pursued, for box-office success translates readily into personal success. Many ploys are adopted to court such success with a minimum of effort. One conductor made a considerable career by appearing in many concert halls with the Second Symphony of Scriabin, which nobody else played. Invariably he was reengaged, but as he very quickly ran out of repertoire, his return visits soon ceased. Few such narrowly opportunistic approaches to building a career work for long, and no ingenuity of programming can disguise poverty of repertoire. The late George Szell was once told that a certain conductor had made a great hit. "With which program," Szell asked, "*A*, *B*, or *C*?"

The second purpose, educating the public, sounds admirable, yet I am somewhat skeptical of the whole principle. Is this a performer's task? One wins approval in certain circles by making pious declarations, especially when they are followed by highly unpopular programming. (In America it has been the lot of associate conductors to perform the works that the music director feels obliged to include, without any desire to conduct them himself.) The phrase "educating the public" is too often mouthed to explain a repertoire that most listeners will dislike but is likely to produce foundation support. It is often a convenient justification for "young people's concerts" that have not lived up to their claims. If we can emancipate ourselves from cant and high-sounding platitudes, we ought to admit cheerfully that a musician belongs to a wide group known as entertainers. The term need not be identified with cheap amusements. It bears no relation to nightclubs and vaudeville—and the public knows the difference. Nevertheless, all entertainers are subject to one rule: they must please their audiences, at least most of the time.

Over a period of time every performing artist should become aware of his own best repertoire and not insist on doing what does not come naturally. Persistent study will broaden and deepen understanding, and there will then be no problem of inadequate repertory. For many conductors, the choice of program is the biggest stumbling block. It need not be, if the repertoire is large enough to allow for flexibility. Thus, I arrive at the third basic purpose of program making, encompassing the great works. I am fully convinced that knowing the whole output of the great composers will enlarge the possibilities for making good programs. The classics can be selected in a conventional way, by following the long-trodden road of putting together an overture, a concerto, and a symphony, or they can be presented with an element of novelty.

Everybody plays the overture to *Egmont*, but hardly anybody plays the rest of the score. It was written as incidental music to Goethe's drama, not for the concert hall. In fact, an imaginative and knowledgeable conductor can make a most effective and novel forty-minute concert piece of the *Egmont* music. It requires a connecting text, chosen from a variety of sources or even commissioned from a talented writer, but the reward will be great. One can revive the music for *The Ruins of Athens*, albeit not every note. I have pieced together at least a dozen major works (that is, works long enough to fill half a concert program) out of opera scores—adjusting them, cutting parts too dependent on the dramatic action, stressing the instrumental interludes, and thus forging them into pieces of symphonic dimensions. In the search for variety, a conductor should be inventive and also willing to take the risk that an experiment may not find universal favor.

In some instances one can and should try to improve on existing adaptations if they do not meet one's own standards. I always liked Prokofiev's music for the ballet *Romeo and Juliet* and performed the suites from time to time as they were put together by the composer. When I became acquainted with the full score, however, the suites no longer satisfied me, because brief excerpts tend to make programs less substantial. I devised out of the ballet score a suite of my own that continues uninterrupted, making a much broader and more formal work than the small pieces of the older suites.

This method is advisable with excerpts from Wagner. A special problem, however, is that Wagner excerpts are so interwoven with the full music drama that it has been almost impossible to find appropriate concert endings when extracting them. Everybody can play the existing arrangement of "Siegfried's Rhine Journey," with the (bad) concert ending by Humperdinck, and the funeral march at Siegfried's death, again with a not very inventive ending. Yet there is a very simple way to join the "Rhine Journey" with the funeral music without changing a single note. This immediately makes one large and imposing piece out of two and replaces an unsatisfactory ending. To eliminate the second ending, I add to the funeral march the orchestral postlude that follows the immolation of Brünnhilde. The result is a piece in symphonic form that nobody else plays.

By similar methods I have devised a suite from *Der Rosenkavalier* that is more original, in orchestration and sequence, than any other excerpts from that opera. The publishers have the score available, but so far nobody has taken the trouble to do it. Instead, secondhand transcriptions with arrangers' orchestrations of the waltz sequence are performed. There are other scores from which imaginative and industrious conductors with curiosity can make up new symphonic selections. I highly recommend this approach to program making, for it lends a novel element to music of familiar style and character. But the program must risk disapproval by the puritanical critic who will reject anything that is not the full original. In Europe one must take care not to program operatic excerpts, no matter how effective, in towns that have regular opera companies that perform the complete operas in repertoire. This is no problem in the United States. There the great Wagner and Strauss operas can be staged in only four or five cities at the most. This should not prevent other cities, including several with great symphony orchestras, from hearing parts of the *Ring* cycle. A "suite from *Die Walküre*" is no different in principle from the suite from *Petrouchka*. (It is imperative not to tamper with the vocal parts of an operatic score. The great Wagner and Strauss operas have enough instrumental sections to make a substantial contribution to the concert repertoire.)

The most popular works of the classical "hit parade," such as the symphonies of Beethoven and Brahms, should be sparingly programmed and only when there is the chance to prepare them well. Nothing and nobody is served by rehashing the Brahms First Symphony with one rehearsal with an orchestra that is below the very top level. On the other hand, a conductor should be quite sure of "his" Brahms First before doing it with a top orchestra, which can give the best rendition with the minimum of rehearsal time.

It is my conviction that a conductor who is able to read music as called for in chapter 1 will within a few years master a very large repertoire. At that point program making will be easy, because there will no longer be the fear of having too little time to learn those works outside the standard repertoire to which one may be committed by necessity, if not by conviction. I have been informed by a talent agent of long experience that the single most frequent cause of conflict between regular and guest conductors is program selection. Since in a decade of guest conducting with some fifty orchestras I have never been in such a conflict, I preach here only what I have practiced myself. No matter what selection is submitted by a conductor for guest appearances, it may be refused for a variety of very good reasons. If one has a large repertoire, it is easy to come up with alternatives. If, however, one has a narrow repertoire and is prepared to give only three or four different programs per season, then the situation can become very awkward and embarrassing.

Special consideration should be given to programming when one takes an orchestra on a tour. For the smaller cities in either America or Europe, hearing a great orchestra is an event that comes only once or twice a season; therefore, the most representative works for a symphony orchestra should be put on the program. At the same time, care must be taken not to duplicate what has been played too often by previous visitors. Here again local experts should be consulted. The primary requirement, again, is a large and catholic repertoire.

Finale

My overall purpose in these chapters has been to wean professional musicians from learning their music through the ear and guide them toward an independent and more reliable method of learning through the eye and the mind. In their artistic infancy musicians are nourished through the ear. Every musical child who is lucky enough is treated to a diet of recordings and model performances by accomplished musicians. This is a necessary stage of learning music, as nursing is to an infant's growth. The problem is that too many professionals today don't get weaned and stay well into their dotage being "breast-fed" through the ample teats of tapes and discs. They remain unready to undertake a personal search for the deeper truths in great music.

In my own musical life I have been spared one stage of a typical career: the ladder of the operatic circuit. Climbing these rungs is the customary way for young maestros to earn their spurs, but it is beset by a danger that I try everywhere to combat: the imitation of one's elders. A young conductor in a provincial European opera house begins as assistant to the principal chef, to be given occasional assignments at popular-priced matinees of *Der Freischütz* or *Die Zauberflöte*. At these he must do exactly as his boss does. Every ritard and every nuance must be copied, with very little leeway for personal expansion or interpretation. This unenviable yet indispensable step in the career of European music life is called by the unbeautiful and untranslatable word *Nachdirigieren*, meaning to conduct precisely after somebody else without making changes. I had one such opportunity when I was twenty-four, acting as assistant to a German maestro in Bologna. After I had showed myself to be a bad risk the impresario had me on the carpet. I was told to either leave my opinions at the hotel or quit. This might have been my fate again a year later, when I joined the Metropolitan Opera Company as assistant conductor, had it not been for the generosity of Artur Bodanzky, who wanted a relief conductor far more than a sycophant. From my first performance, two weeks before my twenty-sixth birthday, I could assert my own readings with the full moral support of the chef.

When, thirty-five years later, I began to think seriously of writing about the

209

subjects treated here, I became aware of my independent ways. They may have given me some trouble over the years, but I have never had to resort to the alibi that I was copying Big Brother. I hope that my readers will risk following their own minds, their own judgment, their own reading of the great masters, based on the most thorough knowledge. The noblest goal is a *radical orthodoxy*. I take my definition from Larousse's dictionary: "Radical: qui appartient à la racine"; "Orthodoxe: conforme à une doctrine considérée comme seule vraie." In short, one must go back to the roots to find the only truth.

Just as these concluding paragraphs were being written, by good fortune I located Felix von Weingartner's out-of-print book, *Über das Dirigieren*, in a secondhand music store. The famous conductor, whose performances in opera and concert I heard as a very young man, begins: "Richard Wagner published in 1869 his well-known treatise [*On Conducting*]. The unvarnished frankness with which he went at the notable conductors of his day brought him the grimmest hostility."[1] Weingartner, whose text was first printed in 1905, had his own *bête noire*, a "superstar" in a day when that word had not yet been coined: the conductor-pianist Hans von Bülow. So it seems that, every few decades, it becomes necessary to remind a new generation of musicians that there are many types of prominent and successful practitioners and that not all are doing the composers' bidding—at least not all of the time. It is not an accident that Bülow appears also in the letter from Richard Strauss, which I quoted earlier. There, even more than in Weingartner's highly critical accounts, Bülow's "vanity" is mentioned.

In the final analysis, talent is composed not only of knowledge and imagination; it needs for the greatest unfolding a personal character free of arrogance. This word, again in a Larousse definition, means "s'attribuer quelque chose sans y avoir droit"; that is, in our context, to assume to oneself that which is the composer's prerogative.

Weingartner writes what he demands of the conductor:

> 1. That he be true to the work, to himself, and to the public. When opening a score he should not think "What can I make of it" but rather "What did the composer want to say with it?"
> 2. That he should always have the feeling of being the most important, most responsible person in the musical life of the community. With good and stylish renditions he may elevate the artistic sensibilities of the public, whereas with bad ones, humoring his vanity, he may spoil the atmosphere for genuine artistic activity. His own greatest triumph is the success of the composer.[2]

Had I come into possession of Weingartner's little essay earlier, I would have been tempted to reprint it in its entirety.

---

1. Felix von Weingartner, *Über das Dirigieren*, 5th ed. (Leipzig: Breitkopf und Härtel, 1920), p. 3 (my translation).
2. Ibid., p. 58 (my translation).

When all is said and done, the conclusion seems inescapable that when we have truly learned to read the scores of the great musical masterpieces, we find there the most exact and explicit directions for their performance. Perhaps one can sum up all I have tried to say in a brief formula: *The absolute is subject to constant change; the relative is permanent.*

Index

Adorno, Theodor, 42
Alpensinfonie (Strauss), 197
Also Sprach Zarathustra (Strauss), 176
André, Maurice, 64
Ansermet, Ernest, 160–62
Armstrong, Louis, 64
Art of Fugue (Bach), 4

Bach, Carl Philipp Emanuel, 67
Bach, Johann Sebastian, 23–26, 27–28, 51; and clefs, 4, 5; and conducting technique, 170; dynamics and, 195, 196; languages and, 9; symbols used by, 11, 33–34; and tempo, 37, 164; tradition and, 70, 74–75, 77, 79, 86, 88–89, 97–99; variations by, 37
Barber of Seville, The (Rossini), 57, 103
Bärenreiter editions, 5, 25–26; and tempo, 104, 112, 118, 119, 124
Bartók, Bela, 49, 78, 128, 165, 197
Beaumarchais, Pierre de, 103
Beethoven, Ludwig van, 23, 49, 103, 179, 204; bowing and, 181–82, 183, 185–86; dynamics and, 194–95, 196, 197, 198, 199–200; economy used by, 45–46; editing of, 189–90, 191, 193, 198; and poetry, 10; rehearsal for, 176; rote playing of, 180; and tempo, 60–62, 63*n*, 101, 106, 125–66 passim; tradition and, 65–96 passim, 201; variations by, 27–40 passim, 147
—First Symphony, 37; and dynamics, 194–95, 197; and tempo, 141, 143, 157; tradition and, 70–72
—Second Symphony: and bowing, 182, 185; and dynamics, 194–95, 197; tempo in, 63*n*; tradition and, 72
—Third Symphony. See *Eroica* Symphony
—Fifth Symphony, 23, 32; and dynamics, 198;

rehearsals of, 176; and tempo, 141, 157–60; tradition and, 72
—Sixth Symphony. See *Pastoral* Symphony
—Ninth Symphony, 11, 32–33, 46; and dynamics, 198; editing of, 193, 198; and tempo, 135–41, 142, 153–55, 166; and tradition, 65, 69
Beethoven Quartets, The (Kerman), 162
Berg, Alban, 44, 204–05
Bizet, Georges, 163
B-minor Mass (Bach), 23–26, 28, 98–99
Bohème, La (Puccini), 100, 149
Bolero (Ravel), 78
Boris Godunov (Moussorgsky), 11, 37, 59, 192–93
Boston Symphony, 169, 181, 204
Boulez, Pierre, 206
Bourgeois gentilhomme, Le (Strauss), 145–46, 147
Brahms, Johannes, 2, 103, 179, 182; dynamics and, 194, 195, 196, 197, 199–200; editing of, 188–89, 193; and poetry, 10; in program selection, 205–06, 208; in rehearsals, 176, 177, 178; and tempo, 102, 129–30, 131, 143–44, 147–48, 164, 165; and variations, 28–37 passim, 61*n*
—First Symphony: and dynamics, 194; rehearsal time for, 208; and tempo, 143–44; variations in, 31
—Second Symphony: and dynamics, 197; editing of, 188–89, 193; rehearsal time for, 176
—Third Symphony, 33, 176, 178, 179
Brandenburg Concertos (Bach), 70, 88, 197
Breitkopf and Härtel editions, 1, 25–26; and bowing, 187; and tempo, 112, 115–16, 118, 119, 124, 156
Broude Brothers editions, 104

213